HOW TO STUDY LAW

AUSTRALIA
Law Book Co.
Sydney

CANADA and USA
Carswell
Toronto

HONG KONG
Sweet & Maxwell Asia

NEW ZEALAND
Brookers
Wellington

SINGAPORE and MALAYSIA
Sweet & Maxwell Asia
Singapore and Kuala Lumpur

How to Study Law

Fifth Edition

Anthony Bradney, LL.B., B.A.
Professor of Law, University of Sheffield

Fiona Cownie, LL.B., LL.M., B.A.
Barrister, H.K. Bevan Professor of Law, University of Hull

Judith Masson, M.A., Ph.D.
Professor of Law, University of Warwick

Alan C. Neal, LL.B, LL.M, D.G.L.S.
Barrister, Professor of Law, University of Warwick

David Newell, LL.B, M.Phil.
Solicitor, Director, The Newspaper Society

THOMSON

™

SWEET & MAXWELL

Published in 2005 by
Sweet & Maxwell Limited of
100 Avenue Road London NW3 3PF
http:/www.sweetandmaxwell.co.uk
Typeset by Servis Filmsetting Ltd, Manchester
Printed in England by Ashford Colour Printing Ltd, Gosport, Hants

A CIP catalogue record for this book is available from the British Library

ISBN 0421 893 80X

No natural forests were destroyed to make this product, only farmed timber
was used and re-planted.

ACKNOWLEDGEMENTS

We are particularly grateful to the Law Society, Council of Legal Education, General Council of the Bar, and UCAS for their help with Chapter 8.

The authors and publishers wish to thank the following for their permission to reprint material from publications in which they have copyright:

R v Jackson [1999] 1 All E.R. 572 and *Tomlinson v Congleton Borough Council and another* [2003] 3 All E.R. 1122 CA; [2003] 3 All E.R. 1122 HL reproduced by permission of LexisNexus Butterworths.

Blackwell Publishing for the article "Doctors as Good Samaritans: Some Empirical Evidence Concerning Emergency Medical Treatment in Britain", by Kevin Williams in the Journal of Law and Society.

Contents

Preface   xi

Part 1

1. Sources of the law

Discovering the Law   3
Parliament   4
Legislation in practice   5
Judge-made law   6
Common law and equity   7

2. Divisions of law

Introduction   11
Criminal law and civil law   11
National, international and European Union law   14
National law   14
International law   14
European Union law   16
Public and Private law   17
Criminal law and Civil law   20

3. Law in action/law in books

Introduction   21
Different questions mean different answers   22
Which kind of question am I asking?   23
Are there really different questions?   24
Answering questions   24
Seeing the law in action   25

Part 2

4. Finding cases and statutes

Finding cases   31
Using full law library non-electronic research facilities   31
Using law reports   33
Updating cases   35
Using limited library facilities   37
Using electronic retrieval facilities   38
Finding and updating statutes   39
How to use Encyclopedias   40
Finding and using material on the law of the European Communities, the European
   Union and the European Economic Area   41
Legislation   42
Information and notices   42
Other materials   43
European Union materials on the internet   43
Community legislation transposed into United Kingdom law   43

5. Reading cases and statutes

Reading a case   45
How to read a statute   53
The different parts   57
Using a statute   58
Statutory Instruments   60

Exercise 1—Statutes I   61
Dealing in Cultural Objects (Offences) Act 2003

Exercise 2—Statutes II   62
Protection from Harassment Act 1997

Exercise 3—Cases I   76
David L Donachie v The Chief Constable of the Greater Manchester Police

Exercise 4—Cases II   92
Tomlinson v Congleton Borough Council and another (CA)
Tomlinson v Congleton Borough Council and another (HL)

6. Reading research materials

Record reading   139
Interviews and questionnaires   139
Observation   140

Sampling   141
Research findings   141

Exercise 5—Research findings   145
Doctors as Good Samaritans

7. Study skills

Studying effectively   169
Independent learning   169
Managing your time   170
Lectures – listening and notetaking   172
Tutorials and seminars   175
Researching a topic for an essay/problem, tutorial or seminar   177
Reading for research   180
Recording your research   182
Writing assignments (essays and problem answers)   184
Exams and assessment   189
International students   192
Further reading   193

Exercise 6—Study skills   194
Essay evaluation   195

Part 3

8. Where next?

Law courses   201
Law as a profession   205
Solicitors and barristers   206
Education and training of solicitors   209
Education and training of barristers   215
Practical points: solicitors and barristers   218
Qualifying as a solicitor in Scotland   219
Qualifying as an advocate (barrister) in Scotland   221
Qualifying as a solicitor in Northern Ireland   221
Qualifying as a barrister in Northern Ireland   223

Appendix I – Careers directory   225
Appendix II – Abbreviations   245
Appendix III – Further reading   247
Appendix IV – Exercise answers   249

x   Contents

Exercise 1   249
Exercise 2   250
Exercise 3   252
Exercise 4   253
Exercise 5   254

Index   257

Preface

The changing learning environment in the twenty-first century law school puts ever more emphasis on the students' ability to make use of primary materials, even at the very beginning of their undergraduate studies. Knowing how to find material and knowing the different techniques for reading material are as important as understanding the content of material. Students need to be active researchers from their first day in the law school. Students also need a basic map of the legal system and the different divisions of law so that they can put their study into context. This new edition of "How to Study Law" builds on previous editions in helping students to learn how to find and read the statutes, cases and socio-legal studies they will use in their substantive courses. It also gives an elementary guide to the legal system and an indication of the careers that are open to law graduates. In this edition we have slightly changed the structure of the book by putting exercises that test the student's knowledge of research techniques immediately after the chapters that discuss those techniques. Legal skills are a vital part of a students learning. We hope this book will help students acquire those skills more easily and more quickly.

Part 1

1 Sources of the law

Discovering the law

We could begin by asking "What is law?". Ordinary people regularly make law for their own circumstances. Freely-negotiated commercial contracts may bind them to behave in particular ways. By becoming members of a sports club or a trade union they agree to comply with a set of rules. Sometimes these forms of law will use the courts to enforce their arrangements. In other cases privately-instituted adjudication bodies are established; a third party being appointed to decide whether an agreement or rule has been broken or not. These kinds of arrangements may seem very different from the normal idea of law, especially if law is thought of mainly in terms of the criminal law. However, it is possible to see law simply as a way of regulating behaviour, of deciding what can be done and what cannot be done.

Most laws are not about something dramatic like murder but are, rather, about the everyday details of ordinary life. Every time a purchase is made, a contract is created. Both parties make promises about what they will do; one to hand over the goods, one to pay the price. In this and other ways, everybody is involved in law every day of their lives. In some cases the state steps in to say what people can do, perhaps by saying how they can contract or, more dramatically, by saying when they can kill each other. This is the kind of law, that which comes from the state, we most frequently think about. Most courses involving law are interested only in this one kind of law and that is what this book is about.

There are many generally acknowledged sources of English law. Some are more obvious than others. Thus, "the Queen in Parliament" (the House of Commons, the House of Lords and the monarch) is a vital source of modern English law. Here proposals for legislation (*Bills*) are presented to, debated by, and voted upon by the House of Commons and the House of Lords, finally receiving the assent of the monarch and thus becoming legislation (*Statutes* or *Acts*). It is also indisputable that judges are significant sources of law, since the English legal system places great emphasis upon judgments in previous legal cases as guidance for future judicial decision-making. There are, however, less obvious sources of English law. Some are direct: for example, in some circumstances the European Union may make law for England and Wales. Others are more indirect: thus the customs of a particular trade may be incorporated into the law by the judges or Parliament or international law (the law between states) may be a basis for national law.

All of the above are sources of *legal rules*. What precisely it is that is meant by the term legal rules is a subject much debated by philosophers of law. Generally speaking, when the term is used it indicates that a particular course of action should, or should not, be followed. Legal rules are said to be *binding*. This means if they are not followed some action in the courts may result. Some of the questions about the nature of law are discussed in Chapter 5, "*Law in Action/Law in Books*".

It will suffice for present purposes if we consider just two of these sources of law: Parliament and the judiciary. In so doing, we will discover the central positions occupied within the English legal system by "*statute law*" and "*judge-made law*". There is a further explanation of international law and the law of the European Union in Chapter 2.

Parliament

Parliament creates law but not all the law that is created through Parliament is of the same kind. There is a need, in particular, to distinguish between various levels of legislation.

The legislation with which most people are familiar is statute law. Bills proposed in Parliament become Acts. These Acts may either be *General* or *Personal and Local*. Both of these are sometimes known as *primary legislation*. General Acts apply to everybody, everywhere within the legal system. In this context it is important to remember that there are several different legal systems within the United Kingdom; one for England and Wales, one for Scotland and one for Northern Ireland. A legal rule in a statute can only be changed by another statute. Any statute, no matter how important it seems, can be changed in the same way as any other.

Some Acts apply to all the legal systems; many apply only to one or two of them. Personal and local Acts apply either to particular individuals or (more usually) to particular areas. Thus, before divorce was part of the general law, it was possible to get a divorce by Act of Parliament. The most common example of local legislation is that which applies to individual cities. The law in Sheffield is sometimes not the same as the law in London. General legislation is much more common than personal and local legislation.

Most legislation consists of a direct statement about how people should behave or indicates the consequences of certain behaviour. For example, a statute may define a crime and say what the punishment will be for that crime. Sometimes Parliament cannot decide exactly what the law should be on a particular point. It may not have the necessary expertise or it may be that the area is one where frequent changes are needed. In such cases Parliament may pass an Act giving somebody else the power to make law in the appropriate area. Such power is often given to government ministers or to local authorities. This is the most common example of what is known as *delegated* or *secondary legislation*. A person or body to whom legislative power is delegated cannot, as can Parliament, make law about anything. The Act (sometimes called *the parent Act*) will determine the area in which law can be made, it may say something about the content of the law, but the details of that law will be left to the person or body to whom legislative power is delegated. They may also have the power to change that law from time to time. Most delegated legislation is published as a *statutory instrument*. Although people are frequently unaware of this type of legislation it is very important, affecting most people's lives. For example, much of the social security system is based on delegated legislation.

The final type of legislation that we have to consider is the range of directives, circulars, and guidance notes produced by various state agencies and bodies such as the Inland

Revenue. Some of these documents bind the people to whom they are addressed to behave in particular ways. Many are not legally binding. They do not compel people in the way that statutes or statutory instruments do. Even so, such documents are often very influential. In practice officials receiving them may always act in the way they indicate. Thus we might consider them all as a form of legislation.

In Chapter 4 you will find an explanation of how to find statutes and statutory instruments and in Chapter 5 an explanation of how you use them to find out where the law stands about something.

Legislation in practice

Even if we can find a statute the question still remains, "What will be its effect?". What will happen when somebody acts in a way that is contrary to the statute?

At this stage it is important to appreciate the relationship between the judges and statute law. The judiciary are bound by and, legally, must apply legislation, whether it is primary legislation or secondary legislation. However, an Act or piece of delegated legislation may be unclear or ambiguous. In some cases the difficulty will be resolved by applying one of the general Interpretation Acts. These are Acts that give a definition of words commonly found in legislation. Thus, for example, one Interpretation Act, the Interpretation Act 1978, says that where a piece of legislation uses the word "he" or "she" this should be taken to mean "he or she" unless it is plain from the context that this should not be so. Some Acts have their own interpretation section, in which certain important words or phrases used in the Act are defined. However, if a difficulty cannot be resolved by such an Act or section; if the ambiguity or lack of clarity remains, it is for the judiciary to decide what the legislation means.

In order to discover the way in which legislation should be applied, the judges have developed a complex network of principles for statutory interpretation, which are designed to assist in the proper application of the law. These principles of statutory interpretation seek, it is said, to combine an interpretation of the natural meaning of the English language used to frame the particular statutory provisions with common-sense meaning and an avoidance of inconsistency. In particular, where primary legislation is involved, it is said that it is not the task of the judges to make law but merely to apply it. Nevertheless, there have been numerous occasions when the judges have been accused of "perverting the true intention" of Parliament. It must be evident that the very process of statutory interpretation always carries with it the risk of divergence between Parliament and the courts in the eventual conclusion reached.

Some of the principles that the judiciary use are very narrow. For example, they might apply only to the meaning of one phrase in a particular type of statute. Others are much broader. Books are written analysing the judicial approach to the interpretation of difficult legislation. At this point it is sufficient for you to know three broad principles. First, judges normally apply the actual words in the legislation not the words the legislator might have intended to use. Secondly, faced with ambiguity, the judges choose the least absurd meaning. Thirdly, when a statute is designed to remedy a problem, the statute will be interpreted in the light of that intent. Plainly these principles will leave many problems unresolved, including that of when to apply one rather than another principle. Leaving aside the difficulties caused in deciding what these principles of interpretation might mean, it is a matter of controversy whether they act as rules deciding what the judges do or provide rationalisations for what the judiciary have already decided.

Judge-made law

Not all legal rules are laid down in an Act of Parliament or some other piece of legislation. A number of fundamental rules are found in the statements of judges made in the course of deciding cases brought before them. A rule made in the course of deciding cases, rather than legislation, is called a rule of *common law*. A common law rule has as much force as a rule derived from statute. Many important areas of English law, such as contract, tort, criminal law, land law and constitutional law, have their origins in common law. Some of the earliest common law rules still survive, though many have been supplemented or supplanted by statute. Common law rules are still being made today, though as a source of new legal rules common law is less important than statute. Strictly speaking, the term common law is confined to rules that have been developed entirely by judicial decisions. It excludes new rules made by judges when they interpret statutes. The term case law covers both kinds of new rules.

The application of case law is easiest to understand when the issue presently before the court has been raised in some previous analogous case. In such a situation the court will look to see if there is a potential applicable rule in the reports of previously decided cases. Then they will decide whether they have to, or should, apply that rule. It is therefore vital that accurate and comprehensive records be kept of past court decisions and judicial pronouncements. Thus the importance of the numerous and varied series of Law Reports can be appreciated. Anybody entering a law library in England can hardly help being impressed at the volume of materials falling within this category of Law Reports. Row upon row of bound volumes, containing the judgments in thousands of past cases, dominate the holdings of any major English law library.

More information about the various kinds of Law Reports and how to use them can be found in Chapter 4. An explanation of how cases should be read is found in Chapter 5.

Cases are decided in court. Different kinds of legal disputes are decided in different kinds of courts. Sometimes it is possible to bring a legal dispute before two or more different kinds of court. In some situations, once a court has given judgment, it is possible to appeal against that judgment to another court. Some courts only hear appeals.

Not every judgment in every case is of equal importance. The weight that is to be given to them as guidelines for future judicial activity will depend upon two things. One is the level of the court in which that case was decided. In English law there is a principle of a *hierarchy of precedents*. Judgments given by superior courts in the hierarchy are binding on inferior courts.

A brief overview of the court structure seen from this hierarchical view appears below on page 7.

The highest, and thus most important court is the House of Lords. The results of cases heard in the House of Lords and in the Court of Appeal will normally be fully reported in the series of Law Reports as a matter of course. Other courts' judgments will either be reported only when they are considered important by those compiling the reports or, in the case of very lowly courts, will not be reported at all.

Even if a previous case is said to be binding, only some parts of the judgment are important. Lawyers distinguish two parts of a judgment: (a) the *ratio decidendi* and (b) the *obiter dicta*. Put most simply, the *ratio decidendi* is that part of reasoning in the judgment which is necessary in order to determine the law on the issue in the particular case before the judge. It is this that is *binding* on other courts in the hierarchy. The *obiter dicta*, on the other hand, is a term used to describe the remainder of the judgment. This is not binding but may be *persuasive*. In the absence of a binding *ratio decidendi* the court may be influenced by *obiter dicta*. These two terms are commonly shortened to *ratio* and *obiter*. There is a further discussion of this and other topics at this point in Chapter 5.

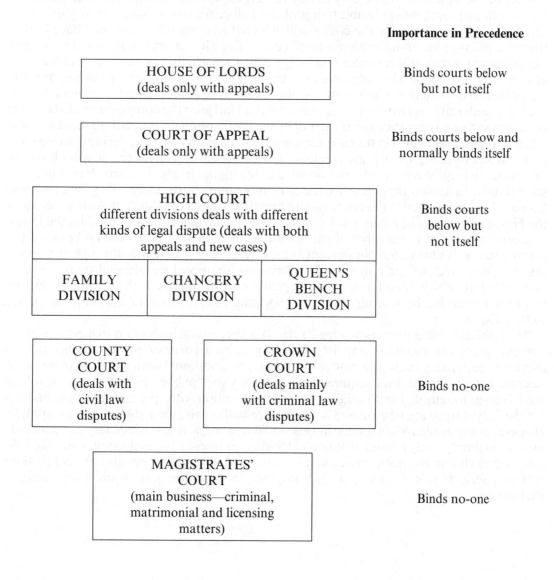

Importance in Precedence

HOUSE OF LORDS (deals only with appeals)	Binds courts below but not itself
COURT OF APPEAL (deals only with appeals)	Binds courts below and normally binds itself
HIGH COURT different divisions deals with different kinds of legal dispute (deals with both appeals and new cases) / **FAMILY DIVISION** **CHANCERY DIVISION** **QUEEN'S BENCH DIVISION**	Binds courts below but not itself
COUNTY COURT (deals with civil law disputes) **CROWN COURT** (deals mainly with criminal law disputes)	Binds no-one
MAGISTRATES' COURT (main business—criminal, matrimonial and licensing matters)	Binds no-one

Thus, in asking whether a particular judgment is "important" from the point of view of influencing future decisions, and so representing the "state of the law" on any particular matter, we need to consider both its importance in terms of the court which delivered the judgment and whether the *ratio decidendi* of the case is sufficiently clear and relevant to future issues of law arising in later cases. The identification of the *ratio decidendi* is not always an easy matter. There is also great debate amongst academics as to what importance the *obiter dicta* in a previous case may or should have. Some academics, whilst accepting that terms like *ratio* and *obiter* are used in judgments, and whilst accepting that at least some judges think they construct their judgments on the basis of *ratio* and *obiter* in previous judgments, believe that important influences on decisions made by judges are to be found in the nature of matters such as the social background of judges, the economic circumstances of the time or even the very nature of language itself. In some instances there will be no binding precedent applicable to a problem before the court. No court may have been faced with the same issue or the courts which were faced with the issue may have been at the same point or lower in the hierarchy of courts. Even if a court is not bound by a previous judgment it may still consider that judgment to see whether or not it provides a good answer to the problem. The judgment may be persuasive. The importance of the previous case will then depend not simply on its position within the court hierarchy but upon factors such as the identity and experience of the individual judge or the composition of the bench of judges sitting to hear the case, the detail of the legal arguments put before the court, and whether the line laid down in the case has since been adopted by courts deciding subsequent cases. When looking for the law created and developed by the judges, it will clearly be important to look at reports of cases decided in the higher levels of courts. Nevertheless, it should not be assumed that these are the only important courts. Only a very small proportion of all cases handled in the court system find their way to the Court of Appeal, let alone the House of Lords. The magistrates' courts are very much more important than the House of Lords in terms of the number of cases with which they deal. Nor would it be correct to assume that it is always the "important" cases which work their way through the appeal system, since much of the motivation for bringing an appeal will depend upon financial considerations which are often totally independent of the merits of the dispute in relation to which the case has been brought or the importance or complexity of the law to be applied to that dispute.

The legislature plainly makes new legal rules. Whether or not, in an effort to meet new developments, problems, and shifts in society's values, genuine departures from established rules of common law actually occur, is a matter of debate. The traditional notion is that common law rules do not alter to meet the requirements of society (or "public opinion"); it is the role of the legislator to remedy this through statutory intervention with specific legislation, and not for the judges to create new rules. The legislature makes law; the judiciary merely apply it. However, many academics and some judges would now argue that the judiciary sometimes do more than simply apply existing law; that in looking for rules of law in previous cases the judiciary subtly change the rules, consciously or otherwise, so that they produce the conclusions that they seek. If this is correct the judiciary are, in this sense, just as much legislators as Parliament.

Common Law and Equity

In the section above the term "common law" is used as a synonym for rules of law derived from judicial decisions rather than statute. This is a proper and common usage of the phrase. However, another equally frequent sense of the word is as an antonym to "equity". English law has deep historical roots. The opposition of common law and equity refers to the system of rules that originally develop in different courts within the legal system. Common law rules arose first. Later, these rules were seen as being over-formal and concerned too much with the way a case was presented rather than with the justice in the issues at stake. Thus a less strict system of equitable rules was developed. In time, the rules of equity also became formalised. Eventually, the different courts were merged and now all courts can apply both the rules of common law and equity.

2 Divisions of law

Introduction

Legal rules can be divided up in many different ways. This chapter introduces some common ways of classifying law. Not all legal rules are of the same type. They show differences in purpose, in origin and form, in the consequences when the rules are breached, and in matters of procedure, remedies and enforcement. The divisions described below are of the broadest kind, chosen to highlight these kinds of differences in legal rules. One kind of division of legal rules has already been introduced, that between statute and case or common law. This division and the others now described overlap. For example, the legal rule defining murder originates in common law, not statute. It is a rule of criminal law rather than civil law; of public law rather than private law and of national law rather than international law.

There are ways other than those discussed here of dividing up the law. One way is to take the legal rules relating to a given topic, grouping them under a title such as "housing law" or "accountancy law". Categorising rules in this way can be very useful: for example, it is not necessary for a personnel manager to know the whole of the general law of contracts before becoming proficient in essential employment law. However, such subject groupings can also be confusing without some understanding of the basic differences between the rules.

Criminal and Civil Law

One of the most fundamental divisions in law is the division between criminal and civil law. Newcomers to the study of law tend to assume that criminal law occupies the bulk of a lawyer's caseload and of a law student's studies. This is an interesting by-product of the portrayal of the legal system by the media. Criminal law weighs very lightly in terms of volume when measured against non-criminal (civil) law. There are more rules of civil law than there are of criminal law; more court cases involve breach of the civil law than involve breach of the criminal law. Law degree students will find that criminal law is generally only one course out of 12 to 15 subjects in a three-year law degree, although some criminal offences may be referred to in other courses.

Criminal law means the law relating to crime only. Civil law can be taken to mean all the rest. The distinction relies not so much on the nature of the conduct that is the object of a legal rule but in the nature of the proceedings and the sanctions that may follow. Some kinds of conduct give rise to criminal liability, some to civil liability and some to both civil and criminal liability. The seriousness of the conduct does not necessarily determine the type of liability to which it gives rise; conduct that is contrary to the criminal law is not always "worse" than conduct that is against the civil law. Few people would consider every criminal offence a moral wrong (except, perhaps, in the sense that every breach of the law might be thought to be a moral wrong). Equally, some actions that are purely breaches of the civil law might be considered breaches of morality. Nor is harm, in the sense of damage done to individuals, something that is found to a greater degree in the criminal law as against the civil law. The person who parks on a "double-yellow line" breaches the criminal law. The company that fails to pay for the goods that it has bought, thereby bankrupting another company, commits only a breach of the civil law. Who has done the greater harm? Concepts of morality have had some influence on the development of English law but historical accident, political policy and pragmatic considerations have played just as important a part in developing our law.

Some conduct which might be considered "criminal" gives rise only to civil liability or to no liability at all and some conduct which you may consider "harmless" may rise to both criminal and civil liability. It will be easier to see that "harm," "morality" and the division between criminal and civil law do not follow any clear pattern if you consider some fictitious examples. In considering them, ask yourself whether or not the conduct described should give rise to any legal liability; if it should, what form should that liability take and what should the legal consequences be which flow from the conduct described? Should any of the people be compensated for the harm done to them and, if so, by whom and for what? Should any of the characters be punished and, if so, for what reason and how? Who should decide whether or not legal proceedings of any variety should be instigated against any of the individuals? The probable legal consequences that follow from each example are found at the end of the chapter. Do not look at these until you have thought about the examples yourself.

Examples

1. Norman drinks 10 pints of beer. He drives his car into a queue at the bus station injuring a young woman and her child.
2. Sue, who is pregnant, lives with Chris. She smokes 50 cigarettes a day. Sue is also carrying on an occasional affair with Richard.
3. Robert agrees to pay Usha, a professional decorator, £500 if she paints his house. She completes the work to a very high standard. Robert, who is a millionaire, refuses to pay her.

Even when a person's actions clearly infringe either the criminal law or civil law, it does not necessarily mean that any actual legal consequences will follow. In criminal and civil cases persons with the legal right to take any legal action have a discretion as to whether or not they initiate legal proceedings. There is a difference between *liability* and *proceedings*. Conduct gives rise to liability. It is for someone else to decide whether or not to take the matter to court by starting proceedings.

In criminal proceedings a *prosecutor* prosecutes the *defendant*. The case is heard in the magistrates' court or the Crown Court, depending on the seriousness of the offence. The prosecutor will have to prove to the court, *beyond all reasonable doubt*, that the defendant committed the offence charged. The court will have to determine whether or not the defendant is guilty. In the magistrates' court it will be for the magistrates to determine this question, in the Crown Court it will be for the jury to decide questions of fact and for the judge to decide questions of law. A finding of "not guilty" will lead to the defendant's acquittal. A finding of "guilty" will lead to a conviction and may lead to a sentence of imprisonment or some other form of punishment such as a fine or probation.

One of the major objectives of the criminal law is to punish the wrongdoer for action that is deemed to be contrary to the interests of the state and its citizens. Criminal proceedings do not have as a major objective the provision of compensation or support for the victim of crime. It is significant that the exercise of the discretion to prosecute is seldom carried out by the victim of the crime. Criminal proceedings are normally initiated by the state or its agents and brought in the name of the Queen or the prosecuting official.

In civil proceedings it is generally the *plaintiff* (the party harmed) (since April 1999 known as the *claimant*) who sues the *defendant*, although in some areas of the civil law other terms are used. For example, in the case of a divorce the petitioner sues the respondent. The case will usually be heard in either the county court or the High Court, depending on the nature of the case and the size of the loss involved. The plaintiff usually has to prove, on *the balance of probabilities*, that the events took place in the manner claimed. This is a lower standard of proof than in criminal cases. If the plaintiff proves their case, the court will make some kind of order. What this will be, will depend upon the kind of case and what the plaintiff has asked for. The basic choice before the court is whether to order the defendant to compensate the plaintiff for their loss by awarding damages, or to order the defendant to act, or refrain from acting, in some specific way in the future, or to make both kinds of orders. The function of civil law is to provide individuals with remedies that are enforceable in the courts where they have suffered a wrong that is recognised by a statute or decided cases. The civil law creates a framework that delineates the rights and obligations of individuals in their dealings with one another. It is primarily founded on the law of contract and tort, which are mainly areas of common law. The law of contract determines which forms of agreement entered into between individuals are legally binding and on whom they will be binding. The law of tort covers categories of civil wrong, other than breach of contract, which may give rise to legal causes of action. It includes the law of negligence, trespass and libel and slander. Just as a set of facts can give rise to conduct that may result in both civil and criminal proceedings, so a set of facts can give rise to actions in contract and in tort. Most plaintiff's primary motivation for bringing civil proceedings will be to obtain an effective remedy for the civil wrong which has been perpetrated. The fact that there is liability will not necessarily mean that they will take action. For example, there may be no point in suing a person for damages if you know they have no money.

The emphasis of the civil law has changed over the last hundred years with an increase in the role of the state and the importance of legislation as opposed to case law as the major source of law. Civil law does not just regulate relations between individuals covering such matters as their property transactions, but also deals with relations between the state and individuals. It covers unemployment and social benefit entitlement, tax and planning questions, and council tenants' relationships with their local authorities. All of these areas are covered by statute law that has created new rights and obligations. These are often enforced in tribunals as opposed to courts.

Statutory provisions have also been enacted in order to minimise the common law rights that have resulted from the judicial development of contract law and the notion of freedom of contract. For example, employment protection and landlord and tenant legislation give employees and tenants statutory rights that will often modify or override terms in their contracts that give their employers or landlords specific rights to dismiss or evict them.

National, International and European Union Law

The term "national" or "municipal" law is used to mean the internal legal rules of a particular country, in contrast to international law that deals with the external relationships of a state with other states. In the United Kingdom, national law is normally unaffected by international legal obligations unless these obligations have been transferred into national law by an Act of Parliament. European Union law, however, cuts across this conventional notion that national and international law operate at different and distinct levels. It is a form of international law in that it is in part concerned with legal relations between Member States, but European Union law may also directly affect the national law of Member States. It will therefore be considered separately from both national and international law.

National Law

The system of national law has already been considered in Chapter 1.

International Law

Public international law regulates the external relations of states with one another. It is a form of law very different from national law. There is no world government or legislature issuing and enforcing laws to which all nations are subject. The international legal order is essentially decentralised and operates by agreement between states. This means that the creation, interpretation and enforcement of international law lies primarily in the hands of states themselves. Its scope and effectiveness depends on the capacity of states to agree and the sense of mutual benefit and obligation involved in adhering to the rules.

International law is created in two main ways: by treaty and by custom. Treaties are agreements between two or more states, and are binding on the states involved if they have given their consent to be so bound. Customary law is established by showing that states have adopted broadly consistent practices towards a particular matter and that they have acted in this way out of a sense of legal obligation. International law is neither comprehensive nor systematic. Few treaties or customary rules involve the majority of world states. Most are bilateral understandings or involve only a handful of parties to a multilateral agreement.

Disputes about the scope and interpretation of international law are rarely resolved by the use of international courts or binding arbitration procedures of an international organisation. This is because submission to an international court or similar process is entirely voluntary and few states are likely to agree to this if there is a serious risk of losing their case of where important political or national interests are at stake. Negotiation is far more common. International courts are used occasionally, for example where settlement is urgent, or protracted negotiations have failed, where the dispute is minor or is affecting other international relations; in other words, in cases where failure to settle is more damaging than an unfavourable outcome. Where international law has been breached, an injured state must rely primarily on self-help for enforcement. There is no effective international institutional machinery to ensure compliance when the law is challenged. This means that in practice powerful states are better able to protect their rights and assert new claims.

Breaching established rules is one, rather clumsy, way of changing international law. In a decentralised system, change can only be affected by common consent or by the assertion of a new claim being met by inaction or acquiescence by others. The lack of powerful enforcement machinery does not mean that international law is widely disregarded. On the contrary, legal rules are regularly followed, not least because states require security and predictability in the conduct of normal everyday inter-state relations.

International law also plays an important role in the promotion of common interests such as controlling pollution, restricting over fishing, or establishing satellite and telecommunication link-ups.

A large number of global or regional international organisations have been established for the regulation and review of current inter-state activity. The best-known example, though perhaps not the most effective, is the United States, whose primary function is the maintenance of international peace and security.

In the United Kingdom, international law has no direct effect on national law and, on a given matter, national law may in fact be inconsistent with the United Kingdom's international obligations. The Government has authority to enter into treaties which may bind the United Kingdom *vis-à-vis* other states. However a treaty will not alter the law to be applied within the United Kingdom unless the provisions are adopted by means of an Act of Parliament. Customary international law may have been incorporated into national law but will enjoy no higher status than any other provision of national law and is, therefore, liable to be superseded by statute. However, it is a principle of judicial interpretation that, unless there is clear legal authority to the contrary, Parliament does not intend to act in breach of international law. In some other countries, international law is accorded a different status. In the Netherlands and Germany, for example, international law takes effect in municipal law and, where these conflict, international law prevails. The lack of direct application should not be taken to mean that international law is of no importance in United Kingdom courts or for United Kingdom citizens. National courts regularly decide domestic cases having presumed the existence and application of international law. For example, under the Vienna Convention of 1961, diplomats enjoy immunity from criminal prosecution. If a defendant claims immunity, a court must decide whether the defendant falls within the terms of the treaty before proceeding further. Secondly, individuals may have rights under international law, enforceable not through national courts but through international institutions. The European Convention on Human Rights gives individuals the right to complain of breaches of the Convention to the European Commission on Human Rights which may then refer the case to the European Court of Human Rights. (These institutions should not be confused with European Union bodies: they are quite separate.) Although the United Kingdom ratified the Convention in 1951, it was only in 1966 that the United Kingdom agreed to the articles of the treaty that recognised the right of individual petition and the compulsory jurisdiction of the Court. The Human Rights Act 1998 gives an individual the right to enforce certain rights found in the Convention against public authorities.

European Union Law

In joining the European Communities in 1973, the United Kingdom agreed to apply and be bound by Community law, accepting that Community law would override any conflicting provisions of national law. Unlike other forms of international law, European Community law is capable of passing directly into national law; it is applicable in the United Kingdom without being adopted by an Act of Parliament. These principles were given legal effect by the passage of the European Communities Act 1972. The European Communities are made up of three organisations: the European Economic Community (EEC), the European Coal and Steel Community (ECSC) and the European Community for Atomic Energy (Euratom). Since the United Kingdom's entry the European Communities have been further enlarged. There are now 25 member states. Moreover, the European Communities are now part of the European Union, following the Treaty on European Union, signed at Maastricht (since added to by the Treaty of Amsterdam and that of Nice). This section will concentrate on the implications of membership of the European Union for United Kingdom law.

The European Union is an international organisation established and developed by treaty between Member States. The basic framework is set out in the EEC Treaty of 1957 ("Treaty of Rome"), which defines the objectives of the Community, the powers and duties of Community institutions, and the rights and obligations of Member States. This treaty goes much further than just creating law that binds both Member States and Community institutions. It contains many detailed substantive provisions, some of that create rights for individuals that are enforceable directly in national courts. The EEC Treaty, and certain others which have followed it, are thus primary sources of Community law. The European Union has a number of major institutions: the Council of European Union, the Commission, the Assembly (or European Parliament), the Court of Justice (and the Court of First Instance) and the Court of Auditors. The terms of the various treaties give the European Union a powerful legislative, administrative and judicial machinery. The Treaty provides that further legislation may be made by the Council of Ministers and the Commission. This is called secondary legislation and takes three forms.

Regulations, once made, pass into the law of a Member State automatically. Regulations are "directly applicable", that means that Member States do not have to take any action (such as passing an Act of Parliament) to implement them or to incorporate them into national law. Regulations are intended to be applied uniformly throughout the Community, and override any conflicting provisions in national law.

Directives are binding on Member States as to the result to be achieved, but leave each Member State with a choice about the method used to achieve that result. Member States are given a transitional period in which to implement the directive. This may involve passing a new law, making new administrative arrangements, or, where national law already conforms with the directive, taking no action. The Commission can initiate proceedings against a Member State if it believes the steps taken do not achieve the desired result. Although directives are addressed to Member States, in some circumstances an individual may be able to rely directly on certain parts, whether or not the Member State has taken implementing action. This is when the relevant part lays down an unconditional obligation and grants enforceable individual rights.

Decisions can be addressed to Member States, individuals or companies. They are binding only on the person to whom they are addressed and take effect on notification.

European Union law is applied in Member States by their system of national courts and tribunals. When a point of European Union law is crucial to a court's decision, the court may refer the case to the Court of Justice for a preliminary ruling on the interpretation of the point in question. Courts against whose decision there is no appeal, (*e.g.* the House of Lords) must make a reference to the Court of Justice when the case hinges on European Union law unless the Court has already ruled on that particular issue. Once the Court of Justice has given a preliminary ruling, the case is referred back to the national court from which it originated, which must then decide the case. The Court of Justice will only answer questions put to it about the interpretation of European Union law; it will not rule on national law or on conflict between national and European Union law or apply its interpretation to the facts of the case. These are all matters for national courts. The Commission may bring an action in the Court of Justice against a Member State for breach of an obligation, such as the non-implementation of a directive. Proceedings may be taken against the Commission or the Council for failing to act where the EEC Treaty imposes a duty to act. There are also provisions for annulling legislation adopted by the Commission or Council, for example, where the action has exceeded the powers laid down by treaty.

Public and Private Law

Another distinction that may be drawn between different types of law is the division between "public" law and "private" law. Public law is concerned with the distribution and exercise of power by the state and the legal relations between the state and the individual. For example, the rules governing the powers and duties of local authorities, the operation of the National Health Service, the regulations of building standards, the issuing of passports and the compulsory purchase of land to build a motorway all fall within the ambit of public law. In contrast, private law is concerned with the legal relationships between individuals, such as the liability of employers towards their employees for injuries sustained at work, consumers' rights against shopkeepers and manufacturers over faulty goods, or owners' rights to prevent others walking across their land. The division of law into public and private law and civil and criminal law are two clear examples of categories that overlap. Thus, for example, some public law is civil and some is criminal.

The significance of the public/private law distinction operates at two levels. First, it is a very useful general classification through which we can highlight some broad differences, such as those in the purpose of law, in sources and forms of legal rules, and in remedies and enforcement. This is the way the idea of public/private law will be discussed here. However, the distinction is also used in a second, narrower sense; as a way of defining the procedure by which claims can be raised in court.

One way of thinking about a legal rule is to consider its purpose. The primary purpose underlying most private law rules is the protection of individual interests, whereas the aim of most public law provisions is the promotion of social objectives and the protection of collective rather than individual interests. The methods used to achieve these purposes also differ. A characteristic feature of public law is the creation of a public body with special powers of investigation, decision-making and/or enforcement in relation to a particular problem, whereas private law achieves its ends by giving individuals the right to take action in defence of their interests.

Many problems are addressed by both public and private law. Sometimes a single statute may include both private rights and liabilities alongside public law provisions. This can be seen both by looking at statutes characteristic of public law and by looking at an example in practice. The Equal Pay Act and the Sex Discrimination Act both came into force in 1975. These Acts made it unlawful to discriminate on the grounds of sex in many important areas such as employment, education and housing. For the individual who had suffered discrimination, the Acts created new private rights to take complaints to industrial tribunals or county courts and claim compensation or other appropriate remedies. At the same time, the Equal Opportunities Commission was set up, with public powers and duties to investigate matters of sex discrimination and promote equal opportunities.

Example

Ann lives next door to an industrial workshop run by Brenda. The machinery is very noisy and the process discharges fumes that make Ann feel ill. This sort of problem is tackled by both public and private law in a number of different ways.

(i)   As a neighbour, Ann may bring a private law action in nuisance, which is a claim that Brenda's activities unreasonably interfere with the use of Ann's land. Ann could claim compensation for the hard she has suffered and could seek an injunction to stop the harmful process continuing.

(ii) There are also public law rules that may be invoked whether or not an individual has or may be harmed, aimed at preventing the problem arising in the first place or controlling the situation for the public benefit. For example, when Brenda first started her workshop she would have needed to get planning permission from the local authority if her activities constituted a change in the use of the land. Planning legislation thus gives the local authority an opportunity to prevent industrial development in residential areas by refusing planning permission, or control it by laying down conditions. Other legislation gives the local authority powers to monitor and control various kinds of pollution and nuisances in their area, including noise and dangerous fumes. A further complex set of private rights and public regulations govern the working conditions of the workshop employees, who would also be affected by the noise and smells.

Public and private law also show differences in their origins and form. Some of the most important principles of private law are of ancient origin and were developed through the common law as individuals took their private disputes to court and demanded a remedy. The rules of private rights in contract, over land and inheritance, to compensation for physical injury or damage to property or reputation, were all first fashioned by judges in the course of deciding cases brought before them. In contrast, most public law rules are of comparatively recent origin first originating in stature, not judicial decisions. There are obvious exceptions. Criminal law and the criminal justice system itself are prime examples where standards of behaviour are set by the state and enforced by a network of public officials with powers of arrest, prosecution, trial and punishment. Much of the early development of this field of public law lies in common law. An important function of public law has its roots in constitutional theory. The actions of public bodies are only lawful if there is a legal rule granting the body authority to act in a given situation. A private individual needs no legal authority merely to act. It is assumed that a person acts lawfully unless there is a legal rule prohibiting or curtailing that behaviour. Public law therefore has a facilitative function, for which there is no equivalent in private law, permitting a public body to take action that would otherwise be unlawful. A feature of much recent public law is a shift towards the grant of broad discretionary powers to public bodies. This means that the same legislative framework can be used more flexibly, accommodating changes in public policy as to the purposes to which the powers should be put or the criteria for the exercise of these powers. This characteristic form of modern public law contrasts quite sharply with the relatively specific rights and duties to be found in private law, and in turn affects the way public and private law can be enforced. All private law is enforced by granting individuals the right to take action in defence of a recognised personal interest. For example, a householder may make a contract with a builder over the repair of a roof, and may sue the builder if the work or materials are of a lower standard than was specified in the contract. Not all public law can be enforced by way of individual action.

The enforcement of public law can be viewed from two perspectives. First, public law can be enforced as when as official ensures that individuals or companies comply with standards set in statutes or delegated legislation, *e.g.* public health officials making orders in relation to or prosecuting restaurants. Secondly, the enforcement of public law can also be seen as the matter of ensuring public authorities themselves carry out their duties and do not exceed their legal powers. Here, the form of public law statutes, mentioned above, rarely ties a public body to supplying a particular standard of service, as a contract may tie a builder, but gives a wide choice of lawful behaviour.

Even where legislation lays a duty on a public authority, there may be no corresponding right of individual action. For example, under the Education Act 1996, local education authorities are under a duty to ensure that there are sufficient schools, in numbers, character and equipment, for providing educational opportunities for all pupils in their area. However, nobody can sue the authority if the schools are overcrowded or badly equipped. The only remedy is to complain to the Secretary of State, who can make orders if satisfied that the authority is in default of their duties. The mechanism for controlling standards of public bodies is generally by way of political accountability to the electorate or ministers rather than the legal process.

Some parts of public law do create individual rights and permit individual enforcement. In social security legislation, for example, qualified claimants have a right to certain benefits and may appeal against decisions of benefit to a tribunal. There is a procedure, special to public law, called "judicial review of administrative action" (often referred to simply as *judicial review*), whereby an individual may go to the High Court alleging unlawful behaviour on the part of a public body. However, in order to go to court, the individual must show "sufficient interest" in the issue in question (this being legally defined) and the court has a discretion whether to hear the case or grant a remedy. This is quite different from proceedings in private law, where a plaintiff does not need the court's permission for the case to be heard but has a right to a hearing if a recognised cause of action is asserted and also a right to a remedy of some kind if successful.

Criminal Law and Civil Law

Legal consequences in questions 1–3:

1. Norman's actions may give rise to both criminal and civil proceedings. He may be prosecuted for drink driving and related road traffic offences and, if convicted, will have a criminal record. All road traffic offences, including parking offences, are just as much part of the criminal law as murder is. He may also be sued by the woman or child who would wish to recover damages for the personal injuries they have suffered. Such an action would be a civil action. The same set of facts may give rise to both criminal and civil liability.
2. Sue has committed no criminal offence. Neither the unborn child nor Richard have any right of civil action for any harm they may consider Sue has done to them.
3. Robert has not committed any criminal offence. He is in no different a position in law to the person who has no money. Usha will be able to commence civil proceedings against him. She will be able to sue him for breach of contract. Robert's wealth makes it more likely that Usha will consider it worth suing him as she is more likely to be able to recover any damages. However she will also have to remember that Robert will, if he wishes be able to hire the best lawyers so as to delay Usha's inevitable court victory.

3   Law in action/law in books

Introduction

This chapter is about the different kinds of questions that arise when studying law and the different techniques you need when studying them. You might think that studying law is purely a matter of learning a large number of legal rules. If this were the case only one kind of question would ever arise—what is the content of any particular legal rule? However, simply learning a large number of legal rules is not always a very useful way of learning about law. Learning the rules is like memorising the answers to a set of sums. It is of no help when the sums change. If all you do is learn a set of legal rules, when the rules change, when the law is altered, you are back where you started. At the very least, to use your legal knowledge, you also need to know how to find legal rules and how to find out if they have been changed. Thus, to the question "What is the content of the legal rule?" are added questions about how to find them.

Not everyone interested in law is interested in questions about the content of legal rules. For example, we might ask whether it is ever right to disobey the law. This is a question of ethics that might, in part, relate to the content of a legal rule but is much more about the nature of moral judgement. Equally questions about how the legal system works in practice are only partially concerned with the content of legal rules. Legal rules are about what should happen. Questions about practice are concerned with what does happen.

The various questions above are not merely different questions; they are different kinds of questions. Because they are questions about different things and because the different questions demand different techniques to answer them, they are often put into separate categories. The terms for these categories vary. Some terms are more precise than others. We have taken one commonly drawn distinction, that between the law in action and the law in books, as the title for this chapter. This is because the distinction is a very basic one that can be applied to most areas of law. The law in action is that which actually happens in the legal system and is concerned with people's behaviour. The law in books is the system of legal rules that can be deduced from reading cases and statutes. A question about how defendants are treated in court is a question about the law in action. A question about the definition of theft in English law is a question about the law in books.

The distinction between the law in action and the law in books is both easy to see and useful to use but it also has its limitations. Some questions about law seem to fit into neither category. For example, is our earlier question about disobedience to law a question about the law in action or the law in books? Information about that actually happens in the legal system will only tell us what people do, not whether their action is morally correct. Equally, being told what the legal rule says is of little help in helping us assess whether we are correct to obey it or not. The question does not appear to fall into either category.

The distinction between the law in action and the law in books is broad but crude. More sophisticated categories provide narrower, more precise distinctions. Thus questions about the nature of law that can include whether or not one has a duty to obey it can be grouped together under the title the philosophy of law or jurisprudence. Such categories are not firmly fixed and may be defined by different people in different ways. Thus some people would use the term the sociology of law to refer to all questions about the operation of the legal system in practice. Others would distinguish between questions about the relationship between law and other social forces and questions about how effective a legal rule is. They would see the first kind of question as falling within the sociology of law and the second as coming under the heading socio-legal studies. It is more important to be able to identify the different kinds of questions than give them the labels.

Different questions mean different answers

Knowing that there are different kinds of questions asked when studying law is of intellectual interest but does it have any further significance? What happens if you fail properly to identify the kind of question that you are asking? We can answer these questions by looking at one way in which different kinds of questions are commonly confused.

For many years it was assumed that legal rules that laid down what should happen were an accurate guide to what actually happened. The law in action was thought to be a reflection of the law in books. It was accepted that there were divergencies but these were thought to be on a small scale and of no importance. However, academics have now shown that there is often a very great difference between legal rules and the practice in the legal system. One example of this can be seen in the area of criminal justice, when people are arrested and taken to the police station for questioning.

The Police and Criminal Evidence Act 1984 (generally referred to as "PACE") lays down a large number of rules relating to the treatment of suspects who are detained in police stations. The purpose of these rules is to try and provide a balance between providing safeguards for the person who is being questioned and enabling the police to carry out a thorough investigation. One of the rules that PACE contains is that the suspect must be told of his/her right to seek legal advice. However, researchers have found that most people do not receive legal advice at the police station. This can happen because many suspects do not appreciate how important it is to have legal advice at an early stage in criminal investigations. However, another significant reason influencing suspects in their decision not to seek legal advice is that the police may use a number of "ploys" to discourage suspects from taking advice, including minimising the significance of what is happening by saying the suspect will only be there for a short time, or emphasising what a long time the detainee will have to wait until their legal adviser arrives. Merely looking at the law in the books could only tell us what is supposed to happen; that suspects are entitled to be told about their right to seek legal advice. It is only when we look at the law in action that we can understand how the law really works in practice; in this case, we come to understand that merely giving a right to people does not mean that they will understand how important it is to exercise that right, nor does giving a right ensure that it will necessarily be implemented in the way it was intended.

The difference between the law in action and the law in books in this area is important for several reasons. First, confusing the different kinds of questions resulted in an inaccurate description. People accepted the wrong kind of material as evidence for their answers, and as a result thought that the law worked in practice in much the same way as the legal rules suggested it should. Secondly, because of that misdescription, those involved in advising others on the law may have given misleading advice. Finally, those involved in considering whether or not the law and legal system are effective and just looked not at the real legal system but, instead, at a shadowy reflection of it.

Which kind of question am I asking?

Somebody has been divorced and you are asked, how will their financial affairs be settled by the courts? Are you being asked what the relevant rules are, or what will actually happen in court, or both? Outside your course of study it may be very difficult to sort out what kind of question you are being asked. For study purposes the task will generally be simpler. The kind of question that you are being asked is likely to be indicated by the nature of your course as a while. The title of your course may give you a clue. A course on "the sociology of law" is unlikely to be much concerned with questions about the content of legal rules. Some kinds of courses are more usually taught with one kind of question in mind than another. For example, courses on "land law" or the "law of contract" are more often concerned with the law in books than the law in action. These kinds of courses are sometimes termed *"black-letter law"* courses. Courses on 'family law' often include a great deal of material that tells us about the law in action. This kind of course is often described as *"socio-legal"*.

Even when it is clear what kind of question your course is generally concerned with problems may still arise. It is not only important to know the kind of question that you are interested in. You must also be able to identify the kind of question that the author of a book or article that you are using is interested in. Are they trying only to analyse the legal rules, the cases and statutes in a particular area of law, or are they also interested in exploring how the law works in practice? If you know the type of answer they are trying to give you will be in a better position to judge the quality of their argument and, thus the value of their work. Even when you have identified the kind of question an author is most interested in you will also have to be careful to see that other kinds of question are not introduced. For example, it is not uncommon to find a book largely devoted to discussion of the content of legal rules also including a few remarks on the value or justice of those rules. There is nothing wrong with this if the author realises that a different kind of question is being addressed and uses the appropriate material to answer it. Unfortunately this is not always so.

Are there really different questions?

There are some people who would argue that it is misleading to distinguish between different questions in the way we have done above. Some would argue that all the distinctions drawn are wrong. Others would argue that only some of them are invalid. Are there really different questions? One argument that might be advanced is about the distinction between the law in action and the law in books. The Court of Appeal has laid down strict rules about when people accused of offences can receive a lesser sentence if they plead guilty (a practice known as plea-bargaining). Research in this area has suggested that these rules are not followed in practice. If we assume that the practice of all courts is not to follow these rules, and if this practice continued for many years, what would it mean to say that the legal rule was that which had been laid down by the Court of Appeal? People would only be affected by what happened in practice that would always be different from that which the legal rules said should happen. Could we really say that the legal rule had any significance? If the legal rule has no significance, then surely all we ought to study is what happens in practice, ignoring questions about the law in books?

Other more complicated forms of the above argument exist. Some people would argue that when a judge makes a decision that decision is influenced by the judge's social background, political views and education. The result of any case is therefore not solely determined by the neutral application of legal rules but by factors personal to the particular judge in the case. If this is so, then what kinds of questions will discussion about the content of legal rules answer? If we are to advise people how to act so as to win cases in court what we need to discuss is not only the content of legal rules but also who the judges are and what their background is. If we want to find out what the law is we have to ask a whole series of questions other than those about ratios or statutes.

In a similar fashion not everyone accepts that questions about the morality of law and questions about the content of law are different. For these people, the very idea of an immoral law is a contradiction in terms. They think that all law must have an irreducible minimum positive moral content. Without that content the "law", in their view, is merely a collection of words that make a command which may be backed by the physical power of the state but do not have the authority of law.

The authors of this book would accept that the distinctions drawn in previous sections are open to question. The relationship between the different questions, if there are different questions, may be more complicated than the simple divisions above. However most books and most courses in law draw the kinds of distinction outlined. At this early stage in your study of law it will be enough if you understand them. Even if later you come to reject all or some of them, you will still find yourself reading material that is based upon them.

Answering questions

This chapter has drawn a distinction between three types of question; those concerned with the nature of law, those concerned with the content of legal rules and those which address the operation of law and legal system in practice. Each type of question has a technique appropriate for answering it.

Questions about the nature of law are those that are most difficult to answer. The questions are basic ones, appearing to be very simple. For example, how is law different from other types of command? What is the difference between a gunman telling me to do something and the state, through law, telling me to do something? Are both simply applications of power or is there something fundamentally different between them? Neither the content of particular legal rules nor the operation of the law in practice provide any answer. Arguments in this area are abstract and philosophical. In advancing and judging such arguments it is necessary to see that all the terms are explained and that the argument is coherent. Arguments used here must also match the world they purport to explain. In practice these simple conditions are very difficult to meet.

The ultimate source for answers to questions about the law in books is the law reports and statutes that have already been discussed in Chapter 1. Only these sources will give you a definitive answer to any question you are asked. You are told how to find these materials in Chapter 4 and how to use them in Chapter 5. In some cases you may not have either the time or the resources to consult original materials. In such instance you can look at some of the various commentaries on the law. These vary in size, depth of coverage and price. Different commentaries serve different purposes. Some are student texts. Others are written for specific professions or occupations. Most cover only a limited area of law. However there are some general guides to the law and some encyclopedias of law. The best encyclopedia of general English law is *Halsbury's Laws of England*. This has a section on almost every area of law. Most good reference libraries will have a copy of this, and your library may also contain some of the other commentaries that are available. All commentaries try to explain legal rules. You should select one suitable to your interests. However, always remember that a commentary is one person's opinion about the law. It may be wrong. You can only be sure what the rule is if you consult the original cases and statutes.

Finding out how the law works in practice is frequently much more difficult than deciding what a legal rule means. It is easy to find opinions about how things work. Almost everybody who has contact with the law, even if only through reading about it in the newspapers, has an opinion on such questions. However, such opinions have little value. At best they are the experience of one person. That experience may be unusual or misinterpreted by that person. What we are trying to understand is how the legal system works, not the anecdotes of one person. Thus, to answer this kind of question, we need to turn to the materials and techniques of the social scientist.

Seeing the law in action

One obvious source of detailed information about the legal system is statistical analyses. "You can prove anything with statistics" is a hostile comment suggesting that nothing at all can be proved with statistics. However, is this so? What use are statistics to anyone studying law?

Information about the number of cases handled by a court shows in specific terms what the court's workload is. Changes from year to year may indicate some effects of changes in the law and practice. Statistics here can be used descriptively to provide a clearer picture than general phrases such as "some", "many" or "a few". Statistical tests can also establish that there is a relationship, a correlation, between different things. For example, the length of a sentence for theft may correlate with the value of the items stolen or the experience of the judge who heard the case. This means that the sentence will be longer if, for example, more items are stolen or the judge is more experienced. Statisticians have produced tests to show whether, given the number of examples you have, there is a strong correlation or not. Where this correlation fits with a theory (sometimes termed a hypothesis) it provides evidence tending to confirm the theory. Such confirmation is important; without it we have little to establish the effect the law has, being forced to rely on personal knowledge of individual instances of its application and having to assume that these have general truth. Empirical study of the operation of law may reveal areas for improvement. It can also confirm that, measured by particular standards, the courts are working well.

If we want to use statistics, where will we get them from? Government departments collect and print a large number of statistics relating to their operations. A comprehensive index to these, the *Guide to Official Statistics*, is published by the Office for National Statistics (ONS). Some of these official statistics provide background information for the study of the operation of law. Thus the ONS publishes details of the size, composition and distribution of the United Kingdom population. This information is essential if one is to be sure that other changes do not merely reflect population changes. The Department for Work and Pensions provides figures for the number of social security claimants and the Department of Health provides figures for the number of children in the care of local authorities. The Home Office produces the annual criminal statistics as well as information about the police forces and immigration. The Department for Constitutional Affairs produces the civil judicial statistics that contain figures for the work of the civil and all appellate courts. Most official statistics are collected from returns filed by local offices of the relevant departments. The content of these is determined by what the department needs to know about its activities and also by what Parliament has asked it to report on. Even minor changes in the collection of official statistics means that it is often impossible to make comparisons over a period of years. The information collected in one year is about something slightly different from that in other years. Moreover, because of the way in which information is collected and the purpose of collecting it, these statistics can only answer a few of the questions about the way the law operates. For example, the judicial statistics list the number of cases brought each year in the County Court, broken down according to the type of claim. They provide little or no information about the applicants, the specific point of law relied on or whether the judgment was successfully enforced.

Official statistics, as a source of information, are limited. They provide information about things of importance to those who collected them. These are not necessarily the things that are important to the researcher. Government departments, the research councils and some private bodies sponsor research into specific areas of law. Small-scale research is often undertaken without sponsorship. Although this research may be based upon official statistics it may involve first collecting the necessary statistics and then deciding what they mean. The researchers must collect the data they need for each project. They have to design the study, that is to select the methods they will use and choose the sample to ensure that they have all the information relevant to their chosen topic. There is a more detailed discussion of some of these issues in Chapter 6, "Reading Research Materials".

The collection of statistics is only one way of describing law and the legal system. Statistics are useful for describing things like numbers of events but are poor for describing things like motivations. If researchers want to find out more about the reasons *why* the law affects people in certain ways, or *how* it affects them, they will have to carry out different types of research. This may involve interviewing people or even directly observing what is happening in the area in which they are interested. In each case the researchers must decide how they can carry out their research so as to ensure that the material they collect is an accurate reflection of the world as a whole.

Socio-legal research has enabled us to understand in a whole range of situations the way in which the law works in practice. It has revealed, for example, how barristers' clerks affect the working lives of barristers, why business-people often prefer to avoid taking their disputes to court, and how the practice of environmental health officers affects the way in which Local Authorities deal with industrial pollution. Socio-legal research offers us the opportunity to extend our knowledge of the law and the legal system far beyond the boundaries of the law in the books, showing us how legal rules are affected by the political, economic and social contexts in which law operates.

Whatever kind of question you are dealing with it is important that *you* decide what the answer is. Merely being able to repeat a passage from a book on legal philosophy, a paragraph from a judgment or the conclusion to a survey is not the same as knowing the answer. If you do not understand the answer you will neither be able to remember nor apply it.

Part 2

4   Finding cases and statutes

In Chapter 1 the importance of cases and statutes as sources of law was explained. This chapter explains how you find reports of cases and copies of statutes and how you make sure that they are up-to-date. As has been explained, these materials are sources of law. From them it is possible to derive the legal rules in which you are interested. Chapter 5 will explain in more detail how this is done.

Finding cases

In the following, the task of discovering case reports will be considered for three different sets of circumstances:

(a) where a well-stocked and supported library is available;
(b) where some research or library facilities are available, but without access to a fully-equipped law library;
(c) with the aid of on-line computerised retrieval facilities.

Most readers will have different facilities available at different times. For example, a reader who has access to a fully-equipped law library can only use it during opening hours. Equally, even if computer facilities are available it may not always be appropriate to use them. It is important that you are aware of the different ways in which to find cases so that you can decide which is the best method to use at any particular time.

Using full law library non-electronic research facilities

The traditional, and still the most comprehensive, form of research in relation to law reports is performed in law libraries containing a wide selection of materials and a variety of support systems, indexes, catalogues, etc. designed to assist the researcher in the task of locating and using particular items. Such libraries are found in academic institutions, such as universities, as well as in professional institutions such as the Inns of Court. In many cases, it is possible to use such libraries even if you are not a member of the institution. What follows in this chapter is an attempt to introduce the reader to the major series of law reports, and to indicate basic methods of locating and checking up-to-date material and of up-dating earlier materials. A helpful guide for those interested in more sophisticated use of the whole range of facilities made available in major law libraries is to be found in *How to Use a Law Library*, by J. Dane and P. Thomas. In particular, that work contains detailed explanations of how to use the various indexes and catalogues available in such libraries, and thus provides a more comprehensive guide on the "mechanics" of locating and using legal materials than is offered here. Law reports go back over 700 years, although most of the case reports you will find in a normal law library have been decided during the last 150 years. Reports are divided into different series. These series do not necessarily reflect any systematic attempt to present the reports of decided cases, (*e.g.* by subject-matter covered), but tend, instead, to indicate the commercial means by which such reports have been made available. Thus, older cases can be found in series which bear the title of the name (or names) of the law reporter(s). Such a series is the nineteenth century series of Barnewall and Alderson (Bar & Ald). (All law reports have abbreviations that are customarily used when discussing them. Whenever a series is first mentioned here its usual abbreviation will be given, in brackets, as above. Appendix II to this book is a list of useful abbreviations, including those to the main law reports.) The only necessary coherence these cases have is that the reporter thought it was worthwhile to print them. The range and variety of these older cases is enormous, although some help has now been provided to modern legal researchers with some of the old series reprinted in a new collection under the title of *The English Reports* (E.R.). In 1865, the Incorporated Council of Law Reporting introduced *The Law Reports*, a series that was divided according to the different courts of the day. The Council has continued these reports though the current divisions of the reports are different. Today one can find the following divisions:

(a) Appeal Cases (A.C.) - reports of cases in the Court of Appeal, the House of Lords and the Privy Council;
(b) Chancery Division (Ch.) - report of cases in the Chancery Division of the High Court and cases appealed from there to the Court of Appeal;
(c) Queen's Bench (Q.B.) - reports of cases in the Queen's Bench Division of the High Court and cases appealed from there to the Court of Appeal;
(d) Family Division (Fam.) - reports of cases in the Family Division of the High Court and cases appealed from there to the Court of Appeal. (Until 1972 the Family Division was the Probate, Divorce and Admiralty Division (P.).)

This series is the closest to an "official" series of case reports. If a case is reported in several different series and there is a discrepancy between the different reports it is *The Law Reports* that should normally be followed. There is, nowadays, a wide range of privately-published law reports. Most of these series concentrate upon a particular area of legal developments, (*e.g.* the law relating to industrial relations, or the law concerning road traffic). However, there are two series that publish cases dealing with decisions affecting a wide range of legal issues. These general series, with which most students of law will quickly become familiar, are the *Weekly Law Reports* (W.L.R.) and the *All England Law Reports* (All E.R.). Each of the series above reports fully any case contained in its volumes. There are, in addition, some sources that provide a short summary of, or extracts from, judgments given. In addition to these general series, it is possible to find short reports of case developments in a variety of sources. The most up-to-date of these sources are those newspapers that print law reports. Most of the quality daily newspapers contain law reports as well as news items on matters of legal interest. *The Times* has contained such reports for the longest time and is regarded as being the most authoritative source of such reports. Case-note sections published in legal periodicals such as the *New Law Journal* (N.L.J.) or the *Solicitors' Journal* (S.J. or Sol. Jo.), are also a good source of such summaries. There have always been specialist series of reports concerned either with one area of law or one type of occupation. In recent years, the numbers of such series has increased. If your interest is not in law as a whole but in particular areas of law, one of these series of reports may be a valuable tool. Indeed, sometimes such series are the only source for a report of a particular case. However, such series should be used with caution. First, these reports may not be as accurate as the series discussed above. Secondly, they represent not reports of the law but reports of such law as the publishers of the series think important. Their greater selectivity may be useful in giving you a guide as to what is important, but dangerous if you think cases not reported in the series must be irrelevant. Helpful lists of such reports can be found in law dictionaries.

Using law reports

Every case which is reported in a series of law reports can be referred to by way of the names of the parties concerned in the action. Thus, where a court action is brought by somebody called Harriman in dispute with somebody called Martin, the case can be referred to as *Harriman v Martin*. However referring to a case in this way is of limited usefulness. The reference does not tell the reader the date of the case nor does it indicate the series of reports in which it is found. It does not even tell us to which case involving a Harriman and a Martin the reader is being referred. There may be several. Thus, in addition to its name, each reported case possesses a unique reference indicator. This normally includes (although not always in the same order):

1. a reference to the title of the series of law reports in which the report is to be found;
2. a date (year) reference. Some series have a volume number for each year. Where the date reference tells you the year in which the case was decided the date is normally enclosed in square brackets;
3. a reference to the volume number (if there is more than one volume of the particular law reports series in the year concerned);
4. a reference to the page or paragraph number at which the report of the case may be located.

If the case of *Harriman v Martin* is reported in the first volume of the *Weekly Law Reports* for 1962, at page 739, the reference would be [1962] 1 W.L.R. 739. This is sometimes called the citation for the case. Knowing this reference or citation, it is possible to go directly to the shelves of the law library which house the volumes containing that reference and to turn directly to the report of the case.

Increasingly people are turning to the web as a source of law reports. This has led the House of Lords, the Court of Appeal, the High Court and the Immigration Appeal Tribunal to create a system of *neutral citation*. Under this system, which first began in 2001 for the Court of Appeal, 2002 for the High Court and 2003 for the Immigration Appeal Tribunal, the court or tribunal has its own abbreviation and each case is given a unique official number by the courts. Within judgments, each paragraph has its own number.

An Immigration Appeal Tribunal reference would look like this:

[2003] UKIAT 1

The references for the High Court look like this:

Chancery Division	[2003] EWHC 123(Ch)
Patents Court	[2003] EWHC 124(Pat)
Queen's Bench	[2003] EWHC 125(QB)
Administrative Court	[2003] EWHC 126(Admin)
Commercial Court	[2003] EWHC 127(Comm)
Admiralty Court	[2003] EWHC 128(Admlty)
Technology and Construction Court	[2003] EWHC 129(TCC)
Family Division	[2003] EWHC 130(Fam)

References for the Court of Appeal look like this:

Court of Appeal (Civil)	[2003] EWCA Civ 1
Court of Appeal (Criminal)	[2003] EWCA Crim 1

References to the House of Lords look like this:

House of Lords	[2003] UKHL 1

Where it is necessary to refer to a precise passage in a judgment by using a paragraph number the paragraph number is put in square brackets. Where a neutral citation is available it is put first before the more traditional citation to a printed hardcopy version of the judgment.

If you know only the names of the parties in the case, you will need first to ascertain the specific reference. Although it would be possible to search the indexes for each individual series of law reports for the names of a case, this would be an inefficient and time-consuming approach. Normally, therefore, recourse is had to a general reference manual, which is known as a case citator. Such a case citator is provided with the commercial reference service known as *Current Law*. Other means are also available for locating the references of specific cases but *Current Law* is that which is most readily available. What follows is a brief description of the *Current Law* case citator. The *Current Law* system of citations for cases works through a combination of three separate reference items:

1. three hard-bound citators covering the periods 1947–1976, 1977–1997 and 1998–2001;
2. a laminated volume for 2002 and 2003;
3. "Monthly Parts," which are issued regularly in pamphlet form, for the current year. These are subsequently replaced by a bound volume for the year.

The importance of using all three items to complement one another will appear when we consider the problem of locating up-to-date references (see below). Entries in the *Current Law Case Citator* are listed by title of case, arranged alphabetically. Thus, to find the law reports reference to the case of *Harriman v Martin* you need to turn to the alphabetical heading under "Harriman".

This reads: *Harriman v Martin* [1962] 1 W.L.R. 739; 106 S.J. 507; [1962] 1 All E.R. 225, CA . . . Digested 61/1249: Referred to, 72/2355.

From this information, we discover not only the law report's reference to the first volume of the *Weekly Law Reports* for 1962, at page 739, but also that there are reports of the same case in:

106 S.J. 507 *i.e.* the 106th volume of the *Solicitors' Journal* at page 507 and:
[1962] 1 All E.R. 225 *i.e.* the first volume of the *All England Reports* for 1962 at page 225.

We are also told that the court that delivered the decision reported at those locations was:

CA, *i.e.* the Court of Appeal.

Next, we are told that a "digest" (a brief summary) of the case has been included in a companion volume to the *Current Law Case Citator* at:

62/1249, *i.e.* in the companion year volume of *Current Law* for 1962 at paragraph 1249.

Finally, we are told that the case was "referred to" (in another case) and that that case is to be found at:

72/2355, *i.e.* in the companion year volume of *Current Law* for 1972 at paragraph 2355.

It now only remains to locate one of these volumes in the law library, and to turn to the appropriate page for a report on the case of *Harriman v Martin*. The above is not only a method for finding the reference to a case. If you already have a reference to a case, but you find that volume already in use in the library, you can use the method above to find an alternative citation for the case.

Up-dating cases

It is not enough to know merely what was said in a particular case in order to know the importance that should be attached to that case. It is also necessary to know whether such an earlier case has been used or referred to subsequently by the judges, or, indeed, whether it has been expressly approved or disapproved of by a later court. If a case is approved by a court that is further up the hierarchy of courts than the court originally giving judgment (and that approval is part of the ratio of that later case) then the case will take on the status of the later decision. Thus a decision of the High Court approved by the Court of Appeal will take on the status of the Court of Appeal. Even if the approval forms part of the *obiter* within the later judgment this will be significant, indicating the way in which the court is likely to give judgment once the matter becomes central in a decision at that level. Disapproval of a case will be important in a similar fashion. Such information can be discovered by using the *Current Law Case Citator*. We can regard a case as reliable (or, at least, not unreliable) where we are informed that it has been "referred to", "considered", "explained", "followed", "approved" or "applied". On the other hand, considerable care must be taken with a case that has been "distinguished", while cases that have been "disapproved" or "overruled" are unlikely to prove reliable for future purposes.

Example

1. **From the *Current Case Citator* for 1977–97**
   Fort Sterling Ltd v South Atlantic Cargo Shipping NVC (The Finrose) [1994] 1 Lloyd's Rep. 559, QBD..*Digested* 95/**4504**

   This tells us the location of the report of the case as explained above. It also that the case was decided in the QBD (*i.e.* the Queen's Bench Division) and we are told that there is a digest of the case in the *Current Law Year Book* for 1995 at para. 4504.

2. **From the *Current Case Citator* for 1998–2001**
   Fort Sterling Ltd v South Atlantic Cargo Shipping NVC (The Finrose) [1994] 1 Lloyd's Rep. 559, QBD..*Digested* 95/**4504**. *Applied, 00/244; Considered 00/569.*

   This gives us both the information that we had before and also tells us that the case has been applied in another case and considered in yet another case. In both instances we are given the reference to the appropriate Current Law Year Book that will enable us to look these two new cases up. If we look up the 2000 Year Book we find that the case at paragraph 244 is

   Thyssen Inc v Calypso Shipping Corp SA [2000] 2 All E.R. (Comm) 97 David Steel J. QBD (Comm Ct)

   This gives us the name of the case that applied *Fort Sterling Ltd v South Atlantic Cargo Shipping NVC (The Finrose)*, a reference to the law report where we can find the case reported (note that All E.R. (Comm) mentioned here is a different series of law reports to the more common All E.R. that we have dicussed elsewhere in this book), the name of the judge in the case and the court where it was heard, the Commercial Court in the Queen's Bench Division. The paragraph also gives a short description of the judgment. Looking up paragraph 569 gives up similar information about *Bua International Ltd v Hai Hing Shipping Co Ltd*.

   Looking up year volumes and monthly parts for 2002, 2003, 2004 and 2005 gives us no further reference to *Fort Sterling Ltd v South Atlantic Cargo Shipping NVC (The Finrose)* so we now have a complete history of the case.

Using limited library facilities

The problems of finding and using cases and law reports where limited resources are available are significant. Clearly, it will not be possible to find reports of all the cases that you may need, since the available reports may only be found in series which are not at your disposal. By the same token, you may not have access to sufficiently comprehensive reference manuals, such as a case law citator or similar. You may have access to one of the general series of law reports. This will often be a set of *All England Law Reports*. Many public reference libraries possess a set of these law reports. If this is the case, some searching for cases can be done using the index contained in those volumes, though this will, of course, be time consuming. Alternatively, if you are concerned only with a limited specialist area you may have access to a specialised series of law reports. Whatever your source of available material, however, it is of paramount importance that you familiarise yourself with the specific indexing and cross-referencing system adopted by that source. If you do this, you will be able to use the material at your disposal, limited though it may be by comparison with the resources of a fully-equipped and supported law library, in the most efficient manner. It will also be important to discover whether you can obtain access to some means for updating the material contained in your available sources. The use of a citator, as explained above, is clearly of major benefit, for the consolidation of information within one reference item avoids the necessity of searching through a range of separate volumes and series. Amongst possible sources of updated information might be the general legal periodicals, such as the *New Law Journal* or the *Solicitors Journal* (both of which have been referred to above). Many public libraries subscribe to one of these, or to other relevant periodicals. Where your needs related to a specific area, the periodicals available in relation to that area may be of assistance in obtaining up-to-date information. Thus, for example, many human resource management journals contain information about cases decided by the courts in relation to employment law. All of these will probably refer you to sources of information that you do not have but they will also enable you to make the most efficient use of those sources that are available. A further common source of information will be text-books on the subject about which you are seeking information. The important rule here is to check that you have access to the latest possible edition of the book, and to bear in mind the possibility that case-law developments may have overtaken the legal position as it was stated at the time of writing of the book. Most books dealing with the law will contain a statement in the "Foreword" stating the date on which the information given in the book is said to be current. In some instances, you may have access to a case-book. This term is something of a misnomer since case-books frequently contain not just cases but also statutes and comments on the law. Such books are generally concerned with a specific topic, for example "contract law", and contain edited material relevant to the area. These books can be a very useful source where you have access only to limited library facilities. However, they suffer from several deficiencies. First, the reader relies on the editor of the volume to select the most appropriate material. There is no way in which the quality of the work can be checked. Secondly, the material presented may only be given in part. Again, the reader must trust that the editor has not given misleading extracts. Finally, the reader has no means of up-dating the material. In some areas of law encyclopedias are produced. These are similar to case-books, although they are generally more detailed. Publishers of this kind of work often supply an up-dating service. Increasingly, encyclopedias are produced in a loose-leaf form and the reader will substitute new pages as supplements are issued.

Using electronic retrieval facilities

To complete this section on finding and using reports of cases, mention must be made of the important and fast-developing range of computerised information retrieval systems.

"On-line" Services

There are two major, commercially marketed, legal data-bases which are widely used in universities and by practitioners, LEXIS and WESTLAW. Both databases cover a number of different jurisdictions and contain not just cases but also legislation and law journals. To use either of these systems effectively requires some training in the way that material is organised and the methods used to search them.

In general both LEXIS and WESTLAW contain the full text of judgments though the format is somewhat different to that in traditional printed law reports. As well as providing access to a large collection of published legal material LEXIS and WESTLAW also include unreported cases *i.e.* cases that have been decided but which have not yet been published in hard-copy form and in some cases never will be published in that form.

Searching for a case using electronic retrieval systems is generally done using key words. The user asks whether a specific term or set of words is to be found in the data-base. The user is then given a list of the cases that contain the item that is being searched for and can then look at the cases that have been found. The user will find that on the one hand if they use only very general terms for their search they will be given a very large list of cases to look at, most of which they will find irrelevant to their needs. If on the other hand they use a very precise term the list provided will not contain any case that is relevant but which uses slightly different terminology in its judgment. The skill in using databases like LEXIS and WESTLAW lies in steering a course between these two extremes.

Databases such as LEXIS and WESTLAW are highly effective ways of finding cases, finding citations for cases and for seeing if a case has been referred to in any other judgment.

Cases on the Net

There are many internet sites which discuss law or legal issues or provide material about law. A number of these provide free access to legal materials.

A wide range of material relating to law is available on the British Government's web site: *www.open.gov.uk*

This is arranged by department and organisation. All decisions of the Judicial Committee of the House of Lords made since 1996 are published free on the internet on the day the judgment is given. They can be found at:

www.parliament.the-stationery-office.co.uk

Selected judgments from the Court of Appeal and the High Court are to be found at: www.courtservice.gov.uk

Both *The Times* and the *Law Society Gazette* provide their law reports on their free web-sites:

www.the-times.co.uk

www.lawgazette.co.uk

Cases of the European Court of Human Rights are available on its website:

www.echr.coe.int

Finding and up-dating statutes

Statutes are published individually but law libraries and some public libraries have bound collections that include all the statutes for a particular year. Statutes passed since 1988 are available on the internet at:

http://www.hmso.gov.uk/legislation/about_legislation.htm

With statutes there are three main problems. Is the statute in force? Has the statute been repealed by Parliament, (*i.e.* replaced by some other statute)? Has the statute been amended by Parliament, (*i.e.* had part of its contents altered by Parliament)? Starting with a provision in an Act of Parliament it is necessary to use one of the "citator" systems in order to discover the most changes (if any) that have affected that provision. The following example shows how to update a relatively recent statutory provision using the *Current Law Legislation Citator*.

Example

Let us take the Children Act 1989 s.8(4). In its original form this provision was set out as follows:

Residence, contact and other orders with respect to children

8- (1) ...

(2) ...

(3) ...

(4) The enactments are-

(a) Parts I, II and IV of this Act;

(b) the Matrimonial Causes Act 1973;

(c) the Domestic Violence and Matrimonial Proceedings Act 1976;

(d) the Adoption Act 1976;

(e) the Domestic Proceedings and Magistrates' Court Act 1978;

(f) sections 1 and 9 of the Matrimonial Homes Act 1983;

(g) Part III of the Matrimonial and family Proceedings Act 1984.

If we assume that in January 2004 we want to discover whether there have been changes to the wording of section 8(4) it is first necessary to turn to the volume of the *Current Law Legislation Citator* that covers the period following the enactment of the Children Act 1989. This is the volume for 1989–1995.

The *Current Law Legislation Citator* is arranged in chronological order by year and by chapter number for each Act. Chapter numbers are fully explained at page 57. For the Children Act 1989 this is Chapter 41. We now need to look for our provision, section 8(4). The entry gives us details of many cases but makes no reference to any amendments. Our search must be continued in later volumes.

In the *Current Law Legislation Citator* for 1996–1999 there are the following entries:

s.8, amended: 1996 c.27 Sch. 8 para. 41, Sch. 8 para. 60, 1998 c. 37 s.119. Sch. 8 para. 68
s.8, repealed (in part): 1996 c. 27 Sch. 10

We now know that the section was amended by Schedule 8 of the statute whose reference is 1996 Chapter 27 and also by the statute whose reference is 1998 Chapter 37. It was also repealed in part by Schedule 10 of the statute whose reference is 1996 Chapter 27.

We now need to continue our search beyond 1999 by checking the more recent volumes of the *Current Law Legislation Citator* for 2000–2001, 2002 and that for 2003. There are no further references to section 8 in those volumes.

We can now look up the statutes that we have found and see what changes have been made section 8(4).

How to use encyclopedias

Encyclopedias are not a source of law (although they may contain sources of law). Cases and statutes are sources of law. They are what will be used when judges are deciding what the outcome of a case is to be. However, for some people encyclopedias will be the only material they have available. Thus it is important to consider how they can be used most effectively. Different examples of encyclopedias vary in form and content. They do not all contain the same kind of material nor are they ordered in the same way. Therefore it is not possible to give a series of rules saying how encyclopedias should be used. What follows are points that a reader should consider when first using any encyclopedia. The first thing to look at is the kind of material that the encyclopedia contains. One advantage of an encyclopedia can be that it brings together a wide variety of material about particular subject matter. Thus, you may find the encyclopedia which you are reading contains all the statutes in a particular area, all the statutory instruments, government circulars and other non-statutory material, references to relevant cases (with some description of their contents) together with some discussion of the application of legal rules in the area. On the other hand the encyclopedia may contain only some of the material or may extract some of it. Thus, for example, instead of having all of a statute you may find that you have only parts of it. Even if the encyclopedia claims to be fully comprehensive, remember that it is no more than a claim. The editors of the encyclopedia may feel that they have included all relevant statutes; others may disagree with them. It is always as important to be aware of what you do not know as what you do know. Relying on an encyclopedia means that there may be gaps in your knowledge of the particular area of law. However, you may feel it worth relying on the encyclopedia because it is the only source available. Equally, you may find it quicker to use an encyclopedia and consider the advantage of speedy access more important than any element of doubt in your knowledge of the area. Most encyclopedias extract at least some of the material that they cover. That is to say that they contain extracts of a statute, statutory instrument, or whatever, rather than the whole. Here the problem is that, in extracting their material, the editors of the encyclopedia limit your knowledge of the law. You rely on them to extract that which is relevant and cannot check the matter for yourself. As a source of law, the less comprehensive an encyclopedia is the less useful it will be. However, the more comprehensive an encyclopedia is the slower it may be to use. Before using the encyclopedia you need to consider the kind of question that you are trying to answer. If the question is a very broad and general one about the framework of some area of law you may find an encyclopedia with less detail easier to use. However, if you are trying to answer a very detailed point, perhaps applying the law to a very precise factual situation, you need the most comprehensive encyclopedia that you can find. Most encyclopedias, and increasingly many other books about law, are now issued in loose-leaf form. This means that the publisher issues supplements to the encyclopedia on a regular basis. These supplements, which contain descriptions of changes in the law, are then substituted for the pages that discuss the out-of-date law. The advantage of the loose-leaf form over ordinary books is that it means the encyclopedia is more likely to be accurate. When using loose-leaf encyclopedias before looking up the point of law that interests you always see when it was last up-dated. You will usually find a page at the front of the first volume of the encyclopedia that tells you when it was last up-dated. The technique for finding out about points of law in an encyclopedia will vary depending upon the encyclopedia being used. Some are organised according to different areas of law within the subject of the encyclopedia. Others have different volumes for different kinds of material; one volume for statutes, one for discussion of the law and so forth. Most will have both indexes and detailed contents pages. Most encyclopedias have a discussion of how they should be used at the beginning of their first volume. Always consult this when first using an encyclopedia.

Finding and using material on the law of the European Communities, the European Union, and the European Economic Area

All basic material in relation to the European Communities, the European Union, and the European Economic Area is published in English. However, some material is not made available in all of the official languages of the European Communities immediately. What is said here refers specifically to English language versions of such material. *The Official Journal of the European Communities* is the authoritative voice of the European Communities, and is used to publish daily information. The Official Journal (the O.J.) is divided into two major parts (the L and C series). There are also separately published notices of recruitment, notices and public contracts and the like, which are published in a Supplement and in Annexes. Twice a year the O.J. issues a Directory of Community legislation in force and other acts of the Community institutions.

Legislation

The L series (Legislation) contains the text of Community legislation. The series is arranged by Volume, starting in 1958, and by issue number sequentially throughout the issue year. Thus, the text of Council Directive 95/45/EC of 22 September 1994 on the establishment of a European Works Council or a procedure in Community-scale undertakings and Community-scale groups of under takings for the purposes of informing and consulting employees is to be found in the Official Journal of September 30, 1994.

  The Volume number for 1994 is Volume 37
  The issue number of the OJ L series for 30 September 1994 is L 254
  The text of the Directive is set out on page 64 and thus the page reference is p.64
  The official reference for the Directive will be OJ No L 254, 30.9.1994, p.64

Information and notices

The C series (Information and Notices) contains, amongst a host of other items, key extracts ("the operative part") from judgments of the Court of Justice of the European Communities (the ECJ, sitting in Luxembourg) and the Court of First Instance (which also sits in Luxembourg). Where the language of the particular court being reported is not English, the C series will include a "provisional translation": the definitive translation being found in the separately published Reports of Cases before the Court. There is also brief coverage of actions brought before the ECJ by Member States against the Council of the European Communities, as well as questions referred to the ECJ by national courts of Member States. Also, to be found in the C series will be Preparatory Acts in the course of being made into legislation by the European Communities. Thus, for example, the Official Journal for February 19, 1994 contains the text of an Opinion delivered by the Economic and Social Committee on a proposal for a Council Regulation on substances that deplete the ozone layer.

  The Volume Number for 1994 is Volume 37
  The issue of the OJ C series for 19 February 1994 is C 52
  The text of the proposed Decision is item 3 in issue C 52, and so the reference is 03
  The full reference for the Opinion is OJ 94/C 52/03.

Other materials

Whilst the *Official Journal* is the best official source of information about Community law it should be noted that a wide range of documentation does not find its way into the *Official Journal* and other sources may have to be considered for those wanting a comprehensive list of European materials—in particular, mention should be made of so-called "COM" documents, which often contain important proposals for future legislation. These are issued by the Commission with a "rolling" numerical reference by sequence of publication during a particular year. Consequently, there is no systematic numbering of such "COM Docs" a matter which frequently gives rise to criticism about the accessibility of important documentation in the legislative field. By way of example, an important recent Communication concerning the application of the Agreement on social policy, presented by the Commission to the Council and to the European Parliament on December 14, 1993, is simply designated:

COM(93) 600 final

Various other series, apart from the "COM" series, are also to be found in relation to a range of spheres of activity within the European Union. Judgments of the European Court of Justice are reported in two series of law reports. One series is that "formally" published by the European Union itself the *European Court Reports* (E.C.R.). The other series is the privately produced *Common Market Law Reports* (C.M.L.R.). Both can be found in the normal manner. In addition to these specialised law reports series, an increasing number of judgments delivered by the European Court of Justice are now reported as a normal part of general law report series.

European Union materials on the internet

The official internet site of the European Union is found at:

http://www.europa.eu.int

From here it is possible to access all the institutions of the European Union in any of the official languages of the Union.

European Union legislation transposed in to United Kingdom law

Where European Union legislation has been transposed into United Kingdom law by means of Statutory Instruments (SIs), it is now possible to discover the relevant references by using Appendix 1 of the *Current Law Statutory Instrument Citator*.

5 Reading cases and statutes

This chapter will explain how you should use the primary sources for legal rules, cases and statutes. You will find a specimen case report and a specimen statute in each section. In addition, there are further examples of case reports in the exercise section of this book (Cases I and II). Skill in the use of the techniques described here can only be acquired with practice. For this reason the exercises in the book enable you to build a range of experience in handling the material contained in cases and statutes.

Reading a case

The contents of law reports are explained here so that you can start to read cases, understand the law which they contain, and make useful notes about them. You will find the court structure, and how cases are decided, explained in Chapter 1. You will find a copy of a case, *R. v Jackson*, on pp. 46–48. All specific references in this section will be to that case. The copy is taken from the *All England Law Reports,* which are the most commonly available law reports. However, if you have access to other kinds of law reports you will find that they look very much the same as the *All England Law Reports.* By way of example, in the exercises section of this book there are also to be found law reports taken both from the Court Service internet site (in transcript form) and from a law reports series known as the *Industrial Cases Reports.* The techniques discussed here will be just as useful in reading other series of law reports and court transcripts. The different series of law reports and their use has been explained in Chapter 4.

The case is the criminal law case of *R. v Jackson.* Lawyers pronounce this "Regina (or "The Queen" or "King", or "The Crown") against Terry". Most criminal cases are written like this. In civil cases, the names of the parties are usually given, as in *Donoghue v Stevenson*, the case being pronounced "Donoghue and Stevenson".

R v Jackson

a

COURT OF APPEAL CRIMINAL DIVISION
ROSE L.J., BUTTERFIELD AND RICHARDS JJ
28 APRIL, 1998

Criminal law—Appeal—Leave to appeal—Practice—Single judge granting leave on b
some grounds but refusing leave on others—Need for leave of full court to pursue
grounds in respect of which leave refused.

Where, on an application for leave to appeal to the Court of Appeal, Criminal
Division, the single judge grants leave on some grounds but specifically refuses leave
on others, counsel for the appellant must obtain the leave of the full court if he c
wishes to pursue the grounds in respect of which leave has been refused (see
p. 574g. post).

Notes
For appeal against conviction or sentence following trial on indictment, see 11(2) d
Halsbury's Laws (4th edn reissue) paras 1352, 1355.

Cases referred to in judgment
R v Bloomfield [1997] 1 Cr App R 135, CA.
R v Chalkley, R v Jeffries [1998] 2 All ER 155, [1998] QB 848, [19983] WLR 146, CA.

e

Appeal against conviction
Stephen Shaun Jackson appealed with leave of the single judge against his
conviction on 25 July 1995 in the Crown Court at Croydon before Judge Crush
and a jury of theft. The facts are set out in the judgment of the court.

Marc Willers (assigned by the *Registrar of Criminal Appeals*) for the appellant.   f
Hugh Davies (instructed by the *Crown Prosecution Service*, Croydon) for the Crown.

ROSE LJ delivered the following judgment of the court. On 25 July 1997 in the
Crown Court at Croydon, this appellant was convicted by the jury of theft, on the
first count in the indictment. He was acquitted of charges of false accounting on
counts 2, 3 and 4. The trial was a retrial, the jury on an earlier occasion having g
acquitted in relation to certain counts on the then indictment, but failed to agree
in relation to the counts upon which the second jury adjudicated. He appeals
against his conviction by leave of the single judge, which was granted in relation
to the first of the two matters which Mr Willers, on behalf of the appellant, seeks
to canvass before this court.   h
    For the purposes of this appeal, the facts can be briefly stated. The appellant
was the proprietor of a minicab firm. Insurance brokers, Thompson Heath &
Bond (South East) Ltd (to whom we shall refer as 'THB') devised a scheme to
enable minicab drivers to pay for their motor insurance by instalments. That
scheme was underwritten by others.   j
    The scheme allowed the premiums to be collected from the minicab drivers on
a weekly basis, and passed on to THB each month. THB then paid the
underwriters.
    It was the Crown's case against the appellant that, while he acted as agent for
THB, to collect weekly premiums from the drivers, between February 1991 and
March 1994, he failed to declare to THB the full amount that he had collected,

a   and that he kept a sum of money, in the region of £100,000, for himself and spent much of it on luxury items for his own benefit.

While he was acting in this way, the appellant, it was common ground, devised a form called a Bank 1 form, on which to record payments made by him to THB. At the original trial, the judge had ordered disclosure of Bank 1 forms by the prosecution but, save for one example of such a form, which was in the *b*   appellant's possession at the time of the first trial, no such disclosure had been made. Between the first trial and the retrial, however, those documents, which had apparently been in the possession not of the prosecuting authorities but of THB, were disclosed to the defence and were available to them at the time of the retrial.

A submission was made to the trial judge, Judge Crush, by Mr Willers then, as now, appearing for the defendant, that the second trial should be stayed as an *c*   abuse of the process of the court. The ground of that submission was that it would not be fair to try the appellant a second time, because the Bank 1 forms had not been available during the first trial and, if they had been, the first jury might have acquitted. The learned judge rejected that submission. That rejection forms the ground of appeal in relation to which the single judge gave leave and which Mr *d*   Willers has placed in the forefront of his argument in this court.

Mr Willers accepts that, although the judge at the first trial ordered disdosure and no disclosure took place, that was because the documents had simply not at that stage been found, although they were in the possession of THB.

Mr Willers did not, during the course of the first trial, make any further application, non-disclosure not having been made, either for the jury to be *e*   discharged, or otherwise.

Mr Willers does not suggest that, at the first trial or subsequently, there was any bad faith on the part of the prosecution in relation to the non-disclosure. He submits that, during the cross-examination of Det Sgt James at the second trial, it emerged that he had left with THB the responsibility for looking through the vast *f*   number of documents and passing to the police those which they thought relevant. Although Mr Willers does not suggest that gave rise to bad faith by the officer, he submits that it would have been better had the officer looked through the documents himself.

By the time of the second trial, however, Mr Willers accepts that the defence had all the documentation that they required, including all the Bank 1 forms. But, *g*   he submits, if there was a real possibility of acquittal at the first trial had those forms then been available, it was unfair for the second trial to take place, and the judge should have acceded to the defence application to stay the second trial for abuse of process.

Mr Willers accepted that his submission came to this that, despite the fact that *h*   all the relevant material was before the second jury who convicted, this court, in ruling upon the safety of that conviction, should speculate that the first jury, faced with all the relevant material, might have acquitted; and therefore it was unfair to proceed with the second trial. Mr Willers referred to the decision of this court in *R v Chalkley*, *R v Jeffries* [1998] 2 All E.R. 155, [1998] QB 848. In the course of giving the judgment of the court in that case, Auld LJ commented, adversely, on an *j*   earlier decision of this court, differently constituted, in *R v Bloomfield* [1997] 1 Cr App R 135, which had attracted some criticism from the editors of the third supplement to *Archbold's Criminal Pleading, Evidence and Practice* (1997 edn) para 7–45. We make that comment because the argument originally advanced in skeleton form on behalf of the appellant relied, in part, on this court's decision in *R v Bloomfield*.

On behalf of the Crown, Mr Davies submits that the safety of the appellant's
conviction depends on the evidence at the second trial, which was followed by an
admirably succinct summing up by the learned judge, following a trial which, for
reasons which are not manifest, had lasted a considerable number of weeks.

Mr Davies draws attention, in relation to the safety of that conviction, to a
number of letters written by the appellant after these apparent defalcations came
to light, the first of them, it was common ground, on 21 March 1994 to a man
called Andrew Orchard. That letter was written on the day that the defendant left
this country, for a period of some seven months in the Canary Islands. The
appellant also wrote letters to his sister, Jackie, and to his partner, David. Each of
those letter, in various ways, comprises a series of admissions of criminal mis-
behaviour of present materiality, coupled with expressions of regret. In the course of
the thal, the appellant sought to explain those letters away on the basis of a state of
confused mind when he had written them.

In our judgment, it is wholly impossible to accept Mr Willers' submission either
that the judge was wrong to rule as he did in refusing a stay, or that that refusal
gives rise to any lack of safety in this appellant's conviction. It frequently happens
that new evidence comes to light between the time of a first trial when a jury
disagrees and a second trial. Such evidence may be favourable to the prosecution
or to the defence. But the verdict of the second jury does not become unsafe
because it was unfair for there to be a second trial. Indeed, pursuing Mr Willers'
argument to its logical conclusion, wherever fresh evidence appears between a
first and second trial, it would be unfair, at least if the evidence assisted the
defence, to have a second trial at all. That is a submission which we roundly reject.
The learned judge was, in our view, correct to refuse the stay on the basis of the
application made to him. That refusal, in the light of the overwhelming evidence
before the second jury, cannot, in any event, be regarded as rendering the verdict
of the second jury unsafe.

The second matter which Mr Willers sought to canvass related to a criticism of the
learned judge's direction in relation to dishonesty and the character of the defence
case. It is said that the judge misdirected the jury and failed to put the defence case
adequately in relation to the way in which money was spent on luxuries.

It is fair to say that Mr Willers sought the leave of this court to pursue the
interrelated grounds in relation to that aspect of the case, the learned single judge
having refused leave to argue those grounds. For the avoidance of doubt, where,
in granting leave to appeal on some grounds, the single judge has specifically
refused leave to appeal on other grounds, the leave of this court is required before
counsel may argue those other grounds. As we have said, Mr Willers sought the
leave of this court. We have read the passage in the summing up in the transcript
of which he complains. It is to be noted that, in answer to a question from the
jury, the judge gave a dear direction as to dishonesty, relevant to this case, in
identical terms to that which he had given at the outset of his summing up.

Nothing in the passage of the summing up about which complaint is made, in
our view, renders it arguable that there was any misdirection. Accordingly, as to
that aspect of the case, we refused leave to pursue an appeal on that basis.

For the reasons given, this appeal is dismissed.

Appeal dismissed.

Carlone Stomberg   Barrister.

Underneath the name of the case at "**a**" you will see three pieces of information. First, you are told the court in which the case was heard. In this case, it was the Court of Appeal, Criminal Division. It is important to know which court heard a case because of the doctrine of precedent (see pages 6–8 for an explanation of the doctrine of precedent).

The report then gives the names of the judges who took part in the case. This information is used to help evaluate the decision. Some judges are known to be very experienced in particular areas of law. Their decisions may be given extra weight. Finally, you are told when the case was heard and when the court gave its decision. In the House of Lords this process is called "delivering opinions", but in other courts it is known as "giving judgment".

The material in italics, at "**b**" on the first page of the report, is written by the editor of the report. It indicates the subject-matter of the case and the issue which it concerned. The subject index at the front of each volume of law reports includes a similar entry under the first words.

The next section, at "**c**", is called the *headnote*. It is not part of the case proper, and is prepared by the law reported, not by the judges. The headnote should summarise the case accurately giving references to important parts of the court's opinion or judgment and any cases cited. Because it is written when the case is reported, the headnote may stress or omit elements of the case which are later thought to be important. Therefore, care should be taken when using the headnote.

The notes, at "**d**", direct the reader to appropriate volumes of *Halsbury's Laws of England* and/or *Halsbury's Statutes of England*. *Halsbury's Laws* provides a concise statement of the relevant law, subject by subject, including references to the main cases and statutes. *Halsbury's Statutes* gives the complete text of all statutes together with annotations that explain them. Although law students and others may need to research the law using *Halsbury* it is not necessary to turn to reference works when reading every case. In most instances, the background law will be sufficiently explained by the judge. In our case of *R. v Jackson* the reference is confined to *Halsbury's Laws*.

At "**e**" there is a list of all the cases referred to by the judges. In relation to each case, a list of different places where the case may be found is given. Where counsel have cited additional cases to which the judges did not refer, this will be given in a separate list under the heading "cases also cited".

At "**e**" to "**f**" you will find a full history of the proceedings of the case. This indicates all the courts that have previously considered the case before the present one. The final sentence of this section indicates where a full account of the facts of the case may be found.

Below "**f**" you will find the names of the counsel (the barristers) who appeared in the case. In the case of *R. v Jackson* the barristers on both sides were what are known as "junior counsel". Senior counsel are called "Q.C.s" (Queen's Counsel), or "K.C.s" (King's Counsel) when the monarch is a King.

The appellant was Jackson, while the Crown (in other words the state) was the respondent.

Not all series of law reports have marginal letters as this one does. When they do, these letters can be used to give a precise reference to any part of the case. Thus, the beginning of Lord Justice Rose's judgment is [1999] 1 All E.R. 572g.

Whilst the matters above provide an introduction to the case, the substance is to be found in the judgments. Every law case raises a question or series of questions to be answered by the judge(s). In civil cases, some of these will be questions of fact (in criminal cases these will be answered by the jury). For example, it may be necessary to know at what speed a car was travelling when an accident occurred. In practice, the answers to these factual questions are very important. Once they have been settled, the legal issues in the case may be simple. However, when it comes to the study of law, it is only the legal questions that matter.

For the judge(s) in a case, therefore, there are two clearly distinguishable processes which have to be gone through when hearing the matter and reaching a judgment. First, there is the process of making "findings of fact". Then, in the light of those findings of fact, there is the process of making "findings on the law". The key questions that are posed to the judge(s) in this context are referred to as "the issues in the case".

Lawyers and students of law are concerned primarily not with the outcome of a case but with the reasoning that the judge gave for the conclusion. The reasoning is important because within it will be found the *ratio decidendi* (often referred to simply as "the *ratio*"). The *ratio* is that part of the legal reasoning which is essential for the decision in the case. It is the *ratio* which is binding under the doctrine of precedent and which is thus part of the law. The *ratio* and the reasons for the decision are not necessarily the same thing. Not all of the reasons given for the decision will be essential. In courts where there is more than one judge, each may give a separate judgment (as can be seen from the examples in the exercises section of this book). If they do, each judgment will have its own reasons, and thus its own *ratio*. The judges must agree a conclusion to the case (although they may do so only by majority). However, they do not have to have the same reasons for their decision. If they have different reasons the judgments have different *ratios* and, thus, the case itself may have no ratio. Lawyers will rarely agree that a case has no *ratio* at all.

Finding the *ratio* in a case is crucial. It is also the most difficult part of reading cases, particularly when the case involves several judgments. The *ratio* is the essence of the case and, thus, may not be found simply by quoting from a judgment. Discovering the *ratio* involves skills of interpretation — understanding and explaining what judges meant, how they reached their conclusions — in order to see the common ground. Although the *ratio* is the law, it cannot be divorced entirely from the facts. Facts that are essential for a decision provide the conditions for the operation of the rules and are, thus, part of the rule itself. Deciding which are essential, as opposed to subsidiary, facts takes skill and practice. Lawyers frequently disagree on exactly what the *ratio* to a decision is. Some may view it broadly, seeing the decision as having few conditions but laying down a general rule. Others may take a narrower approach, suggesting that only in very limited circumstances would a decision bind a future court. Subsequent cases often help to clarify what the *ratio* of a previous case is accepted as being.

The editors of a law report write what they consider the *ratio* to be in the headnote. They may be wrong. Even if their interpretation is plausible when they write it, a later case may take a different view. For these reasons, statements of law in the headnote cannot be relied on.

If we look at *R. v Jackson* we can see that some of the things that we are told in the judgment are irrelevant for the purposes of constructing the *ratio*. The case before the Court of Appeal concerns a question relating to "leave to appeal". Thus, for example, the fact that the accused collected money on a weekly basis, rather than monthly, is of no account. Similarly, the fact that he failed to declare to the insurance brokers the full amount that he had collected is not significant for the purposes of the Court of Appeal on the question concerning "leave to appeal". However, we will be aware that, for the original trial judge in the Crown Court, when the charges brought against the accused were of "false accounting", this would have been a very significant matter.

You will see that in the case of *R. v Jackson* Lord Justice Rose (Rose, L.J.) delivers a judgment that is the "judgment of the court". This therefore reflects the shared views of himself, Lord Justice Butterfield and Lord Justice Richards. You should compare this with the judgments and opinions set out in the cases contained in the exercises of this book. Having set out the history of the case (at page 572g–h), Lord Justice Rose then gives a brief outline of the relevant facts for the purposes of the appeal (at page 572h–573d). This is followed by a summary of the submissions made by the counsel for each party (at page 573d–574c). You will see that counsel are said to have "submitted" certain things and to have "accepted" other matters during the course of their arguments before the Court of Appeal. Having dealt with these matters by way of preliminary presentation, Lord Justice Rose then moves on to the conclusions of the Court of Appeal. It is here that we look for the reasons and the *ratio* in the case.

The first matter considered (set out at page 574c–e) is the court's view on a proposition put by counsel for the appellant. You will gather that the Court of Appeal has little sympathy for the argument put forward, and in quite strong terms (at page 574e) "roundly rejects" the proposition that "wherever fresh evidence appears between a first and second trial, it would be unfair, at least if the evidence assisted the defence, to have a second trial". This leads the Court of Appeal to the conclusion that (i) the trial judge acted correctly in refusing to "stay" the trial of the accused, and (ii) anyway, given the evidence before the second jury in this case, that the verdict of that second jury could not be regarded as in any way "unsafe" (see page 574e–f). These conclusions are specific to this case, although the first one follows from the view expressed by the court on counsel's (roundly rejected) proposition. The narrow *ratio* of the case may thus be discovered by looking at that view, which was essential for reaching the eventual decision delivered by the Court of Appeal.

However, it is the "second matter" dealt with by the Court of Appeal that has drawn the attention of the law report editor to this case. At page 574f–g you will see that the court is faced with a question of what permission (or "leave") is required in order for an appeal to be made against particular aspects of a case. The eventual decision of the Court of Appeal (not to allow an appeal to be pursued on the basis of an alleged misdirection in the trial judge's summing up) is set out at page 574j, and the reasons for arriving at this decision are explained at page 574h. However, in order to reach that decision, the court has had to decide in what circumstances an appeal such as this may or may not be pursued. In this case the Court of Appeal goes further than to pronounce merely in relation to the specific case before it, relating to Jackson, the accused. Here, the court makes a general statement "for the avoidance of doubt", which is intended to clarify the situation for all future cases where this issue arises (set out at page 574g–h). That *ratio*, indeed, is also the part of the judgment that has been extracted by the editor of the law reports series to form the headnote that we have already looked at (at page 572c).

R. v Jackson contains only a single judgment. That judgment is a short one. If one had a longer judgment (and most judgments are longer) or multiple judgments in the same case, the task of constructing a *ratio* would be much more difficult. When one has to consider one judgment and its obscurities in the light of other judgments the process of analysing the law becomes even more uncertain. In order to appreciate some of the problems of constructing a *ratio* in a less straightforward case, therefore, you should apply the techniques discussed here to the law reports contained in the exercises section of this book.

A court must follow the *ratio* of any relevant case that is binding on it under the doctrine of precedent. Thus, the question arises, when is a case relevant? A case in the same area must be followed unless it can be "distinguished" on the basis of its facts. If the facts of the case cannot be distinguished — if, as it is commonly put, the case is "on all fours" — then it must be followed. The process of distinguishing cases is really just another way of deciding what the *ratio* of the case is. If the material facts necessary for the operation of the legal rule in the first case are not found in the second, or are different, there is no precedent. Just as lawyers differ about what the *ratio* to a case is, so they differ about whether a case is binding in a particular situation or not. Indeed, it is suggested by some commentators that judges sometimes distinguish cases on "flimsy grounds" simply to avoid having to follow precedents which they find unwelcome.

That which is not part of the *ratio* of the case is said to be the *obiter dictum*. This is usually referred to as "the *obiter*". *Obiter* is said to have "persuasive authority". That which was said *obiter* in a court such as the House of Lords may be very persuasive indeed for a relatively inferior court such as a County Court. Moreover, remarks made *obiter* may indicate which way the law is developing, or which kinds of arguments judges find particularly persuasive. Equally, judges are not always very careful about differentiating between *ratio* and *obiter*.

The remainder of this section provides some guidance on how to study cases. The first question a student should ask about a case is "Why has this case been set?" The purpose of studying cases is to obtain an understanding of the relevance of the case to the area of law being studied. Some cases will be more important than others. A leading House of Lords decision will require more time and closer examination than a decision that is merely illustrative of a point mentioned in a lecture or included in a problem. Where a case has developed or defined an area of law it is usually helpful to start by reading what the textbook writers say about it. Where more than one case has to be read on the same point of law, they should, if possible, be read in chronological order and each one digested before moving on to the next. If the subject under consideration is not an area of substantive law, such as tort or contract, but procedure or precedent, different aspects of the case will be important. In reading the case it is essential that the relevance of the case is borne in mind.

A second question to ask when reading cases is, "How much time is available?" Try to spend more time on important decisions and important judgments, even if you have to rely on a headnote or a textbook when it comes to the others. Do not spend the greater proportion of your time reading cases which have been overruled or which have novel or interesting facts but no new point of law. The headnote is helpful when allocating time. Treat judgments in the same way as you treat cases. Do not waste your time reading judgments that merely repeat something you have already read. Spend more time on the leading judgments than on the others. Again, the headnote will be helpful for this. Some judgments are more clearly written than others. Some judgments are shorter than others. Neither clarity nor brevity necessarily means that the judgment is more important. Choose what you read because it is the best for your purposes, not because it is the easiest!

Notes on any case should start with the case name and any references. They should then include:

1. a brief statement of the facts of the case;
2. the history of the case;
3. the point of law under consideration;
4. the decision with the reasons for it, together with any names of cases relied upon.

One side of A4 paper should provide enough space for this basic information, leaving the reverse side free for individual notes from judgments and, where necessary, any comments.

Some students prefer to keep notes of cases on file cards. These are easier to refer to quickly, but less can be put on them.

When reading judgments in order to make notes, look for agreement and disagreement on each of the points relevant to your study. It is often useful to make separate notes on each of the points raised by the case and then see what different judges said about them. In particular, too, do not forget to make it clear in your notes whether a judge was dissenting or not.

How to read a statute

This section will explain how you should read statutes. The way in which statutes are created is explained on pages 4–5. Looking for a particular legal rule in a statute can be confusing. Some statutes are over 100 pages long, although most are shorter. The language they use often appears complicated and obscure. If you understand the structure of a statute and follow a few simple rules in reading them, statutes will become much clearer.

A copy of a statute, the House of Lords Act 1999, is reproduced below. All subsequent references here are to this statute.

You can find statutes in a number of different ways. Not all of the statutes that you find will look the same as the one that we have reproduced for you. One way to find a statute is to buy it from Her Majesty's Stationery Office, the official stockist for Government publications, or one of its agents. These copies look much the same as the one that we have reproduced, but they have, in addition, a contents list at the beginning. This is also the case in relation to statutes which you may find on the internet. Statutes are also printed in a number of different series with different volumes for each year. The copy of the House of Lords Act 1999 which you are referring to is taken from such a series published by the Incorporated Council of Law Reporting. Some series of statutes are printed in an annotated form. This means that the statute is printed with an accompanying explanatory text, telling you what the statute does. If you use an annotated statute, remember that only the words of the statute are definitive. The explanatory text, although often helpful, is only the opinion of the author.

ELIZABETH II

House of Lords Act 1999　　①

1999 Chapter 34　　②

An Act to restrict membership of the House of Lords by virtue of a hereditary peerage; to make related provision about disqualifications for voting at elections to, and for membership ③ of, the House of Commons; and for connected purposes.

[11th November 1999]　④

BE IT ENACTED by the Queen's most Excellent Majesty, by and with the advice and consent of the Lords Spiritual and Temporal, and Commons, in this present Parliament assembled, and by the authority of the same, as follows:—

⑤

1. No-one shall be a member of the House of Lords by virtue of a hereditary peerage.

Exclusion of hereditary peers.

⑥

Exception from section 1.

2.—(1) Section 1 shall not apply in relation to anyone excepted from it by or in accordance with Standing Orders of the House.

(2) At any one time 90 people shall be excepted from section 1; but anyone excepted as holder of the office of Earl Marshal, or as performing the office of Lord Great Chamberlain, shall not count towards that limit.

(3) Once excepted from section 1, a person shall continue to be so throughout his life (until an Act of Parliament provides to the contrary).

(4) Standing Orders shall make provision for filling vacancies among the people excepted from section 1; and in any case where—

(a) the vacancy arises on a death occurring after the end of the first Session of the next Parliament after that in which this Act is passed, and
(b) the deceased person was excepted in consequence of an election,

that provision shall require the holding of a by-election.

(5) A person may be excepted from section 1 by or in accordance with Standing Orders made in anticipation of the enactment or commencement of this section.

(6) Any question whether a person is excepted from section 1 shall be decided by the Clerk of the Parliaments, whose certificate shall be conclusive.

Removal of disqualifications in relation to the House of Commons.

3.—(1) The holder of a hereditary peerage shall not be disqualified by virtue of that peerage for—

(a) voting at elections to the House of Commons, or
(b) being, or being elected as, a member of that House.

(2) Subsection (1) shall not apply in relation to anyone excepted from section 1 by virtue of section 2.

Amendments and repeals.

4.—(1) The enactments mentioned in Schedule 1 are amended as specified there.

(2) The enactments mentioned in Schedule 2 are repealed to the extent specified there.

Commencement and transitional provision.

5.—(1) Sections 1 to 4 (including Schedules 1 and 2) shall come into force at the end of the Session of Parliament in which this Act is passed.

(2) Accordingly, any writ of summons issued for the present Parliament in right of a hereditary peerage shall not have effect after that Session unless it has been issued to a person who, at the end of the Session, is excepted from section 1 by virtue of section 2.

(3) The Secretary of State may by order make such transitional provision about the entitlement of holders of hereditary peerages to vote at elections to the House of Commons or the European Parliament as he considers appropriate.

(4) An order under this section—

(a) may modify the effect of any enactment or any provision made under an enactment, and
(b) shall be made by statutory instrument which shall be subject to annulment in pursuance of a resolution of either House of Parliament.

Interpretation and short title.

6.—(1) In this Act "hereditary peerage" includes the principality of Wales and the earldom of Chester.

(2) This Act may be cited as the House of Lords Act 1999.

SCHEDULES

SCHEDULE 1

AMENDMENTS

Peerage Act 1963 (c.48)

1. In section 1(2) of the Peerage Act 1963 (disclaimer of certain hereditary peerages) for the words from "has" to the end there shall be substituted the words "is excepted from section 1 of the House of Lords Act 1999 by virtue of section 2 of that Act".

Recess Elections Act 1975 (c.66)

2. In section 1 of the Recess Elections Act 1975 (issue of warrants for making out writs to replace members of the House of Commons whose seats have become vacant), in—

    (a) subsection (1)(a), and

    (b) paragraph (a) of the definition of "certificate of vacancy" in subsection (2),

    for the words "become a peer" there shall be substituted the words "become disqualified as a peer for membership of the House of Commons".

SCHEDULE 2

REPEALS

Chapter	Short title	Extent of repeal
1963 c.48.	The Peerage Act 1963.	In section 1(3), paragraph (b) and the word "and" immediately preceding it.
		Section 2.
		In section 3, in subsection (1)(b), the words from "(including" to "that House)" and, in subsection (2), the words from "and" to the end of the subsection.
		Section 5.

The different parts

① This is the *short title* of the Act, together with its year of publication. When you are writing about a statute, it is normal to use the short title and year of publication to describe the statute. Sometimes, when a statute is referred to constantly, the short title is abbreviated. Thus, the Disability Discrimination Act 1995 is often referred to as "the D.D.A. 1995". If you work in a particular area of law, you will quickly learn the standard abbreviations for that area.

② This is the official *citation* for the statute. Each Act passed in any one year is given its own number. This is known as its *chapter number*. Thus you can describe a statute by its chapter number and year. The citation "1999 Chapter 34" could only mean the House of Lords Act 1999. "Chapter" in the official citation may be abbreviated to "c.", as in the top right hand corner of your copy of the statute. This form of official citation began in 1963. Before that, statutes were identified by the "regnal year" in which they occurred, followed by their chapter number. A regnal year is a year of a monarch's reign. Thus, "30 Geo 3 Chapter 3" refers to the Treason Act 1790, which was passed in the 30th year of King George III's reign. It is much easier to remember and use the short title of an Act rather than its official citation.

③ This is the *long title* of the Act. The long title gives some indication of the purpose behind the Act. It may be of some use in deciding what the Act is all about. However, the long title may be misleading. For example, the long title of the Parliament Act 1911 indicates that the Act is part of a process of abolishing the House of Lords — although, nearly nine decades later, that institution is still in existence, even though the House of Lords Act 1999 has introduced restrictions upon membership of the institution by virtue of a hereditary peerage. Long titles are sometimes vague and may conflict with the main body of the Act. In the event of such a conflict, the legal rule is that expressed in the main body of the Act.

④ This indicates when the *royal assent* was given and the House of Lords Bill 1999 became an Act. Statutes become law on the date when they receive the royal assent *unless the Act says otherwise*. The statute itself may say that it becomes law on a fixed date after the royal assent, or it may give a Government Minister the power to decide when it becomes law. When a Minister brings a statute into effect after the date on which it has been passed a "commencement order" must be made. This is a form of delegated legislation. Statutes do not have a retrospective effect unless the Act expressly says so.

⑤ This is known as the *enacting formula*. It is the standard form of words used to indicate that a Bill has been properly passed by all the different parts of the legislature.

⑥ By each section you will find a short explanation of the content of that section. These *marginal notes* may help you to understand the content of the section if it is otherwise unclear.

The main body of the statute that follows is broken up into numbered *sections*. Each section contains a different rule of law. When you refer to a rule of law contained in a statute, you should say where that rule of law is to be found. This enables others to check your source and to see whether or not they agree with your interpretation of the law. Instead of writing "section", it is usual to abbreviate this to "s.". Thus, "section 1" becomes "s.1". Sections are often further subdivided. These sub-division are known as *subsections*. When you wish to refer to a subsection, you should add it in brackets after the main section.

Example

Q. How many people are excepted from s.1 of the House of Lords Act 1999?
A. 90 people at any one time. See s.2(2) House of Lords Act 1999.

In larger statutes, sections may be grouped together into different *Parts*. Each Part will deal with a separate area of law. Looking for the correct Part will help you to find the particular legal rule that you want.

Some statutes have one or more *Schedules* at the end. The content of these varies. Some contain detailed provisions that are not found in the main body of the act. Others are merely convenient reminders and summaries of legal rules, and changes to legal rules, found elsewhere in the Act.

In the House of Lords Act 1999, for example, there are two Schedules. The first Schedule says which sections of previous statutes have been changed (amended) by the 1999 Act. This Schedule sets out the detailed effect of the amendments, which are given their legal effect by virtue of s.4(1) of the Act. The second Schedule sets out which sections of a previous statute have been repealed by the 1999 Act. Those repeals are given their legal effect by virtue of s.4(2) of the Act.

References to Schedules are often abbreviated as "Sched.". Where a Schedule is divided up, the divisions are known as *paragraphs*, and can be abbreviated as "para.".

Using a statute

Your use of statutory material will vary. Sometimes you will be referred to a particular section or sections of a statute in a case, article, or book that you are reading. In other instances, a new statute will be passed which you need to assess as a whole in order to see how it affects those areas of law in which you are interested. In either case, when first reading statutory material, you may be able to gain some help in deciding what it means from commentaries.

Commentaries are explanations of the law written by legal academics or practitioners. Annotated statutes, which were discussed earlier, are one useful source of such commentaries. You may also find such commentaries in books and articles on the area of law in which the statute falls. Always remember that a commentary represents only one author's opinion of what the statute says. In the case of a very new statute there will probably be no commentary. Therefore, you will need to be able to read a statute yourself, so that you can assess the value of other people's opinions and form your own view when there is no other help available.

When reading a statute, do not begin at the beginning and then work your way through to the end, section by section. Statutes do not necessarily use words to mean the same things that they do in ordinary conversation. Before you can decide what a statute is about you need to know if there are any special meanings attached to words in it. These special meanings can be found in the Act, often in sections called *definition* or *interpretation sections*. These are frequently found towards the end of the Act. For example, in the House of Lords Act 1999, there is a guide in s.6(1) to the interpretation of the expression "hereditary peerage" when used in the context of the Act. An Act may have more than one definition section. Sometimes, Parliament, when laying down a particular meaning for a word, will say that the specified meaning will apply in all statutes in which that word appears. Unless a statute specifically says this, however, you should assume that a definition in a statute applies only the use of the word in that statute.

You are now in a position to decide what new legal rules the statute creates. Some people begin this task by reading the long title of the Act to give themselves some idea of the general aim of the statute. Although this can be helpful, as we saw above in the section on the different parts of the Act, it can also be misleading.

Statutes should be read carefully and slowly. The general rule is that a statute means precisely what it says. Each word is important. Because of this, some words that we use loosely in ordinary conversation take on special significance when found in a statute. For example, it is important to distinguish between words like "may" and "shall", one saying that you *can* do something and the other saying that you *must* do something. Conjunctives, such as "and", joining things together, must be distinguished from disjunctives, such as "or", dividing things apart.

Example

Section 26A(1) of the Race Relations Act 1976 provides that:

"It is unlawful for a barrister or barrister's clerk, in relation to any offer of a pupillage or tenancy, to discriminate against a person —

    (a) in the arrangements which are made for the purpose of determining to whom it should be offered;

    (b) in respect of any terms on which it is offered; or

    (c) by refusing, or deliberately omitting, to offer it to him."

As a result, a barrister or a barrister's clerk will discriminate unlawfully if they do *any one* of the acts spelled out in (a) *or* (b) *or* (c).

This would be a very different provision if it had said that it was necessary for all three of the acts (a) *and* (b) *and* (c) to be present before discrimination occurred. As the law stands, any one of the acts listed will make the actor guilty of unlawful discrimination. If a conjunctive were substituted, then it would be necessary to show all three acts in order for unlawful discrimination to be established.

So far, the emphasis has been upon closely reading the particular statute. You should also remember that the statute should be read in the context of the general Acts, rules and principles of statutory interpretation discussed in Chapter 1.

One further thing to remember when reading a statute is that the fact that it has been printed does not mean that it is part of the law of the land. It may have been repealed. It may not yet be in force. Re-read pages 39–40 if you cannot remember how to find out if a statute has been repealed. Go back and read about the royal assent on page 57 if you cannot remember how to find out if a statute is in force.

Statutory instruments

What statutory instruments are, the way in which they are created, and the purposes that they have, are discussed on page 4.

Statutory instruments should be read in the same way as statutes. However, whilst statutes make relatively little reference to other sources, statutory instruments, because of their purpose, make very frequent reference either to other statutory instruments or to their parent statute. The legislative power has been given only for a limited purpose, the statutory instrument is a small part of a larger whole. For this reason, you will find it much more difficult to understand a statutory instrument if you do not have access to the surrounding legislation. Before reading a statutory instrument, it is vital that you understand the legislative framework into which it fits.

Exercise 1

Statutes I

Start by re-reading the appropriate parts of Chapter 5 and then look at the Dealing in Cultural Objects (Offences) Act 2003. Then answer the questions. When answering the questions make sure you include the correct statutory references. Answers to Section A questions for each exercise are to be found in Appendix IV.

Dealing in Cultural Objects (Offences) Act 2003

(2003 c. 27)

An Act to provide for an offence of acquiring, disposing of, importing or exporting tainted cultural objects, or agreeing or arranging to do so; and for connected purposes.

BE IT ENACTED by the Queen's most Excellent Majesty, by and with the advice and consent of the Lords Spiritual and Temporal, and Commons, in this present Parliament assembled, and by the authority of the same, as follows: —

s 1 Offence of dealing in tainted cultural objects

(1) A person is guilty of an offence if he dishonestly deals in a cultural object that is tainted, knowing or believing that the object is tainted.
(2) It is immaterial whether he knows or believes that the object is a cultural object.
(3) A person guilty of the offence is liable —

    (a) on conviction on indictment, to imprisonment for a term not exceeding seven years or a fine (or both),
    (b) on summary conviction, to imprisonment for a term not exceeding six months or a fine not exceeding the statutory maximum (or both).

s 2 Meaning of "tainted cultural object"

(1) "Cultural object" means an object of historical, architectural or archaeological interest.
(2) A cultural object is tainted if, after the commencement of this Act —

    (a) a person removes the object in a case falling within subsection (4) or he excavates the object, and
    (b) the removal or excavation constitutes an offence.

(3) It is immaterial whether —

(a) the removal or excavation was done in the United Kingdom or elsewhere,
(b) the offence is committed under the law of a part of the United Kingdom or under the law of any other country or territory.

(4) An object is removed in a case falling within this subsection if —

(a) it is removed from a building or structure of historical, architectural or archaeological interest where the object has at any time formed part of the building or structure, or
(b) it is removed from a monument of such interest.

(5) "Monument" means —

(a) any work, cave or excavation,
(b) any site comprising the remains of any building or structure or of any work, cave or excavation,
(c) any site comprising, or comprising the remains of, any vehicle, vessel, aircraft or other movable structure, or part of any such thing.

(6) "Remains" includes any trace or sign of the previous existence of the thing in question.
(7) It is immaterial whether —

(a) a building, structure or work is above or below the surface of the land,
(b) a site is above or below water.

(8) This section has effect for the purposes of *section 1*.

s 3 Meaning of "deals in"

(1) A person deals in an object if (and only if) he —

(a) acquires, disposes of, imports or exports it,
(b) agrees with another to do an act mentioned in paragraph (a), or
(c) makes arrangements under which another person does such an act or under which another person agrees with a third person to do such an act.

(2) "Acquires" means buys, hires, borrows or accepts.
(3) "Disposes of" means sells, lets on hire, lends or gives.
(4) In relation to agreeing or arranging to do an act, it is immaterial whether the act is agreed or arranged to take place in the United Kingdom or elsewhere.
(5) This section has effect for the purposes of *section 1*.

s 4 Customs and Excise prosecutions

(1) Proceedings for an offence relating to the dealing in a tainted cultural object may be instituted by order of the Commissioners of Customs and Excise if it appears to them that the offence has involved the importation or exportation of such an object.
(2) An offence relates to the dealing in a tainted cultural object if it is —

(a) an offence under *section 1*, or
(b) an offence of inciting the commission of, or attempting or conspiring to commit, such an offence.

(3) Proceedings for an offence which are instituted under subsection (1) are to be commenced in the name of an officer, but may be continued by another officer.

(4) Where the Commissioners of Customs and Excise investigate, or propose to investigate, any matter with a view to determining —

   (a) whether there are grounds for believing that a person has committed an offence which relates to the dealing in a tainted cultural object and which involves the importation or exportation of such an object, or

   (b) whether a person should be prosecuted for such an offence, the matter is to be treated as an assigned matter within the meaning of the Customs and Excise Management Act 1979 (c. 2).

(5) Nothing in this section affects any powers of any person (including any officer) apart from this section.

(6) "Officer" means a person commissioned by the Commissioners of Customs and Excise under *section 6(3)* of the Customs and Excise Management Act 1979.

s 5 Offences by bodies corporate

(1) If an offence under *section 1* committed by a body corporate is proved —

   (a) to have been committed with the consent or connivance of an officer, or
   (b) to be attributable to any neglect on his part,

he (as well as the body corporate) is guilty of the offence and liable to be proceeded against and punished accordingly.

(2) "Officer", in relation to a body corporate, means —

   (a) a director, manager, secretary or other similar officer of the body,
   (b) a person purporting to act in any such capacity.

(3) If the affairs of a body corporate are managed by its members, subsection (1) applies in relation to the acts and defaults of a member in connection with his functions of management as if he were a director of the body.

s 6 Short title, commencement and extent

(1) This Act may be cited as the Dealing in Cultural Objects (Offences) Act 2003.
(2) This Act comes into force at the end of the period of two months beginning with the day on which it is passed.
(3) This Act does not extend to Scotland.

Section A

1. What criminal offence does this Act create?
2. To which parts of the United Kingdom does it apply?
3. Is it in force?
4. a) In what circumstances can an offence under this Act be prosecuted by a Customs Officer?

b) What other offences relating to dealing in cultural objects can be prosecuted by Customs and Excise?

5. Charles wants to install an antique fireplace in his house. He contacts Bob who tells him that for "the right money" he can find him an original Georgian fireplace. Bob then arranges with Del to remove the fireplace from an empty house without asking the owner's permission.

   a) Do Charles, Bob or Del commit the offence of dealing in a tainted cultural object?
   b) Does it make any difference that all the parties believe that the fireplace is a modern reproduction which has come straight from the maker.

6. The Elgin Marbles are statues and carvings that originally formed part of the Acropolis in Athens and are now in the British Museum in London. They were removed from the Acropolis in 1801 and brought to England by Lord Elgin.

   a) Would Christos commit an offence under the Act if he removed one of the Marbles from the museum and took it back to Greece?
   b) Did the British Museum commit an offence under the Act when if obtained the marbles in the nineteenth century?
   c) If Lord Elgin removed the carvings today with a view to their protection would he commit the offence of dealing in a tainted cultural object? What would Lord Elgin have to do to ensure that he did not commit this offence?

Section B

7. What is the short title of this Act?
8. Why do you think this Act was passed?
9. Peter goes to an old church and steals a 12th century statue of a saint. He sells this to Michael who exports antiques to America. It is well known that items of this kind exist only in churches or in museums. Has Michael committed an offence under the Act?
10. Anita collects old bottles and jars. She pays for her hobby by selling some of what she has found. Recently she has been excavating on the site of an old rubbish dump where she found and removed lots old bottles.

    a) Has Anita committed an offence under the Act?
    b) Would your answer be different if Anita had found the bottles in the wreck of an old ship?

11. Following the war in Iraq in 2003, buildings were looted and ancient ceramic tiles disappeared. Dealers were alerted but specific descriptions were not provided. In January 2004, the Heritage Art company acquired a number of old ceramic tiles from a man who was not known to them but who said he had worked as a security guard in the Middle East. The company then contacted Amer, an expert on Middle Eastern Art who advises various museums on what they should purchase. Amer arranged for the tiles to be bought by the Eastern Cultural Museum in Wales. Assuming the tiles were removed after January 1, 2004, which (if any) of the parties has committed an offence under the Act.

13. Do you think this Act will deter people who trade in antiquities stolen from archaeological sites?

Exercise 2

ELIZABETH II

Protection from Harassment Act 1997

1997 CHAPTER 40

An Act to make provision for protecting persons from harassment and similar conduct.

[21st March 1997]

BE IT ENACTED by the Queen's most Excellent Majesty, by and with the advice and consent of the Lords Spiritual and Temporal, and Commons, in this present Parliament assembled, and by the authority of the same, as follows:—

England and Wales

Prohibition of harassment.

1.—(1) A person must not pursue a course of conduct —

(a) which amounts to harassment of another, and
(b) which he knows or ought to know amounts to harassment of the other.

(2) For the purposes of this section, the person whose course of conduct is in question ought to know that it amounts to harassment of another if a reasonable person in possession of the same information would think the course of conduct amounted to harassment of the other.

(3) Subsection (1) does not apply to a course of conduct if the person who pursued it shows —

(a) that it was pursued for the purpose of preventing or detecting crime,

(b) that it was pursued under any enactment or rule of law or to comply with any condition or requirement imposed by any person under any enactment, or

(c) that in the particular circumstances the pursuit of the course of conduct was reasonable.

Offence of harassment.

2.—(1) A person who pursues a course of conduct in breach of section 1 is guilty of an offence.

(2) A person guilty of an offence under this section is liable on summary conviction to imprisonment for a term not exceeding six months, or a fine not exceeding level 5 on the standard scale, or both.

1984 c. 60

(3) In section 24(2) of the Police and Criminal Evidence Act 1984 (arrestable offences), after paragraph (m) there is inserted —

"(n) an offence under section 2 of the Protection from Harassment Act 1997 (harassment)."

Civil remedy.

3.—(1) An actual or apprehended breach of section 1 may be the subject of a claim in civil proceedings by the person who is or may be the victim of the course of conduct in question.

(2) On such a claim, damages may be awarded for (among other things) any anxiety caused by the harassment and any financial loss resulting from the harassment.

(3) Where —

(a) in such proceedings the High Court or a country court grants an injunction for the purpose of restraining the defendant from pursuing any conduct which amounts to harassment, and

(b) the plaintiff considers that the defendant has done anything which he is prohibited from doing by the injunction,

the plaintiff may apply for the issue of a warrant for the arrest of the defendant.

(4) An application under subsection (3) may be made —

(a) where the injunction was granted by the High Court, to a judge of that court, and

(b) where the injunction was granted by a county court, to a judge or district judge of that or any other county court.

(5) The judge or district judge to whom an application under subsection (3) is made may only issue a warrant if —

(a) the application is substantiated on oath, and
(b) the judge or district judge has reasonable grounds for believing that the defendant has done anything which he is prohibited from doing by the injunction.

(6) Where —

(a) the High Court or a county court grants an injunction for the purpose mentioned in subsection (3)(a), and
(b) without reasonable excuse the defendant does anything which he is prohibited from doing by the injunction,

he is guilty of an offence.

(7) Where a person is convicted of an offence under subsection (6) in respect of any conduct, that conduct is not punishable as a contempt of court.

(8) A person cannot be convicted of an offence under subsection (6) in respect of any conduct which has been punished as a contempt of court.

(9) A person guilty of an offence under subsection (6) is liable —

(a) on conviction on indictment, to imprisonment for a term not exceeding five years, or a fine, or both, or
(b) on summary conviction, to imprisonment for a term not exceeding six months, or a fine not exceeding the statutory maximum, or both.

4.—(1) A person whose course of conduct causes another to fear, on at least two occasions, that violence will be used against him is guilty of an offence if he knows or ought to know that his course of conduct will cause the other so to fear on each of those occasions.

Putting people in fear of violence.

(2) For the purposes of this section, the person whose course of conduct is in question ought to know that it will cause another to fear that violence will be used against him on any occasion if a reasonable person in possession of the same information would think the course of conduct would cause the other so to fear on that occasion.

(3) It is a defence for a person charged with an offence under this section to show that —

(a) his course of conduct was pursued for the purpose of preventing or detecting crime,

(b) his course of conduct was pursued under any enactment or rule of law or to comply with any condition or requirement imposed by any person under any enactment, or

(c) the pursuit of his course of conduct was reasonable for the protection of himself or another or for the protection of his or another's property.

(4) A person guilty of an offence under this section is liable —

(a) on conviction on indictment, to imprisonment for a term not exceeding five years, or a fine, or both, or

(b) on summary conviction, to imprisonment for a term not exceeding six months, or a fine not exceeding the statutory maximum, or both.

(5) If on the trial on indictment of a person charged with an offence under this section the jury find him not guilty of the offence charged, they may find him guilty of an offence under section 2.

(6) The Crown Court has the same powers and duties in relation to a person who is by virtue of subsection (5) convicted before it of an offence under section 2 as a magistrates' court would have on convicting him of the offence.

Restraining orders.

5.—(1) A court sentencing or otherwise dealing with a person ("the defendant") convicted of an offence under section 2 or 4 may (as well as sentencing him or dealing with him in any other way) make an order under this section.

(2) The order may, for the purpose of protecting the victim of the offence, or any other person mentioned in the order, from further conduct which —

(a) amounts to harassment, or

(b) will cause a fear of violence,

prohibit the defendant from doing anything described in the order.

(3) The order may have effect for a specified period or until further order.

(4) The prosecutor, the defendant or any other person mentioned in the order may apply to the court which made the order for it to be varied or discharged by a further order.

(5) If without reasonable excuse the defendant does anything which he is prohibited from doing by an order under this section, he is guilty of an offence.

(6) A person guilty of an offence under this section is liable —

(a) on conviction on indictment, to imprisonment for a term not exceeding five years, or a fine, or both, or
(b) on summary conviction, to imprisonment for a term not exceeding six months, or a fine not exceeding the statutory maximum, or both.

6. In section 11 of the Limitation Act 1980 (special time limit for actions in respect of personal injuries), after subsection (1) there is inserted —

Limitation. 1980 c. 58.

"(1A) This section does not apply to any action brought for damages under section 3 of the Protection from Harassment Act 1997."

7.—(1) This section applies for the interpretation of sections 1 to 5.

Interpretation of this group of sections.

(2) References to harassing a person include alarming the person or causing the person distress.

(3) A "course of conduct" must involve conduct on at least two occasions.

(4) "Conduct" includes speech.

Scotland

8.—(1) Every individual has a right to be free from harassment and, accordingly, a person must not pursue a course of conduct which amounts to harassment of another and —

Harassment.

(a) is intended to amount to harassment of that person; or
(b) occurs in circumstances where it would appear to a reasonable person that it would amount to harassment of that person.

(2) An actual or apprehended breach of subsection (1) may be the subject of a claim in civil proceedings by the person who is or may be the victim of the course of conduct in question; and any such claim shall be known as an action of harassment.

(3) For the purposes of this section —

"conduct" includes speech;
"harassment" of a person includes causing the person alarm or distress; and

a course of conduct must involve conduct on at least two occasions.

(4) It shall be a defence to any action of harassment to show that the course of conduct complained of —

(a) was authorised by, under or by virtue of any enactment or rule of law;
(b) was pursued for the purpose of preventing or detecting crime; or
(c) was, in the particular circumstances, reasonable.

(5) In an action of harassment the court may, without prejudice to any other remedies which it may grant —

(a) award damages;
(b) grant —

(i) interdict or interim interdict;
(ii) if it is satisfied that it is appropriate for it to do so in order to protect the person from further harassment, an order, to be known as a "non-harassment order", requiring the defender to refrain from such conduct in relation to the pursuer as may be specified in the order for such period (which includes an indeterminate period) as may be so specified,

but a person may not be subjected to the same prohibitions in an interdict or interim interdict and a non-harassment order at the same time.

(6) The damages which may be awarded in an action of harassment include damages for any anxiety caused by the harassment and any financial loss resulting from it.

(7) Without prejudice to any right to seek review of any interlocutor, a person against whom a non-harassment order has been made, or the person for whose protection the order was made, may apply to the court by which the order was made for revocation of or a variation of the order and, on any such application, the court may revoke the order or vary it in such manner as it considers appropriate.

1976 c.13.

(8) In section 10(1) of the Damages (Scotland) Act 1976 (interpretation), in the definition of "personal injuries", after "to reputation" there is inserted, "or injury resulting from harassment actionable under section 8 of the Protection from Harassment Act 1997".

Breach of non-harassment order.

9.—(1) Any person who is found to be in breach of a non-harassment order made under section 8 is guilty of an offence and liable —

(a) on conviction on indictment, to imprisonment for a term not exceeding five years or to a fine, or to both such imprisonment and such fine; and

(b) on summary conviction, to imprisonment for a period not exceeding six months or to a fine not exceeding the statutory maximum, or to both such imprisonment and such fine.

(2) A breach of a non-harassment order shall not be punishable other than in accordance with subsection (1).

10.—(1) After section 18A of the Prescription and Limitation (Scotland) Act 1973 there is inserted the following section —

Limitation. 1973 c. 52.

"Actions of harassement.

18B.—(1) This section applies to actions of harassment (within the meaning of section 8 of the Protection from Harassment Act 1997) which include a claim for damages.

(2) Subject to subsection (3) below and to section 19A of this Act, no action to which this section applies shall be brought unless it is commenced within a period of 3 years after —

(a) the date on which the alleged harassment ceased; or

(b) the date, (if later than the date mentioned in paragraph (a) above) on which the pursuer in the action became, or on which, in the opinion of the court, it would have been reasonably practicable for him in all the circumstances to have become, aware, that the defender was a person responsible for the alleged harassment or the employer or principal of such a person.

(3) In the computation of the period specified in subsection (2) above there shall be disregarded any time during which the person who is alleged to have suffered the harassment was under legal disability by reason of nonage or unsoundness of mind."

(2) In subsection (1) of section 19A of that Act (power of court to override time-limits), for "section 17 or section 18 and section 18A" there is substituted "section 17, 18, 18A or 18B".

Non-harassment order following criminal offence. 1995 c. 46

11.—After section 234 of the Criminal Procedure (Scotland) Act 1995 there is inserted the following section —

"Non-harassment orders

Non-harassment orders.

234A.—(1) Where a person is convicted of an offence involving harassment of a person ("the victim"), the prosecutor may apply to the court to make a non-harassment order against the offender requiring him to refrain from such conduct in relation to the victim as may be specified in the order for such period (which includes an indeterminate period) as may be so specified, in addition to any other disposal which may be made in relation to the offence.

(2) On an application under subsection (1) above the court may, if it is satisfied on a balance of probabilities that it is appropriate to do so in order to protect the victim from further harassment, make a non-harassment order.

(3) A non-harassment order made by a criminal court shall be taken to be a sentence for the purposes of any appeal and, for the purposes of this subsection "order" includes any variation or revocation of such an order made under subsection (6) below.

(4) Any person who is found to be in breach of a non-harassment order shall be guilty of an offence and liable —

(a) on conviction on indictment, to imprisonment for a term not exceeding 5 years or to a fine, or to both such imprisonment and such fine; and

(b) on summary conviction, to imprisonment for a period not exceeding 6 months or to a fine not exceeding the statutory maximum, or to both such imprisonment and such fine.

(5) The Lord Advocate, in solemn proceedings, and the prosecutor, in summary proceedings, may appeal to the High Court against any decision by a court to refuse an application under subsection (1) above; and on any such appeal the High Court may make such order as it considers appropriate.

(6) The person against whom a non-harassment order is made, or the prosecutor at whose instance the order is made, may apply to the court which made the order for its revocation or variation and, in relation to any such application the court concerned may, if it is satisfied on a balance of probabilities that it is appropri-

ate to do so, revoke the order or vary it in such manner as it thinks fit, but not so as to increase the period for which the order is to run.

(7) For the purposes of this section "harassment" shall be construed in accordance with section 8 of the Protection from Harassment Act 1997."

General

12.—(1) If the Secretary of State certifies that in his opinion anything done by a specified person on a specified occasion related to —

    (a) national security,
    (b) the economic well-being of the United Kingdom, or
    (c) the prevention or detection of serious crime,

and was done on behalf of the Crown, the certificate is conclusive evidence that this Act does not apply to any conduct of that person on that occasion.

National security, *etc.*

(2) In subsection (1), "specified" means specified in the certificate in question.

(3) A document purporting to be a certificate under subsection (1) is to be received in evidence and, unless the contrary is proved, be treated as being such a certificate.

13. An Order in Council made under paragraph 1(1)(b) of Schedule 1 to the Northern Ireland Act 1974 which contains a statement that it is made only for purposes corresponding to those of sections 1 to 7 and 12 of this Act—

Corresponding provision for Northern Ireland. 1974 c. 28.

    (a) shall not be subject to sub-paragraphs (4) and (5) of paragraph 1 of that Schedule (affirmative resolution of both Houses of Parliament), but
    (b) shall be subject to annulment in pursuance of a resolution of either House of Parliament.

14.—(1) Sections 1 to 7 extend to England and Wales only.

Extent.

(2) Sections 8 to 11 extend to Scotland only.

(3) This Act (except section 13) does not extend to Northern Ireland.

15.—(1) Sections 1, 2, 4, 5 and 7 to 12 are to come into force on such day as the Secretary of State may by order made by statutory instrument appoint.

Commencement.

(2) Sections 3 and 6 are to come into force on such day as the Lord Chancellor may by order made by statutory instrument appoint.

(3) Different days may be appointed under this section for different purposes.

Short title.   **16.** This Act may be cited as the Protection from Harassment Act 1997.

Section A

1. a)   When did section 7 of the Protection from Harassment Act come into force?
    b)   Has this Act been amended?

2.   To what parts of the United Kingdom does this Act apply?
3.   Does the Protection from Harassment Act define "harassment"?
4.   Does the Protection from Harassment Act create criminal or civil liability?
5.   Romeo repeatedly visits the home of his former girlfriend Juliet. He sits outside in his car hoping to catch sight of her, and if he does, attempts to give her a bunch of flowers. On three occasions he has actually put the flowers into her arm or bag.

    a)   Is Romeo guilty of the offence of harassment in section 2?
    b)   Apart from contacting the police, what legal action can Juliet take to stop Romeo annoying her?

6.   Mr MacGregor is a keen gardener with a large garden full of strawberries, plums and apples. Peter and his friends frequently climb over the garden wall and take the fruit. Mr MacGregor has become increasingly angry about this. Whenever he sees the boys in his garden he chases them away, waving garden tools at them and shouting that he will "skin them alive" them. Peter's mother complained to the local police about Mr MacGregor's behaviour. Mr MacGregor has been charged with an offence under the Protection from Harassment Act, s. 4. Advise Mr MacGregor whether he has any defence.
7.   If Mr MacGregor was convicted what powers would the court have to deal with his behaviour and prevent its reoccurrence?
8.   Ed is a fervent animal right's campaigner. He has organised a campaign against Sheila, a dog breeder. On different occasions, various people known to Ed have broken into the yard where Sheila keeps her dogs and let them out. This worries Sheila in case the dogs are injured or mate with non-pedigree dogs. On some occasions the dogs have escaped into the neighbouring property, a children's nursery and terrified the children.

    a)   Is Ed guilty of any offence under the Protection from Harassment Act 1997?
    b)   Can either Sheila or the nursery obtain compensation for the effects of Ed's campaign?

Section B

9. In what circumstances can someone who harasses another be arrested?
10. Why was it thought necessary to enact the Protection from Harassment Act? What sources of information could help you establish the reasons for this legislation?
11. Austin is an under cover agent with the anti-terrorist squad. Recently his duties have involved close surveillance of a suspected terrorist MM. This has included watching him from a neighbouring property, repeatedly telephoning (without speaking) to check whether he is at home, and following him if he leaves home.

    a) Has Austin committed any offence under the Protection from Harassment Act?
    b) A prosecution of Austin would prevent him continuing in the anti-terrorist squad. Is there any action that could be taken to ensure that he is not prosecuted?

12. What are the main differences between the offence under section 2 and the offence under section 4? Why do you think it was considered necessary to have two separate offences in English and Welsh law?
13. David is a prominent politician. He has been having an affair with his research assistant despite his long-standing support for "proper standards of morality". Since rumours about this surfaced a month ago, reporters have been camped outside David's London flat and the home he shares with his wife in his constituency. Each time he has entered or left these premises reporters have taken photographs of him and asked him for interviews. Advise David whether he can use the Protection from Harassment Act 1997 to have the reporters removed.
14. Zina lived with her boyfriend Sol for nearly five years. During this time he repeatedly abused her both physically and emotionally. He prevented her meeting her friends or family and drove her to work, and collected her so that he could control her movements. Six months ago after a particularly nasty attack Zina moved into a woman's refuge and changed her job so that Sol could not find her. Zina remains terrified of Sol. She is sure he is attempting to find her. He has contacted her family and her old employer and left letters for her with them. Zina is so scared that Sol will trace her that she has made no attempt to contact anyone she knows who also knows Sol. Advise Zina whether Sol's behaviour can be controlled by the Protection from Harassment Act 1997.

Drafting Exercises

15. Draft an amendment to the Protection from Harassment Act 1997 which prevents journalists from being charged with harassment if they repeatedly seek to contact a person in connection with a matter of public interest.
16. Assuming Romeo (question 5) is convicted, draft an order which restrains him from contacting Juliet or going within 250 metres of her home or place of work.

Exercise 3

CASE I

Case No: B3/2003/0450

Neutral Citation No: [2004] EWCA Civ 405

IN THE SUPREME COURT OF JUDICATURE

COURT OF APPEAL (CIVIL DIVISION)

ON APPEAL FROM THE MANCHESTER COUNTY COURT

HIS HONOUR JUDGE TETLOW

Royal Courts of Justice

Strand, London, WC2A 2LL

Date: 7th April 2004

Before :

LORD JUSTICE AULD

LORD JUSTICE LATHAM

and

LADY JUSTICE ARDEN

Between :

DAVID L DONACHIE   **Appellant**

– and –

THE CHIEF CONSTABLE OF   **Respondent**

THE GREATER MANCHESTER POLICE

Mark Turner QC (instructed by **Betesh Fox & Co**) for the Appellant

Andrew Edis QC and William Waldron (instructed by **Weightmans**) for the Respondent

Hearing date : 16th February 2004

JUDGMENT : APPROVED BY THE COURT FOR HANDING DOWN
(SUBJECT TO EDITORIAL CORRECTIONS)

Lord Justice Auld:

1. This is an appeal by David Donachie against the order of His Honour Judge Tetlow on 28th February 2003 in the Manchester County Court dismissing his claims in negligence and for breach of statutory duty against the Chief Constable of Manchester for damages for personal injuries when serving as a police officer in the North West Regional Crime Squad. The appeal is against the Judge's rejection of his claims for want of reasonable foreseeability of his injuries, the Judge having found in his favour on the issues of breach of duty and causation. The Chief Constable, by a respondent's notice, seeks to uphold the Judge's finding on the issue of reasonable foreseeability and, by way of cross-appeal to challenge his finding on the issue of causation.

The facts

2. On the evening of 2nd November 1997 Mr Donachie was required, in the course of his duty, to attach a tagging device to the underside of a car that the Crime Squad believed belonged to a gang of criminals. The car was parked in a street behind the public house in which the suspected criminals were drinking. Mr Donachie was one of a group of officers detailed to carry out the operation. Normally, to avoid discovery while attaching the device, they would have done it in the early hours of the morning when the suspects could be expected to be asleep. However, this operation was urgent — hence the unusual and more risky timing of it.

3. The system operated by the officers was that one of them — in this instance Mr Donachie — would attach the device to the underside of the car while the others kept watch from in and around a police "tracking" van against the possibility of the suspects emerging from the public house and catching him in the act. If all had gone well, he should have been able to approach the car, get underneath it and attach the device out of sight and walk away; and the device should have immediately begun recording signals to the tracking van. Unfortunately, and unknown to Mr Donachie and his fellow officers, the device was fitted with a battery, which, although newly fitted and used earlier that day on another vehicle, had failed. When Mr Donachie attempted to attach it to the car, it did not operate so as to give a signal. He had to return to the car, retrieve it and take it back to the van where he and his colleagues attempted to find out what was wrong with it and make it work. They did not know whether the device or Mr Donachie's positioning of it under the car or the battery caused the malfunction. Having examined and fiddled with the device, he then had to go back to the car, get under it again and try again to attach it in a position where it would work. However, again it did not do so, and it continued to fail until after two battery replacements and seven more trips by him to the car. He was eventually successful on the ninth trip in attaching the device in working condition.

4. With every approach that Mr Donachie had to make to the car, he subjected himself to an increased risk of being caught in the act and attacked by the suspects, if they left the public house and saw him underneath or close to the vehicle. On his account, he became increasingly frightened, fearing serious injury or event death if the suspects saw what he was doing. He and all the other officers with him considered that it was the most stressful operation of this sort that they had ever experienced.

5. However, they were not the only officers in the Squad to experience difficulties of this sort with the tagging devices issued to them for such a purpose. There was an established history of problems with the batteries provided with the devices; about 30% of new batteries failed. Those responsible in the Greater Manchester Force for issuing them knew or ought to have known of the problem. But no evidence was called on behalf of the Chief Constable at the trial to suggest that they had done much, if anything, about it, for example by introducing a simple system of checking the batteries before issuing them with the device for a tagging operation.

6. Mr Donachie already suffered from hypertension rendering him particularly vulnerable to stressful conditions, though those for whom the Chief Constable were responsible knew nothing of that. The whole operation, which, as I have said, put him in great fear, aggravated that hypertension causing extreme stress. As a result, on the medical evidence accepted by the Judge, he developed a clinical psychiatric state, leading to an acute rise in blood pressure, which caused a stroke.

7. The Judge found:

> i. that the Chief Constable was negligent in failing to operate a safe system of work and was in breach of statutory duty in failing to provide equipment that was in an efficient state;

> ii. that there was an unbroken chain of causation between those breaches of duty and the stroke, consisting of:

>> a. Mr Donachie's fear of serious physical injury from attack by the suspected criminals should they discover him interfering with their car during the repeated visits to the car necessitated by the breaches;

>> b. the aggravation thereby caused to his already stressed condition;

>> c. consequent clinical psychiatric injury, contributing to

>> d. the stroke;

> iii. but that, as he suffered no physical injury of the sort that he had feared, namely in the form of an attack by the suspected criminals, and as the psychiatric injury giving rise to his stroke was not reasonably foreseeable because of the Chief Constable's non-culpable ignorance of his vulnerability to stress, he had suffered no reasonably foreseeable injury;

his claims in negligence and for breach of statutory duty both failed.

8. Mr Donachie appeals the Judge's finding that his injury was not reasonably foreseeable, maintaining that the Judge applied the wrong test of reasonable foreseeability to the facts of the case. The Chief Constable, by a respondent's notice, seeks to uphold the Judge's dismissal of the claim on that ground and also on the ground that he should not have found causation established. The Chief Constable also raises certain arguments as to the applicability and effect of the relevant statutory provisions, which do not in the event require determination in the appeal.

The issues

9. The appeal raises three issues, all of them overlapping:

   i. whether the Judge, on his own findings, overlooked the fact that there was a reasonably foreseeable risk of *physical* injury and, therefore, wrongly treated Mr Donachie as if he were a secondary victim claiming damages for psychiatric injury for whom it was necessary to establish some sort of an "an event" for which the Chief Constable was culpably responsible, rather than a primary victim whose claim included damages for physical injury for whom proof of such an event was not necessary;

   ii. whether, on the issue of reasonable foreseeability, the Judge wrongly took into account Mr Donachie's particular vulnerability to stress by reason of his pre-existing hypertension; and

   iii. whether, on the issue of causation raised in the respondent's notice, the test of causation of Mr Donachie's injuries, psychiatric and/or physical, were caused by the Chief Constable's negligence and/or breach of duty.

Reasonable foreseeability of injury/proximity

10. Mr Mark Turner QC, on behalf of Mr Donachie, put at the forefront of the appeal that the Judge, on his own findings, overlooked the fact that there was a reasonably foreseeable risk of physical injury. He submitted that the Judge wrongly relied on the test of foreseeability set out by this Court in *Sutherland v. Hatton* [2002] PIQR P221, where the claim failed because, the Court held, there was no reasonably foreseeable risk of injury of any sort. Here, he maintained, the Judge, having accepted that Mr Donachie had suffered a clinical psychiatric condition leading to a physical injury in the form of a stroke as a result of the Chief Constable's negligence, wrongly failed to consider whether he was a primary or secondary victim. He said that if he had done so, he would have been bound by authority, in particular *Page v. Smith* [1996] 1 AC 155, HL, to conclude that he was a primary victim, since the Chief Constable should reasonably have foreseen the possibility of some physical injury whatever the precise mechanics of its causation.

11. In order to follow, and before continuing with, Mr Turner's submissions on the issue of reasonable foreseeability, I should set out, at least in summary form, the main principles established by the House of Lords in *Page v. Smith*, the nature of the factual issue in the case and also a much cited passage from the speech in it of Lord Lloyd of Berwick. The main principles are that:

   i. A defendant owes a duty of care to a person where he can reasonably foresee that his conduct will expose that person to a risk of personal injury.

   ii. For this purpose the test of reasonable foreseeability is the same whether the foreseeable injury is physical or psychiatric or both.

iii. However, its application to the facts differs according to whether the foreseeable injury is physical or psychiatric. In the latter case, if the claimant is not involved in some sort of "event" caused by the negligence, he is a "secondary" victim and liability is more difficult to establish (see the recent discussion by the House of Lords in *Barber v. Somerset County Council* [2004] UKHL 13);

iv. If the reasonably foreseeable injury is of a physical nature, but such injury in fact causes psychiatric injury, it is immaterial whether the psychiatric injury was itself reasonably foreseeable. Equally if, as in this case, the breach of duty causes psychiatric injury causing in turn physical injury, it is immaterial that neither the psychiatric injury nor the particular form of physical injury caused was reasonably foreseeable. Thus, in *Page v. Smith*, the claimant was involved in a road accident caused by the defendant's negligence that caused him no physical injury, but aggravated a pre-accident condition of fatigue syndrome. The House of Lords upheld his entitlement, subject to establishing causation, to claim in damages for negligence. Lord Lloyd, applying the approach that I have just summarised from a passage from his speech at 190C–D, said at 190C–F:

. ". . . the test in every case ought to be whether the defendant can reasonably foresee that his conduct will expose the plaintiff to risk of personal injury. If so, then he comes under a duty of care to that plaintiff. If a working definition of "personal injury" is needed, it can be found in section 38(1) of the Limitation Act 1980; "Personal injuries" includes any disease and any impairment of a person's physical or mental condition . . ." . . . In the case of a secondary victim, the question will usually turn on whether the foreseeable injury is psychiatric . . . In the case of a primary victim the question will almost always turn on whether the foreseeable injury is physical. But it is the same test in both cases, with different applications. There is no justification for regarding physical and psychiatric injury as different "kinds" of injury. Once it is established that the defendant is under a duty of care to avoid causing personal injury to the plaintiff, it matters not whether the injury in fact sustained is physical, psychiatric or both. The utility of a single test is most apparent in those cases . . . where the plaintiff is both primary and secondary victim of the same accident.

Applying that test in the present case, it was enough to ask whether the defendant should have reasonably foreseen that the plaintiff might suffer physical injury as a result of the defendant's negligence, so as to bring him within the range of the defendant's duty of care. It was unnecessary to ask, as a separate question, whether the defendant should reasonably have foreseen injury by shock; and it is irrelevant that the plaintiff did not, in fact, suffer any physical injury."

12. On the associated issue of proximity, Mr Turner criticised the Judge's reliance in rejecting Mr Donachie's claims, on the notion that he had to prove, not only that he had been exposed to a risk of physical injury from being assaulted by the suspected criminals, but also that an "event", say, in the form of such an assault had taken place. He suggested that such an approach was inconsistent with the principles laid down by the House of Lords in *Page v. Smith* and the Court of Appeal decisions following it of *Young v. Charles Church (Southern) Ltd.*, 24th April 1997, QBENF 96/0920/C; and *Schofield v. Chief Constable of the West Yorkshire Police* [1999] ICR 193, CA.

13. Looking at the facts of this case, Mr Turner submitted that it was not a pre-requisite of actionability that the suspected criminals should have intervened to attack Mr Donachie. There was clearly a risk that they would emerge from the public house at any time and that, if they saw him interfering with their car, they would attack him. The fact that, after the event, it is known that they did not do so, he maintained, is immaterial, since Mr Donachie is a primary victim and, as Lord Lloyd of Berwick said in *Page v. Smith*, at page 197F, hindsight has no application to the claims of primary victims:

"In claims by secondary victims it may be legitimate to use hindsight in order to be able to apply the test of reasonable foreseeability at all. Hindsight, however, has no part to play where the plaintiff is a primary victim."

And, on what Mr Turner called a "four square" application of Lord Lloyd's test at 190F, set out above, it was enough to ask whether the Chief Constable should have reasonably foreseen that Mr Donachie might suffer physical injury as result of the negligence, so as to bring him within the range of the duty of care.

14. Mr Turner added that, even if it was necessary to identify some sort of an "event" for this purpose, the Judge's distinction between injury caused by fear that the suspected criminals would emerge from the public house is indistinguishable from fear that Mr Donachie would have felt had they actually done so, save possibly as to degree.

15. Mr Andrew Edis QC, for the Chief Constable accepted that the Chief Constable had a duty to take all reasonable steps to protect Mr Donachie from physical injury caused by violent criminals, by the provision of a reasonable system for checking batteries provided for tracking devices. However, he maintained that:

      i. there was no such duty to protect him from or to reduce work-related stress, since to impose it would fail the foreseeability and the fair, just and reasonable elements of the test in *Caparo Industries plc v. Dickman* [1990] 2 AC 605; and

      ii. although there is a duty of protection, whether from physical or psychiatric injury, which could become actionable in the event of criminals actually causing either or both forms of injury, there was no such event here, simply the claimed effect of stress upon Mr Donachie's body. Thus, he submitted, in the events that did happen, as distinct from those that might have happened, there was no foreseeable risk of injury of any sort; so the Judge correctly applied the rule in *Sutherland v. Hatton*

Thus, he submitted, the notion of proximity raises no separate issue, for if Mr Donachie was negligently exposed to an event that carried a reasonably foreseeable risk of physical injury, there was sufficient proximity; otherwise not.

16. As to the first of his submissions, Mr Edis, whilst acknowledging that the *Page v. Smith* rule is a matter of principle and not, in general, fact sensitive, urged the Court to have in mind the factual context in which it arises for consideration in this case. He had in mind that the job of a policeman is, by its very nature, full of stress. A chief constable puts his officers in the way of danger whenever he sends them out on the beat. Here, Mr Donachie was an

experienced officer in the Regional Crime Squad who had coped with duties in that capacity for many years. He was a man, submitted Mr Edis of whom the Chief Constable could reasonably expect a certain fortitude in the face of physical dangers to which his job exposed him. It was only if, on the facts, there could be said to have been reasonable foreseeability of physical injury from the Chief Constable's breach of duty in relation to the defective batteries that the *Page v. Smith* rule would come into play. He said that there was a risk of physical injury to any officers engaged on such tagging duties, even if the batteries were not defective, a risk that went with the job. The question was whether it could be said that there was reasonable foreseeability that that risk was materially increased by the provision of defective batteries in the sense of exposing him to imminent physical harm, as distinct from "manageable" or controllable risk of such harm. If not, such foreseeability could only relate to psychiatric injury and would justify the Judge's approach in reliance on *Sutherland v. Hatton*. He relied for his proposition as to "imminence" of physical harm for this purpose on a number of authorities, including *Frost v. Chief Constable of Yorkshire* [1999] 2 AC 455 and *W v. Essex County Council* [2001] 2 AC 592, HL.

17. The tagging operation in this instance was not, he submitted one that involved a risk of such imminent physical danger as to constitute an "an event" in the sense of putting Mr Donachie in sufficient proximity to the foreseeable source of harm so as to be able to rely on the psychiatric injury giving rise to physical injury — as was, for example, the pregnant barmaid in *Dulieu v. White & Sons* [1901] 2 KB 669, who suffered nervous shock causing her to give premature birth as a result of the tortfeasor's horse van bursting into her bar from the roadway.

18. The difficulty for Mr Edis in urging the Court to look at this case as one in which the defective batteries did not increase the reasonable foreseeability of physical injury normally inherent in a police tagging operation is that neither the evidence nor the Judge's finding on that evidence supports it. The Judge, having carefully rehearsed the evidence, expressly found that it was reasonably foreseeable that, as a result of the malfunction of the batteries, the existing small risk in the operation would become considerably greater and the consequent stress to Mr Donachie severe or extreme. In paragraphs 30 and 56 of his judgement, he said:

"30. It is suggested by the Defendant that the Claimant is putting it too highly in saying that when he was on his back under the car he feared for his life. Even if his memory has been enhanced by reflection I have no doubt he feared despite the presence of the safety net he might be detected and suffer some unpleasant consequences namely injury if not death."

"56. Was it foreseeable that battery failure or lack of implementation of a system for testing batteries created a foreseeable risk of harm? If there is a system or lack of a system which allows for unpredictable batteries to be deployed in devices under cars then it is to be expected and foreseeable that more than one trip to the target vehicle will be required before the device works. The more often a person has to go under a vehicle to fix a tag and the longer in total he is under that vehicle the greater the risk of discovery and assault even with a safety net in place. That was the more so in the instant case when the suspects were nearby and might approach the vehicle at any time. Therefore the increase in the risk of physical injury due to faulty batteries prolonging the time necessarily to be spent under the target vehicle was foreseeable. Each journey to the car increased the risk of discovery and assault. . . ."

19. In my view, there is no basis on which this Court could go behind those findings, albeit that they are findings of secondary fact. Nor can I see any legal basis for Mr Edis's further and related submission that, even so, it is necessary for Mr Donachie, on a *Page v. Smith* approach, to prove that there is a reasonable foreseeability of *imminent* physical harm, as contrasted with exposure to a "manageable" or controllable risk of harm. None of the authorities to which Mr Edis referred the Court on this point begins to support this suggested qualification of the *Page v. Smith* principle.

20. The Judge, despite his findings on causation, approached the question of reasonable foreseeability of injury on the basis that the relevant injury was psychiatric injury, not physical injury of whatever sort. On that basis and because of his view that there was no "event", in the sense of no assault, to which Mr Donachie had been exposed, and no reason for the Chief Constable to have known of any special vulnerability to stress, he was a secondary victim in respect of whom, reasonable foreseeability of stress giving rise to psychiatric injury was not enough to establish a breach of duty. This is how he put it, at paragraphs 59–61 of his judgment:

"59. The Defendant knew that tagging operations were stressful in general terms. The Defendant would be taken to know that getting under a car to fix a device would be stressful in the sense that there would be apprehension of discovery and more so if the driver and passengers were nearby and would at some stage return to the vehicle. The Defendant would in such circumstances foresee that the stress would be prolonged if not increased every time a return visit to the car was necessary. This throws me back to the case of *Sutherland v. Hatton* and the threshold question namely whether the kind of harm to this claimant was reasonably foreseeable bearing in mind that there are no occupations which should be regarded as intrinsically dangerous to mental health.

60. As I have already found, the Defendant did not know that the Claimant was suffering from hypertension or that it was poorly controlled or, as the cardiologists agree, that such had been the case from 1995 at least. In such circumstances it is difficult to see how the Defendant could be liable for any mental illness or the consequences thereof caused by stress induced by being under the car. Dr Johnson, the psychiatrist retained by the Defendant, accepts that if the Claimant felt intensely that he was at risk of injury whilst under the car such could trigger a psychiatric reaction or illness . . . However, in the absence of knowledge that the Claimant had anything wrong with him which might predispose him to such mental illness it is difficult to see on the basis of *Sutherland* how the Defendant could reasonably foresee this problem arising. It could be argued that here the injury to health attributable to stress was physical not mental, namely stroke and therefore *Sutherland* would be of no assistance. It seems to me even so that the employer would need to know there was something about the Claimant's state of health which would predispose him to such injury. The cardiologists agree that that the risk of stroke for "normal" members of the population is slight. The Defendant therefore could not reasonably foresee a stroke for such a person if he did what the Claimant was doing on 2 November 1997. The cardiologists agree that raised blood pressure increases the risk of having a stroke. . . . I can accept Dr Levy's view that poorly controlled hypertension with prolonged levels of stress meant it was foreseeable that a stroke could follow. That does not avail the Claimant in the absence of knowledge of the Claimant's condition by the Defendant. Dr Levy reached the opinion that an episode of extreme stress could trigger a

stroke even in a person with no history of raised blood pressure. . . . That may be so but I do not think that that makes injury any more reasonably foreseeable in the instant case.

61. I conclude therefore that the Defendant is right in saying that the particular injury is not reasonably foreseeable or that it is too remote. Putting it another way I do not consider this is a *Page v. Smith* case. The event in *Page v. Smith* was a road traffic accident. The equivalent event in this case would have been the arrival of the villains on the scene. It is with some diffidence and reluctance that I have come to the conclusion that damages for this particular injury are not recoverable in negligence."

21. It is plain from *Page v. Smith* and the authorities following it that, in the case of claims for nervous shock or other form of psychiatric injury, the application of the test of reasonable foreseeability differs according to whether the claimant is a "primary" or a "secondary" victim. In the case of the latter the law accepts, but more reluctantly than in the case of the former, the possibility in certain cases of establishing reasonable foreseeability of injury. This reluctance, by the imposition of certain control mechanisms, has — as a response to the "floodgates" argument — its root in the policy of careful scrutiny of claims where the sole injury for which damages are claimed is psychiatric; see *McLoughlin v. O'Brien* [1983] 1 AC 410, HL, especially per Lord Scarman at 431 B–D.

22. However, where the court is satisfied that reasonable foreseeability has been established, whether for physical or psychiatric injury or both, it is immaterial whether the foreseeable injury caused, and in respect of which the claim is made, is caused directly or through another form of injury not reasonably foreseeable. Thus, as Lord Browne-Wilkinson indicated in *Page v. Smith*, at 181A–B, a negligent act may cause physical injury or illness either directly or through a psychiatric route, or it may cause psychiatric injury either directly and/or through direct physical injury or illness.

23. I agree with Mr Turner that the Judge, in the passages from his judgment that I have set out in paragraph 19 above, wrongly relied on *Sutherland v. Hatton*, a claim for occupational stress induced psychiatric injury that failed because there was no reasonably foreseeable risk of injury of any sort. This case was one in which, as I have said, there was a reasonable foreseeability that the Chief Constable's breach of duty would cause physical injury to Mr Donachie, though not of the kind he actually suffered, and via the unforeseeable psychiatric injury actually caused by his negligence. He was thus a primary victim in respect of whom there was a reasonable foreseeability of physical injury and, in consequence, in respect of whom it was not necessary to prove involvement in an "event" in the form of an assault or otherwise. There can be no doubt that the Judge, on his findings of fact that we have set out in paragraph 18 above, was satisfied on the evidence before him that there was a reasonable foreseeability of physical injury.

24. I should add that, even if it had been necessary to look for an "event" in this case sufficient to enable Mr Donachie to rely as a primary victim on reasonable foreseeability of psychiatric, as distinct from physical injury, I would have had sympathy with Mr Turner's submission that the circumstances in which he had been placed as a police officer, coupled with his fear engendered by those circumstances of physical injury, are indistinguishable in principle from occurrence of such injury. If A puts B in a position which A can reasonably foresee that B would fear

physical injury, and B, as a result, suffers psychiatric injury and/or physical injury, B is, in my view, a primary victim. If it were necessary to characterise the onset of the fear causative of such injury as "an event", I would do so. There is all the difference in the world between a person like Mr Donachie, put in such a position by the tortfeasor, and someone who happens to learn from afar and/or a significant time afterwards of an event in which he had no involvement, the discovery of which he claims to have caused him psychiatric injury.

Pre-existing vulnerability

25. This issue is part of the foresee ability issue, but as it was treated as a discrete area of argument by both Mr Turner and Edis, I shall give it the same focus as they did.

26. Mr Turner criticised the Judge's reliance, in paragraphs 59 to 61 of his judgment (see paragraph 19 above), on Mr Donachie's pre-existing hypertension as a symptom of his special vulnerability to stress and its mental or other consequences when considering the issue of reasonable foreseeability of injury. He noted too that there was no evidence that he was susceptible to psychiatric injury. He submitted that any such pre-existing vulnerability, whether to stress or psychiatric injury, was irrelevant to foreseeability, since the test is that a tortfeasor takes his victim as he finds him in cases of psychiatric injury as well as physical injury.

27. Mr Edis submitted that the pre-existing vulnerability of Mr Donachie is relevant to reasonable foreseeability because, unless the Chief Constable knew of it there was no reasonable risk of injury of any kind, and it is only where there is a foreseeable risk of physical injury that the tortfeasor must take his victim as he finds him. In developing that argument, he drew the following analogy from the facts in *Page v. Smith*. Driving a vehicle badly creates a foreseeable risk of injury if an accident occurs. All those involved in the "event", that is, the accident may recover damages, whether for physical or mental injury, or both. But it does not follow from that reasoning that a person not the subject of such an "event", who is, not involved in the accident, can recover damages for stress caused by their fear that there might be an accident.

28. If I am correct in my view that Mr Donachie is a primary victim because the Chief Constable's breaches of duty gave rise to a reasonable foreseeability of physical injury, albeit of a different form from the one caused by those breaches, any pre-existing vulnerability of Mr Donachie to stress causative of psychiatric injury is irrelevant. The Chief Constable must take his victim as he finds him. Lord Lloyd, in *Page v. Smith*, said, at 197E–H:

". . . In claims by secondary victims the law insists on certain control mechanisms, in order as a matter of policy to limit the number of potential claimants. Thus, the defendant will not be liable unless psychiatric injury is foreseeable in a person of normal fortitude. These control mechanisms have no place where the plaintiff is the primary victim. . . . Subject to the above qualifications, the approach in all cases should be the same, namely, whether the defendant can reasonably foresee that his conduct will expose the plaintiff to the risk of personal injury, whether physical or psychiatric. If the answer is yes, then the duty of care is established, even though physical injury does not in fact, occur. There is no justification for regarding physical and psychiatric injury as different "kinds of damage". . . . A defendant who is under a duty of care to the plaintiff, whether as primary or secondary victim, is not liable for damages for nervous shock unless the shock results in some recognised psychiatric illness. It is no answer that the plaintiff was predisposed to psychiatric illness. Nor is it relevant that the illness takes a rare form or is of unusual severity. The defendant must take his victim as he finds him."

29. Accordingly, the fact that the Chief Constable was not, and could not reasonably have been expected to be, aware of any particular vulnerability of Mr Donachie, by reason of hypertension possibly causative of psychiatric injury, is no impediment to Mr Donachie's claim under the heading of reasonable foreseeability or in causation. It follows for this reason too, that the Judge erred in his reasoning in paragraphs 59–61 of his judgment (see paragraph 19 above) that, because the Chief Constable had not been put on notice about Mr Donachie's hypertension, all that followed from his breaches of duty on 2nd November 1997 was not reasonably foreseeable. That reasoning flowed from his basic error in concluding, as he put it in paragraph 61, that this was not "a *Page v. Smith* case".

30. However, if, for the reasons I have given in paragraph 24 above, it had been necessary to consider the validity of the Judge's conclusion that there was no reasonable foreseeability of psychiatric injury on account of Mr Donachie's pre-existing vulnerability, I could not have upheld his finding. There was no evidence that he was vulnerable to psychiatric illness, only that his pre-existing hypertension predisposed him to a stroke, not to psychiatric injury.

31. There is no need to deal separately with the issue of breach of statutory duty, since, as Mr Turner conceded, the issues as to foreseeability in negligence are essentially the same as those arising for consideration under the relevant statutory provisions.

Causation

32. The general rule in personal injury cases remains the "but for" test laid down by the House of Lords in *Bonnington Castings Ltd. v. Wardlaw* [1956] AC 613, as interpreted by the majority of the House in *McGhee v. National Coal Board [1973] 1 WLR 1*, a general rule that Lord Bingham reiterated in paragraph 8 of his speech in *Fairchild v. Glenhaven Funeral Services Ltd*. [2003] 1 AC 32:

"In a personal injury action based on negligence or breach of statutory duty the claimant seeks to establish a breach by the defendant of a duty owed to the claimant, which has caused him damage. For the purposes of analysis, and for the purpose of pleading, proving and resolving the claim, lawyers find it convenient to break the claim into its constituent elements: the duty, the breach, the damage and the causal connection between the breach and the damage. In the generality of personal injury actions, it is of course true that the claimant is required to discharge the burden of showing that the breach of which he complains caused the damage for which claims and to do so by showing that but for the breach he would not have suffered the damage."

33. As Lord Bingham went on to emphasise in paragraph 9 of his speech, the issue in *Fairchild* did not concern the general validity and applicability of that requirement, but

whether in special circumstances such as those in that case there should be any variation or relaxation of it. Those circumstances were that the claimant had contracted mesothelioma following successive employments with two employers, each of whom was in breach of duty in exposing him to excessive quantities of asbestos dust, the only possible cause of his condition. In the state of medical science he was unable to prove which or whether both of his employers, by reason of their breach of duty, had caused his condition. Their Lordships, faced with the injustice of depriving him of recovery of compensation in such circumstances, held essentially on policy grounds that he should be entitled to recover against both employers on the *McGhee* basis that his employer, in exposing him to a risk to which he should not have been exposed, materially contributed to the injury against which his employer had a duty to protect him. Lord Nicholls of Birkenhead observed at paragraph 36 of his speech in *Fairchild* that the real difficulty lies in elucidating in sufficiently specific terms the principle to be applied in reaching that conclusion. And he later observed, at paragraph 43, that considerable restraint is called for in relaxation of the threshold "but for" test of causal connection.

34. The Judge's findings on the issue of causation, which are to be found in paragraphs 53 to 55 and 62 to 71 of his judgment, were, in summary, as follows. The Greater Manchester Police Force had been using tagging devices of the type involved in this case for some two years. There was no evidence that the Force had any system for checking their efficiency or the state of the batteries fitted to them. The Force's experience of using the devices was that they were not reliable and that, on occasion, they would not operate properly. They had a propensity either not to work at all when new — there was about a 30% rate of failure — or to cease working whilst in use and without warning. There was no means of testing whether a battery was defective before fitting it to a device. And, even when fitted, the only way of testing it before attaching it to a vehicle was to walk with it some two or three metres from the tracking police vehicle, something not normally done nor instructed — and not done in this instance. The significance of all this to the issue of causation can be seen from the observations of the Judge in paragraph 56 of his judgment, albeit that he was there dealing with foreseeability. I have already set out part of those observations in paragraph 18 above, but for convenience, I reproduce here the whole of paragraph 56:

"Was it foreseeable that battery failure or lack of implementation of a system for testing batteries created a foreseeable risk of harm? If there is a system or lack of a system which allows for unpredictable batteries to be deployed in devices under cars then it is to be expected and foreseeable that more than one trip to the target vehicle will be required before the device works. The more often a person has to go under a vehicle to fix a tag and hence the longer in total he is under that vehicle the greater the risk of discovery and assault even with a safety net in place. That was the more so in the instant case when the suspects were nearby and might approach the vehicle at any time. Therefore the increase in the risk of physical injury due to faulty batteries prolonging the time necessarily to be spent under the target vehicle was foreseeable. Each journey to the car increased the risk of discovery and assault. In such circumstances it is clear that the duty of care owed to the Claimant included a duty to reduce the time of exposure under the target vehicle by having a system of ensuring that batteries were reliable. The Claimant relies upon the maxim "res ipsa loquitur" Whether that maxim strictly applies or not, it behoves the Defendant to show that he has done all he reasonably could have done in and about the provision of reliable batteries. In the absence of any evidence on that score it right to infer that the Defendant is in breach of duty in that respect."

35. As to whether the Chief Constable was in breach of that duty — that is, "culpable" in exposing Mr Donachie to risk on the occasion in question, the Judge found, in paragraph 69 of his judgment, that he was not in respect of the first of the nine trips to the car, possibly not in respect of the second, to retrieve the device, or the third to attach it for a second time, still with the same battery — presumably because it had been working shortly before this operation began and would have passed any system of testing. However, he found that the remaining six trips were "culpable".

36. The Judge held that causation was established. In paragraphs 62 to 71 of his judgment, he found that Mr Donachie had suffered extreme stress as a result of repeated trips to the car to attach the device, and that such stress caused or materially contributed to the later stroke. In paragraphs 70 and 71 he referred to medical evidence, which he accepted, that the greater the stress the greater the risk of Mr Donachie having a stroke, and that, *but for* the malfunction, there might have been a small risk but it was considerably greater if the stress was a lot greater. He continued:

"70. . . . I agree almost as a matter of common-sense that the greater the number of trips the greater the stress. It is therefore easy to conclude that the excess exposure to stress caused or made a material contribution to the subsequent cerebrovascular accident. If that approach be wrong the Claimant contends that all he has to show is that the additional significant exposure to stress was caused by the culpability of the Defendant. If he does so then he relies upon *McGhee v. The National Coal Board* (1973) 1 WLR 1. That case was discussed and analysed in *Fairchild v. Glenhaven Funeral Services Ltd.* . . . by Lord Bingham at . . . paragraphs 17–21. See also Lord Hoffmann at . . . paragraph 64.

71. In short the "culpable" trips to the motorcar materially increased the risk of stroke occurring and therefore although the Claimant cannot show that but for the culpable trips he would not have suffered the stroke he nonetheless succeeds on establishing causation. That must be right. It follows that if my conclusions as to foreseeability of harm are wrong then causation is established."

37. As I read those paragraphs, the Judge, contrary to the views of Lords Reid, Simon and Salmon in *McGhee* regarded the notion of "material contribution" and that of "material increase in risk" as different and alternative tests. In the light of the analyses of some of their Lordships in *McGhee* and *Fairchild*, I have some sympathy with his approach. But, in any event, despite the indicative, as distinct from conditional, manner in which he referred to the "but for" test in paragraph 71, it is plain that, for the purpose of considering the alternative of "material increase in risk", he was there referring to his preferred conclusion in paragraph 70, namely the "but for" test. It should be noted that he began the second sentence of paragraph 70 with the finding ". . . *but for* the malfunction there might have been a small risk but it was undoubtedly considerably greater" (my emphasis), given, as he had found, that "the stress was a lot greater". And, as can be seen, he went on in that paragraph to find that the excess exposure to stress "caused or made a material contribution" to the subsequent stroke, a finding clearly based on the conclusion on the evidence in paragraph 66 of his judgment:

"I conclude as a matter of fact having heard all the evidence that the stress suffered by the Claimant can be categorised as extreme or severe or even perhaps acute. As said the cardiologists' view is that in those circumstances the stress of the occasion *caused or materially contributed to* the subsequent cerebro-vascular accident. I have no difficulty in accepting their opinion." [my emphasis]

38. Thus, the Judge, who had clearly put his mind to the different tests of causation indicated in the authorities, dealt with it on the *Bonnington* basis. That is, he applied the "but for" test recently reaffirmed as the norm for claims for personal injury in negligence claims by the House of Lords in *Fairchild*. He only turned, in the latter part of paragraph 70 and in paragraph 71, to the material increase in risk test as an alternative. Whether or not, in the light of the equation of the majority of their Lordships in *McGhee* of the notions of "material contribution" and "material increase in risk", he was wrong to treat them as different tests, his clear finding in paragraph 70 was that the excess exposure to stress "caused or made a material contribution to" the subsequent stroke.

39. It follows that the Judge applied the general "but for" rule, not some *Fairchild* relaxation of it, as suggested by Mr Edis. In my view, the Judge was correct in the circumstances to apply the general rule.

40. As to the facts, Mr Edis criticised the Judge's findings that six of the nine trips to the car were "culpable". He relied on the fact that, on the evidence accepted by the Judge, it was not until the fifth trip, that is, after the first battery had failed for the second time, that Mr Donachie tried another battery. So, he argued, the Chief Constable's culpability did not begin until the sixth trip when Mr Donachie had to retrieve the device from the car for the third time. It followed, he said that about half the total stress to which Mr Donachie was exposed was not "culpable", a consideration relevant to causation as well as foreseeability, since Mr Donachie had to prove that the extra stress was a material contribution to his subsequent stroke. To do that, Mr Edis submitted, he had to prove that he would not have suffered his injury but for those "culpable" trips to the car.

41. Mr Edis, in addition to what he maintained was "substantial non-culpable stress" on the day in question, pointed to earlier features of Mr Donachie's mental state, including: evidence that the Judge accepted of his change of mood in the previous six weeks and Mr Donachie's own attribution of his condition to a sudden recall from holiday, his normal workload and a meeting with an informer two days later. No culpability on the part of the Chief Constable had been established in respect of such matters, but, said Mr Edis, they were relevant to the issue of causation. He maintained that in a case such as this, a single wholly exceptional event and with such contributory factors, the "but for" test remains the general rule in tort, as acknowledged their Lordships in *Fairchild*.

42. Mr Turner accepted that Mr Donachie's first trip to the car would have been necessary to attach the device even if it had been in proper working order. However, he maintained that all of the following eight trips were caused by the Chief Constable's breach of duty, given the evidence, accepted by the Judge, that, despite the Force's two years' experience of a high failure rate of the batteries and the risk that such failure created for officers using them, it had done nothing about it, by investigation, instruction or warning or otherwise.

43. As to the correctness of the test of causation adopted by the Judge, Mr Turner relied on the fact that the Judge had found, on the evidence before him, not only that stress for which the Chief Constable was culpably responsible had increased the risk of Mr Donachie suffering from a clinical psychiatric condition and stroke, but that such stress had caused, in the sense of materially contributed to, both those conditions. Accordingly, he submitted, Mr Donachie succeeded before the Judge on that basic *Bonnington* test of "material contribution" to the injury without need for recourse to the "material increase in risk" alternative derived from *McGhee* and *Fairchild*.

44. The only question is whether the Judge, in his application of the *McGhee* test, could properly find on the evidence before him that the Chief Constable had caused or materially contributed to Mr Donachie's injuries, given the various factors contributing or capable of contributing to his extreme stress at the material time and to the impossibility for him of proving their relative contributions.

45. I do not see on what basis the Court could properly interfere with the Judge's finding in paragraph 70 that the excess culpable exposure by the Chief Constable of Mr Donachie to extreme stress in the circumstances that he found proved, "caused or made a material contribution" to his stroke. As Mr Edis acknowledged in argument, this is primarily a factual matter on which the Judge has made clear findings of primary fact.

46. Accordingly, I would allow Mr Donachie's appeal on the issue of reasonable foreseeability and, to the extent if at all it is a separate consideration, the issue of pre-existing vulnerability, and dismiss the Chief Constable's cross-appeal on the issue of causation.

Latham LJ:

47. I agree.

Arden LJ:

48. I also agree.

The following questions relate to the law report reproduced above for the case of *David L Donachie v The Chief Constable of the Greater Manchester Police*. When noting your answers to the questions, you should include reference(s) to the appropriate points in the judgment from which you have drawn your information.

SECTION A

    1. Who brought the initial complaint in the case of *David L Donachie v The Chief Constable of the Greater Manchester Police?*

    2. Give a short statement of the issues raised by the *Donachie* case before the Court of Appeal.

    3.   (a) In which courts was the case of *David L Donachie v The Chief Constable of the Greater Manchester Police* heard?

     (b) Were these criminal or civil proceedings?

     (c) What was the decision in each of the hearings?

     (d) Was the decision in the hearing of the case at first instance overturned on appeal?

4. What were the grounds upon which the appeal was brought by Mr Donachie before the Court of Appeal?

5. What was the response of the Chief Constable of the Greater Manchester Police to Mr Donachie's appeal?

6. What were the issues identified by the Court of Appeal in the case?

SECTION B

7. Discover whether the case of *David L Donachie v The Chief Constable of the Greater Manchester Police* has been reported in any of the published series of law reports.

8. Has the case of *David L Donachie v The Chief Constable of the Greater Manchester Police* been appealed beyond the Court of Appeal?

9. What view does the Court of Appeal express in relation to the proposition by counsel (Mr. Turner), which is referred to in paragraph 10 of the decision, as to the application of "the test of foreseeability" in *Sutherland v Hatton?*

10. Why does the Court of Appeal consider that this was not "a *Page v Smith* case"?

11. What does the Court of Appeal confirm to be "the general rule" on causation in personal injury cases?

Exercise 4

Case II

Tomlinson v Congleton Borough Council and another

[2002] EWCA Civ 309, [2003] UKHL 47

a

COURT OF APPEAL, CIVIL DIVISION
WARD, SEDLEY AND LONGMORE LJJ
16 JANUARY, 14 MARCH 2002

b

HOUSE OF LORDS
LORD NICHOLLS OF BIRKENHEAD, LORD HOFFMANN, LORD HUTTON, LORD HOBHOUSE
OF WOODBOROUGH AND LORD SCOTT OF FOSCOTE
23, 24 JUNE, 31 JULY 2003

c

Occupier's liability – Common duty of care – Nature of duty – Reasonable care – Lake open to the public – Occupier posting notices prohibiting swimming – Occupier aware of further steps which could minimise likelihood of swimming – Claimant running into lake, diving, and suffering injury – Whether occupier having taken such care as in all the circumstances was reasonable to see that claimant would be reasonably safe – Occupiers' Liability Act 1957, s 2.

d

The defendants owned, occupied and managed a public park. In the park was a lake formed from a disused sand extraction pit. The lake had sandy beaches and was a popular recreational venue where yachting, sub-aqua diving and other regulated activities were permitted, but swimming was not. Notices reading 'Dangerous water: no swimming' were posted but they had little or no effect. The unauthorised use of the lake and the increasing possibility of an accident was of concern to the defendants. A plan to landscape the shores and plant over the beaches from which people swam had been approved, but work had begun only shortly before 6 May 1995. On that date the claimant went to the lake. He ran into the water and dived, striking his head on the sandy bottom with sufficient force to cause him an injury which resulted in paralysis from the neck downward. He brought proceedings for damages claiming that the defendants, as occupiers, owed him the common duty of care set out in s 2(2)[a] of the Occupiers' Liability Act 1957, which was a duty to take such care as in all the circumstances was reasonable to see that a visitor would be reasonably safe in using the premises for the purposes for which he was permitted to be there. At trial it was conceded that he had seen and ignored the warning signs so that when he entered the water he had ceased to be at the park for purposes for which he had been invited and permitted by the defendants to be there, and had accordingly ceased to be a visitor and had become a trespasser. As such he was owed a lesser duty of care under the Occupiers' Liability Act 1984. The judge found against the claimant, holding inter alia that the danger and risk of injury were obvious, and that an occupier was not under a duty to warn against such a risk. The claimant appealed. The majority of the Court of Appeal allowed his appeal, holding that the gravity of the risk of injury, the frequency with which park users came to be exposed to the risk, the failure of warning signs to curtail the extent to which the risk was being run and the attractiveness of the location led to the conclusion that

e

f

g

h

j

---

a   Section 2, so far as material, is set out at [6], below

All England Law Reports 3 September 2003

CA   Tomlinson v Congleton BC   1123

a the occupiers were reasonably to be expected to offer some protection against the risks of entering the water. The posting of notices, shown to be ineffective, had therefore not been enough to discharge the duty. The authorities should have carried out the landscaping and planting which had been recommended to them. The defendants appealed.

b **Held** – The majority of the Court of Appeal appeared to have proceeded on the oversimplified basis that if there had been a foreseeable risk of serious injury the defendants had been under a duty to do what was necessary to prevent it. Even assuming that the circumstances of the instant case were such that a duty had been owed to a lawful visitor under s 2(2) of the 1957 Act, and that there had been a risk attributable to the state of the premises rather than to the acts of the c claimant, the question of what amounted to 'such care as in all the circumstances of the case is reasonable' depended not only on the likelihood that someone might be injured and the seriousness of the injury which might occur, but also on the social value of the activity which gave rise to the risk and the cost of preventative measures. Those factors had to be balanced against each other. It d would be extremely rare for an occupier of land to be under a duty to prevent people from taking risks which were inherent in the activities they freely chose to undertake upon the land. He would be entitled to impose conditions prohibiting risky activities, as the defendants had done in the instant case by prohibiting swimming. But the law did not require him to do so. There was an important question of freedom at stake. It would be unjust if the harmless recreation of e responsible people upon the beaches were prohibited in order to comply with what was thought to be a legal duty to safeguard irresponsible visitors against dangers which were perfectly obvious. That such people took no notice of warnings could not create a duty to take other steps to protect them. Local authorities and other occupiers of land were ordinarily under no duty to incur f such social and financial costs as had been incurred in the instant case to protect a minority, or even a majority, against obvious dangers. Accordingly, in the instant case, even if swimming had not been prohibited, and the defendants had owed a duty under s 2(2) of the 1957 Act, that duty would not have required them to have taken any steps to prevent the claimant from diving or warning him against dangers that were perfectly obvious. It followed that there could have g been no duty owed under the 1984 Act. The appeal would therefore be allowed (see [1], [34], [40]–[42], [45], [46], [48], [50]–[52], [65], [83], [84], [94], below (House of Lords judgment)).

Dictum of Lord Phillips of Worth Matravers MR in *Donoghue v Folkestone Properties Ltd* [2003] 3 All ER 1101 at [53] approved.

h
Notes
For the common duty of care to visitors and an occupier's duty of care to persons other than visitors, see 33 *Halsbury's Laws* (4th edn reissue) paras 631–634, 640.

For the Occupiers' Liability Act 1957, s 2, see 31 *Halsbury's Statutes* (4th edn) j (2000 reissue) 466.

Cases referred to in judgments and opinions
Addie (Robert) & Sons (Collieries) Ltd v Dumbreck [1929] AC 358, [1929] All ER Rep 1, HL.
Bartrum v Hepworth Minerals and Chemicals Ltd (29 October 1999, unreported), QBD.
Bolton v Stone [1951] 1 All ER 1078, [1951] AC 850, HL.

British Railways Board v Herrington [1972] 1 All ER 749, [1972] AC 877, [1972] 2
    WLR 537, HL.

Bucheleres v Chicago Park District (1996) 171 Ill 2d 435, Ill SC.

Calgarth, The, The Otarama [1927] P 93, CA.

Coggs v Bernard (1703) 2 Ld Raym 909, 92 ER 107, [1558–1774] All ER Rep 1, DC.

Corp of the City of Glasgow v Taylor [1922] 1 AC 44, HL.

Cotton v Derbyshire Dales DC [1994] CA Transcript 753, (1994) Times, June 20.

Darby v National Trust [2001] EWCA Civ 189, [2001] PIQR P372.

Donoghue v Folkestone Properties Ltd [2003] EWCA Civ 231, [2003] 3 All ER 1101,
    [2003] 2 WLR 1138.

Donoghue v Stevenson [1932] AC 562, [1932] All ER Rep 1, HL.

Hastie v Magistrates of Edinburgh 1907 SC 1102, Ct of Sess.

Hillen v ICI (Alkali) Ltd [1936] AC 65, [1935] All ER Rep 555, HL.

Hughes v Lord Advocate [1963] 1 All ER 705, [1963] AC 837, [1963] 2 WLR 779, HL.

Jebson v Ministry of Defence [2000] 1 WLR 2055, CA.

Jolley v Sutton London BC [2000] 3 All ER 409, [2000] 1 WLR 1082, HL.

Overseas Tankship (UK) Ltd v Miller Steamship Co Pty, The Wagon Mound (No 2)
    [1966] 2 All ER 709, [1967] 1 AC 617, [1966] 3 WLR 498, PC.

Ratcliff v McConnell [1999] 1 WLR 670, CA.

Reeves v Metropolitan Police Comr [1999] 3 All ER 897, [2000] 1 AC 360, [1999] 3
    WLR 363, HL.

Scott v Associated British Ports, Swainger v Associated British Ports [2000] All ER (D)
    1937, CA.

Smith v Leech Brain & Co Ltd [1961] 3 All ER 1159, [1962] 2 QB 405, [1962] 2 WLR 148.

Staples v West Dorset DC (1995) 93 LGR 536, CA.

Stevenson v Corp of Glasgow 1908 SC 1034, Ct of Sess.

Vancouver-Fraser Park District v Olmstead (1974) 51 DLR (3d) 416, Can SC.

Whyte v Redland Aggregates Ltd [1997] CA Transcript 2034, CA.

Cases also cited or referred to in skeleton arguments and in list of authorities

*Fairchild v Glenhaven Funeral Services Ltd, Dyson v Leeds City Council, Pendleton v
    Stone & Webster Engineering Ltd, Babcock International Ltd, National Grid Co, Fox
    v Spousal (Midland) Ltd, Matthews v Associated Portland Cement Manufacturers
    (1978) Ltd* [2001] EWCA Civ 1881, [2002] IRLR 129, [2002] 1 WLR 1052; *rvsd*
    [2002] UKHL 22, [2002] 3 All ER 305, [2003] 1 AC 32, [2002] 3 WLR 89.

Ferguson v Welsh [1987] 3 All ER 777, [1987] 1 WLR 1553, HL.

Glasgow Corp v Muir [1943] 2 All ER 44, [1943] AC 448, HL.

Heaven v Pender (1883) 11 QBD 503, CA.

Indermaur v Dames (1865–66) LR 1 CP 274, CCP; *affd* (1866–67) LR 2 CP 311, Ex
    Cham.

Letang v Ottawa v Electric Railway Co [1926] AC 725, PC.

Nagle v Rottnest Island Authority (1993) 177 CLR 423, HC Aust.

Osborne v London and North Western Rly Co (1888) 21 QBD 220, DC.

Parker v PFC Flooring Supplies Ltd [2001] PIQR P115.

Romeo v Conservation Commission of the Northern Territory (1998) 151 ALR 263, Aust HC.

White v Blackmore [972] 3 All ER 158, [1972] 2 QB 651, [1972] 3 WLR 296, CA.

Appeal

The claimant, John Peter Tomlinson, appealed from the decision of Jack J on 21
March 2001 in the Manchester District Registry holding (i) that the defendants,
Congleton Borough Council and Cheshire County Council, were not liable for

a damages for breach of their duty of care under s 1 of the Occupiers' Liability Act 1984 to the claimant who had suffered accidental injury as a trespasser in a park which the defendants together owned, occupied and managed; and (ii) that the claimant's contributory negligence amounted to a proportion of two-thirds. The facts are set out in the judgment of Ward LJ.

b *Bill Braithwaite QC* and *Gerard Martin QC* (instructed by *Paul Ross & Co*, Manchester) for the claimant.

Raymond Machell QC (instructed by *James Chapman & Co*, Manchester) for the councils.

Cur adv vult

c

14 March 2003. The following judgments were delivered.

WARD LJ.

d [1] This appeal concerns an accident with very severe consequences which happened on 6 May 1995 to the claimant, John Tomlinson. He was 18 years old at the time and he was one of many hundreds of people who regularly went to Brereton Heath Park near Congleton in Cheshire. The park was owned and occupied by the borough council (the first defendant) and managed for them by the county council (the second defendant). They have resolved their initial *e* differences and now defend jointly as occupiers.

[2] The centrepiece of the park is a lake. It is not a natural mere but a disused quarry, about 40 feet deep at its deepest point towards which the shore shelves at varying degrees. It was an extremely popular venue where yachting, sub-aqua diving and other regulated activities were permitted, but swimming and diving were not. The prohibition was made clear by notices reading 'DANGEROUS *f* WATER: NO SWIMMING', which had little or no effect. A succession of disclosed internal documents, to which I shall have to refer in detail later, shows the local authorities to have been fully alive to this and the need to do what they could about it. A scheme was in fact developed to plant the shores from which people swam with vegetation which would make them inaccessible, but by the *g* date of the accident the budgetary bids for the relatively modest cost of doing this work had been repeatedly turned down. Since the accident, planting has been carried out and has proved effective.

[3] May 6 1995 was the Saturday of a bank holiday weekend and a hot day. The claimant went there after work with some friends in the early afternoon. He *h* went in and out of the water, like others, to cool off, diving or plunging within his depth. At one point of the afternoon Mr Tomlinson dived from a standing position in water which came no higher than his mid-thigh. Somehow—it has never become clear how, but the judge saw no reason to attribute it to a submerged object—Mr Tomlinson struck his head with sufficient force to drive *j* his fifth cervical vertebra into the spinal canal. The injury paralysed him from the neck down, and in the time since he has made only a limited recovery of the use of his hands and arms.

[4] His case against the local authorities is that as occupiers it was their breach of their duty of care towards him which was the cause of his accident. Their case is that the risk of danger was, as he knew, an obvious one and he willingly accepted it.

[5] Jack J, who tried the issue of liability in Manchester on 21 March 2001, set
out the history in careful detail. At the end of it he said:

> 'I conclude this section by noting that there was nothing about the mere at
> Brereton Heath which made it any more dangerous than any other ordinary
> stretch of open water in England. Swimming and diving carry their own
> risks. So, if the mere at Brereton was to be described as a danger, it was only
> because it attracted swimming and diving, which activities carry a risk.'

[6] As to the occurrence of the accident, the judge found:

> 'Mr Tomlinson waded into the water until it was a little above his knees,
> probably at or no deeper than mid-thigh level. He could not see the bottom.
> He then threw himself forward in a dive or plunge. He intended it to be a
> shallow dive. But it went wrong. He went deeper than he intended. His
> head struck the sandy bottom ... I am satisfied that he did not dive towards
> the shore, and I am satisfied that he did not jump into the air and then
> jack-knife to do a vertical dive ... Mr Tomlinson said that he was a strong
> swimmer. It appeared from his evidence that he did not have much
> experience of diving. Somehow on this occasion he just got it wrong, with
> tragic results. He might have been saved by his arms, had they been
> outstretched in from of him, but somehow he was not.'

[7] The judge's findings, which have not been challenged on this appeal, that
the claimant had seen and ignored the signs meant that when he entered the
water, he ceased to be at the park for the purposes for which he was invited and
permitted by the defendants to be there. He accordingly ceased to be a visitor and
became a trespasser. As such, he was owed not the common duty of care under
the Occupiers' Liability Act 1957 but the duty contained in s 1 of the Occupiers'
Liability Act 1984. That Act, replacing the accretion of common law rules,
provides by s 1:

> 'Duty of occupier to persons other than his visitors.—(1) The rules enacted by
> this section shall have effect, in place of the rules of the common law, to
> determine—(a) whether any duty is owed by a person as occupier of
> premises to persons other than his visitors in respect of any risk of their
> suffering injury on the premises by reason of any danger due to the state of
> the premises or to things done or omitted to be done on them; and (b) if so,
> what that duty is.
>   (2) For the purposes of this section, the persons who are to be treated
> respectively as an occupier of any premises (which, for those purposes,
> include any fixed or movable structure) and as his visitors are—(a) any
> person who owes in relation to the premises the duty referred to in section 2
> of the Occupiers' Liability Act 1957 (the common duty of care), and (b) those
> who are his visitors for the purposes of that duty.
>   (3) An occupier of premises owes a duty to another (not being his visitor)
> in respect of any such risk as is referred to in subsection (1) above if—(a) he
> is aware of the danger or has reasonable grounds to believe that it exists;
> (b) he knows or has reasonable grounds to believe that the other is in the
> vicinity of the danger concerned or that he may come into the vicinity of the
> danger (in either case, whether the other has lawful authority for being in
> that vicinity or not); and (c) the risk is one against which, in all the

a   circumstances of the case, he may reasonably be expected to offer the other some protection.

(4) Where, by virtue of this section, an occupier of premises owes a duty to another in respect of such a risk, the duty is to take such care as is reasonable in all the circumstances of the case to see that he does not suffer injury on the premises by reason of the danger concerned.

b   (5) Any duty owed by virtue of this section in respect of a risk may, in an appropriate case, be discharged by taking such steps as are reasonable in all the circumstances of the case to give warning of the danger concerned or to discourage persons from incurring the risk.

(6) No duty is owed by virtue of this section to any person in respect of risks willingly accepted as his by that person (the question whether a risk was

c   so accepted to be decided on the same principles as in other cases in which one person owes a duty of care to another) ...'

[8] Jack J found against the claimant. His essential conclusions were these:

'[27] In his cross-examination Mr Tomlinson accepted that he knew that

d   he should not dive in shallow water where he might hit the bottom. He accepted that he could not see the lake bed, that he assumed that it was sufficiently deep to dive without hitting the bed, and that he should have checked. These were important answers but in reality they were a necessary acceptance of the obvious. In short, Mr Tomlinson took a risk.

[28] A duty arises by reason of s 1(3) of the 1984 Act if three matters are

e   satisfied. First, there must be a risk of which the occupier was aware (or had reasonable grounds to believe existed). The risk here was not the risk of drowning through, for example, exhaustion or cramp, but the risk of injury through diving—which might include drowning consequent on a direct injury. The defendants were aware of this danger: I refer in particular to the

f   two head injuries in 1992. The second is satisfied if the occupier knows that the claimant may come into the vicinity of the danger. That was the case here. The third is that, in all the circumstances of the case, the risk was one against which the occupier may reasonably be expected to offer the claimant some protection. It was submitted on behalf of the defendants that this was not satisfied. Where there is a duty, s 1(4) provides that it is to take such steps

g   as are reasonable in all the circumstances to give warning of the danger concerned or to discourage persons from incurring that risk. In the circumstances of this case at least, consideration of the third requirement under s 1(3) and consideration of the duty under s 1(4) cover much the same ground.

h   [29] In my view the danger and risk of injury from diving in the lake where it was shallow were obvious. That is my conclusion on the evidence in the case. It concurs with the conclusions reached in the cases which I have cited. On the basis of *Darby v National Trust* [2001] EWCA Civ 189, [2001] PIQR P372 that is really the end of the matter. For the essence of that

j   case—a 1957 Act case—and others is, in my view, that an occupier is not under a duty to warn against a risk which is obvious. But, if I take a step further and say that the history showed some protection was required because of the attractions of the lake, then I would hold that the signs were reasonable and sufficient steps to give warning of the danger and to discourage persons from incurring the risk. It can be said that despite the signs people continued to go into the water. That was a decision which they

were free to make: they could choose to accept the risk. I do not think that
the defendants' legal duty to the claimant in the circumstances required
them to take the extreme measures which were completed after the accident
involving the fencing off of the areas where people went into the water and
the planting of the beaches with trees. I should add that I reject the
submission that by putting the warning signs on the beaches the defendants
were inviting swimming elsewhere. That is lacking in realism. If the water
was dangerous off the beaches, it was plainly at least as dangerous elsewhere.

[30] I also consider that an alternative route to the answer in this case is
under s 1(6). For, by diving as he did, Mr Tomlinson willingly accepted the
risk involved ...

[34] Finally, if I am wrong and the defendants were in breach of duty to
the claimant, the question of contributory negligence would arise. In my
view, on the facts and circumstances which I have set out it would be
appropriate to apportion the responsibility for the injury as to one-third to
the defendants and two-thirds to the claimant. I do so on the basis that
Mr Tomlinson dived in very shallow water, knowing of the notices warning
of the danger.'

[9] Mr Braithwaite QC, having taken this court through the authorities which
Jack J had considered in detail, and having drawn attention to the way the dangers
had been considered by the authorities, submitted that if Jack J's decision was
right, an occupier's liability is discharged simply by the display of notices even
where the locus is a public resort, where it is perceptible that the notices do not
have the required effect, and where alternative measures which will be effective
are manifest but are not undertaken. The duty, he submits, was to do what was
practicable to prevent the occurrence of accidents, not merely to warn people
that they might occur. As to contributory negligence, he submits that no more
than one third of the blame can properly rest upon the claimant.

[10] Mr Machell QC submits that in the circumstances found by the judge the
defendants owed the claimant no duty; or that if they did, it was discharged by
the display of warning notices. He relies in particular upon the judge's finding
that there was nothing about this lake which made it more dangerous than any
other stretch of open water, and that the risk of injury from diving where the lake
was shallow was obvious. This was not a case where an unpredictable declivity
in the lake bed had caused a child to lose its footing and drown (which,
Mr Machell accepted, would have attracted liability): this was a case of an adult
choosing to dive into shallow water.

[11] Mr Braithwaite meets this argument initially by submitting that the judge
has adopted two erroneous premises in reaching his conclusion. He has expressly
treated the lake as no more dangerous than any other ordinary open stretch of
water, when the chief reason for keeping swimmers out was precisely that it was
treacherous underfoot. And he has taken the risk to be not the generalised risk
that anybody entering the water might, albeit in a possibly unpredictable way,
have a nasty accident, but as the specific risk of injury through diving. If so, he
argues, the conclusion must be arrived at afresh by this court on a correct factual
and legal basis.

[12] Like the judge, we have reviewed various authorities. I must deal with
them, albeit shortly. The first is *Staples v West Dorset DC* (1995) 93 LGR 536. There
the plaintiff was crouching on a plainly visible dark layer of the algae-covered
slope of the harbour wall to which the public had access as a promenade. He

a slipped and suffered serious injury. His claim was brought under the Occupier's Liability Act 1957 and he contended that the council ought to have erected a sign warning that the cobb was slippery particularly when wet. Kennedy LJ with whom the other members of the court agreed held (at 541):

b 'It is, in my judgment, of significance that the duty is a duty owed by the occupier to the individual visitor, so that it can only be said that there was a duty to warn if without a warning the visitor in question would have been unaware of the nature and extent of the risk. As the statute makes clear, there may be circumstances in which even an explicit warning will not absolve the occupier from liability (see section 4(*a*) above); but if the danger is obvious, the visitor is able to appreciate it, he is not under any kind of *c* pressure and he is free to do what is necessary for his own safety, then no warning is required.'

One should, however, not pass from the judgment without noting Kennedy LJ's further comment (at 544):

d 'Of course, after the accident the position was different. The district council then knew that a visitor had slipped off the edge into the sea, and, as responsible occupiers, they had to do what they could to prevent a recurrence, so they posted warning notices. The fact that they took that action after the accident does not enable me to draw the inference that, in order to discharge the common duty of care to the plaintiff, they should have *e* done so before the accident occurred.'

[13] *Whyte v Redland Aggregates Ltd* [1997] CA Transcript 2034 is an unreported decision of this court handed down on 27 November 1997. The plaintiff hit his head when diving into the water in a disused gravel pit owned by the defendants. Again it was a case on the common duty of care under the 1957 Act. The *f* plaintiff's complaints were that the occupiers had failed to find out about the uneven state of the bottom of the pit and had failed to give proper warnings as to the danger. There had been no previous accidents. Hirst LJ dismissed the appeal after an analysis of the facts. Henry LJ agreed but added this:

g 'In my judgment, the occupier of land containing or bordered by the river, the seashore, the pond or the gravel pit, does not have to warn of uneven surfaces below the water. Such surfaces are by their nature quite likely to be uneven. Diving where you cannot see the bottom clearly enough to know that it is safe to dive is dangerous unless you have made sure, by reconnaissance or otherwise that diving is safe i e that there is adequate depth *h* at the place where you choose to dive. In those circumstances, the dangers of there being an uneven surface in an area where you cannot plainly see the bottom are too plain to require a specific warning and, accordingly, there is no such duty to warn ...'

j Harman J added pungently:

'There is far too much open water in this island where riparian owners are private citizens for a duty of such a wide general nature to be easily imposed by the law.'

[14] *Ratcliff v McConnell* [1999] 1 WLR 670 concerned an inebriated student ignoring all clear warnings, climbing over a locked gate and diving more steeply

into the shallow end of the pool than he intended. Giving a judgment with which
the other members of the court agreed Stuart-Smith LJ said (at 681 (para 37)):

a

'Even if the defendants knew or had reasonable grounds to believe that
students might defy the prohibition on use of the pool and climb over the not
insignificant barrier of the wall or gate, it does not seem to me that they were
under any duty to warn the plaintiff against diving into too shallow water, a
risk of which any adult would be aware and which the plaintiff, as one would
expect, admitted that he was aware. Had there been some hidden
obstruction in the form of an extraneous object in the pool or a dangerous
spike, of which the defendants were aware, the position might have been
different.'

b

Stuart-Smith LJ added two other pertinent comments. First he said (at 680
(para 35)): '... it is important to identify the risk or danger concerned since the
occupier had to have knowledge of it, or reasonable grounds to believe it exists:
section 1(3)(*a*).' He later said (at 683 (para 44)):

c

'The duty, if any, is owed to the individual trespasser, though he may be a
member of a class that the occupier knows or has reasonable grounds to
believe is in the vicinity of the danger. But the danger of and extent of what
it is reasonable to expect of the occupier varies greatly depending on whether
the trespasser is very young or very old and so may not appreciate the nature
of the danger which is or ought to be apparent to an adult.'

d

[15] *Bartrum v Hepworth Minerals and Chemicals Ltd* (29 October 1999,
unreported) is a decision of Turner J. The claimant dived from a ledge on a cliff
and struck his head on the bottom of an old quarry. There was a history of
swimming accidents and signs warning against swimming were being ignored.
Turner J held that the danger of not diving far enough out from the cliff to enter
the deep water was so obvious to any adult that it was not reasonably to be
expected of the defendants that they would offer any protection. Even if there
was a duty, a sign warning 'NO SWIMMING' was—

e

f

'authoritative for the proposition that people were not expected to swim
in that lake, whether they entered it by walking or wading, or by jumping or
diving; the greater must, it seems to me, include the less.'

g

[16] The latest swimming case is *Darby v National Trust* [2001] EWCA Civ 189,
[2001] PIQR P372. The claim was brought under the 1957 Act. There were no
warning signs. A little unusually leading counsel and junior counsel for the
claimant put forward different propositions. Leading counsel accepting the
difficulty that the risk of death by drowning was foreseeable submitted that the
warning should have included a warning against the possibility of contracting
Weil's disease. Junior counsel submitted there was no proper correlation
between the risk of swimming in the sea and of swimming in that particular pond.
The Court of Appeal did not agree with him. May LJ said (at [27]):

h

j

'It cannot be the duty of the owner of every stretch of coastline to have
notices warning of the dangers of swimming in the sea. If it were so, the
coast would have to be littered with notices in places other than those where
there are known to be special dangers which are not obvious. The same
would apply to all inland lakes and reservoirs. In my judgment there was no
duty on the National Trust on the facts of this case to warn against

a   swimming in this pond where the dangers of drowning were no other or greater than those which were quite obvious to any adult such as the unfortunate deceased.'

[17] When giving permission to appeal Henry LJ drew attention to some obiter comments of Simon Brown LJ in *Scott v Associated British Ports, Swainger v Associated British Ports* [2000] All ER (D) 1937 at [20], a decision of the Court of

b   Appeal, to the effect that:

> '... let us postulate (contrary to the facts) that the defendants here had known full well that dozens of youngsters in the 13 to 15 age group routinely surfed on their rails in the manner of these appellants, and that a simple fence would have been wholly effective in eliminating this practice. Could it really
>
c   > then be said that they were under no duty to erect such a fence; or, indeed, that a youth who came to be injured whilst surfing had accepted the risk and therefore was owed no duty of care? I hardly think so. For my part, indeed, I would recognise that on certain facts a comparable duty would be owed by occupiers to trespassers who they know are consciously imperilling
>
d   > themselves on their land to that owed by police or prison officers to those known to be of suicidal tendency in their care: see *Reeves v Metropolitan Police Comr* [1999] 3 All ER 897, [2000] 1 AC 360. All that, however, is for another day and another case.'

Mr Braithwaite submits that today is the day and this is the case.

e   [18] Mr Braithwaite did rely also on *Jebson v Ministry of Defence* [2000] 1 WLR 2055 but I do not find the authority helpful as it concerns a duty of care as carriers to passengers being carried in an army lorry. The case is, however, convenient for its citation of a passage in the speech of Lord Steyn in *Jolley v Sutton London BC* [2000] 3 All ER 409 at 416, [2000] 1 WLR 1082 at 1089:

f   > 'Two general observations are, however, appropriate. First, in this corner of the law the results of decided cases are inevitably very fact sensitive. Both counsel nevertheless at times invited your Lordships to compare the facts of the present case with the facts of other decided cases. That is a sterile exercise. Precedent is a valuable stabilising influence in our legal system.
>
g   > But, comparing the facts of an outcomes of cases in this branch of the law is a misuse of the only proper use of precedent, namely to identify the relevant rule to apply to the facts as found.'

I respectfully agree.

[19] In that search for principle, I have found it useful to trace the

h   development of the law. The extreme position was taken by *Robert Addie & Sons (Collieries) Ltd v Dumbreck* [1929] AC 358 at 365, [1929] All ER Rep 1 at 4 which established the rule that an occupier was only liable to a trespasser if he did 'some act ... with the deliberate intention of doing harm to the trespasser, or at least some act done with reckless disregard of the presence of the trespasser'. The

j   harshness of that rule was ameliorated by *British Railways Board v Herrington* [1972] 1 All ER 749, [1972] AC 877 which discarded the *Addie* test and substituted a test, variously expressed, but usually summed up as the test of 'common humanity'. That prompted the Law Commission's inquiries and their report on *Liability for Damage or Injury to Trespassers and Related Questions of Occupiers' Liability* (Law Com no 75) (Cmnd 6428) was presented in March 1976. The Law Commission proposed steering a path between extending the common duty of

care to trespassers and treating trespassing as an activity to be undertaken at the
trespasser's risk with there being no duty on the occupier to make his land safe   *a*
for persons whom the occupier did not desire to be present on his land at all. The
result was the 1984 Act, the terms of which I have already recited.

[20] Since the 1984 Act defines when an occupier of premises owes a duty to
another, and if so what the standard of care is, it is in my view essential to use the
Act as a template for judgment in each and every case. I do not wish to suggest   *b*
that the decisions in the cases I have recited are wrong but I have found it useful
to warn myself that a finding that a risk was obvious is a statement of a
conclusion, not the application of a principle. For the principle one must look to
the 1984 Act. It is a staged process.

[21] The first stage under s 1(1) is to identify the risk and the danger. The risk
is expressed to be to persons other than visitors suffering injury on the premises   *c*
by reason of any danger due to the state of the premises (or to things done or
omitted to be done on them). In this case there was a risk of injury being suffered
by anyone entering the water because of the dangers due to the state of the
premises, the premises being constituted by the configuration and contents of
this pond created as it was from a disused sand-extraction pit. There was a risk of   *d*
injury through drowning because of the dangers, among others, of the effect of
cold water, being caught in weed, being stuck in the mud or plunging
unexpectedly into deep water. There was the risk of injury through diving
because of the dangers of diving too steeply in shallow water or into an
obstruction. There may have been risks of other injury from other dangers,
e g Weil's disease. These risks of injury arose as soon as one entered the water   *e*
because one did not know what danger lurked, or where it lay hidden. The exact
nature of the hazard may not much matter in the particular circumstances of this
case.

[22] The next stage is to determine whether or not a duty was owed by the
occupier. That question depends solely upon whether the three criteria of s 1(3)   *f*
are satisfied.

[23] The first is whether the occupier was aware of the danger. Here that is
beyond question. But a few of the records will suffice to indicate the extent of the
defendants' knowledge. The Brereton Heath Management Advisory Group was
established in January 1983. At the end of its first year the minutes of
21 November 1983 record that: 'The risk of a fatality to swimmers was stressed   *g*
and agreed by all.' A water safety site visit of 11 May 1990 recorded:

> 'Many instances of swimming during hot spells. During such times up to
> 2,000 people are present with as many as 100 in the water ... Extensive
> "beach" areas are popular with families ... Not unnaturally many will   *h*
> venture into the water for a swim.
>   Hazards.
>   (iii) Long history of swimming activity here (a "known" spot for
> swimming).'

An accident was recorded on 19 May 1992 when a man dived into the lake and   *j*
'hit head on something'. The following week a person was pulled unconscious
from the lake and had to be resuscitated. The management committee reported
on 9 June 1992:

> 'The lake acts as a magnet to the public and has become heavily used for
> swimming in spite of a no swimming policy due to safety considerations. As

a   a result of the general flaunting [sic] of the policy [to ban swimming] there
have been a number of near fatalities in the lake with three incidents
requiring hospital treatment in the week around Whitsun. Whilst the
rangers are doing all they can to protect the public it is likely to be only a
matter of time before someone drowns.'

b   [24] On 23 July 1992 the leisure services department wrote:

'To provide a facility that is open to the public and which contains beach
and water areas is, in my view, an open invitation and temptation to swim
and engage in other waters-edge activities despite the cautionary note that is
struck by deterrent notices etc., and in that type of situation accidents
become inevitable.'

c

The Cheshire Water Safety Committee meeting on 5 October 1993 noted that:
'The site has a history of near drownings.' In a resolution put to the borough
council on 21 November 1999 it was noted that: 'We have on average three or
four near drownings every year and it is only a matter of time before someone

d   dies.' The claimant suffered his injuries six months later.

[25] The second criterion to establish whether a duty is owed is provided by
s 1(3)(b), namely that the occupier knows or has reasonable grounds to believe
that the other person is in the vicinity of the danger concerned. Again this has not
been in dispute. The minutes I have cited establish that and there is more to like
effect. It is quite clear that the park was a very popular venue and despite all

e   efforts to impose the ban on swimming, it was known to the defendants that
many entered the water and were in the vicinity of the dangers concerned.

[26] The third, and in this case crucial, requirement laid down by s 1(3)(c) is
whether the risk was one against which, in all the circumstances of the case, the
occupiers might reasonably be expected to offer the trespasser some protection.

f   Analysing that, the protection is against any such risk as is referred to in sub-s (1),
the risk, that is, of the trespasser suffering injury by reason of the dangers lurking
in the mere. The protection we are looking for is 'some protection'. The question
is whether some protection might reasonably be expected to be offered. The
question is not whether reasonable protection is to be expected. To frame the
question that way is to fail to distinguish between the establishing of the duty

g   under s 1(3) and the standard of care necessary to satisfy the duty which is
provided by s 1(4). These are distinct and separate requirements and I am
concerned that the judge may have failed to keep them separate and distinct
when he said:

h   '[28] ... In the circumstances of this case at least, consideration of the third
requirement under s 1(3) and the consideration of the duty under s 1(4) cover
much the same ground ...

[29] In my view the danger and risk of injury from diving in the lake
where it was shallow were obvious ... an occupier is not under a duty to
warn against a risk which is obvious.'

j   [27] There is a further important phrase in s 1(3)(c): the question is whether
some protection might reasonably be expected to be offered 'in all the
circumstances of the case'. This serves to emphasise Lord Steyn's observation that
cases are 'inevitably very fact sensitive' (see [18], above).

[28] The circumstances of this case are that Brereton Heath Park has for years
been a well-known and well-used leisure attraction. The minutes show that in

1992 160,000 people used the park during the year. During a hot spell   *a*
2,000 people were present with as many as 100 in the water. The lake was a
magnet to the public and the sandy beaches an invitation to swim. Of major
concern to the occupiers was the unauthorised use of the lake and the increasing
possibility of an accident. As minutes of the advisory group held as long ago as
17 March 1988 record:

> 'On busy days the overwhelming numbers make it impossible to control   *b*
> this use (swimming and the use of rubber boats) of the lake, and it is difficult
> to see how the situation can change unless the whole concept of managing
> the park and the lake is revised.'

[29] In discharge of the common duty of care owed to the visitors under the
Occupiers' Liability Act 1957, the authorities placed prominently signs which   *c*
forbade swimming and warned of the 'dangerous water'. In entering the water
against that prohibition, the claimant made himself a trespasser to whom a
different duty was now owed. If the words on the noticeboard 'NO SWIMMING'
qualified the use he was permitted to make of the facility, do the other words
above or below that, 'DANGEROUS WATER' constitute some protection   *d*
against the risk of injury if the person decides to take a swim? I think that maybe
too narrow a view of a warning notice which serves a composite purpose of
turning a visitor into a trespasser and also warning him of a danger. But this case
does not rest there. The misuse of the facility, the extent of the unauthorised
swimming, the history of accidents and the perceived risk of fatality was noted
and acted upon by the occupiers over many years. They did not, as may have   *e*
been the fact in some of the other decided cases, treat the notice as sufficient to
discharge any duty that might be owed. Here the authorities employed rangers
whose duty it was to give oral warnings against swimming albeit that this met
with mixed success and sometimes attracted abuse for their troubles. In addition
to the oral warnings, the rangers would hand out safety leaflets which warned of   *f*
the variable depth in the pond, the cold, the weeds, the absence of rescue services,
waterborne diseases and the risk of accidents occurring. It seems to me that the
rangers' patrols and advice and the handing out of these leaflets reinforced the
ineffective message on the sign and constituted 'some protection' in fact given
and reasonably expected to be offered in the circumstances of this case.
Congleton Beach, as the place was also known, was as alluring to 'macho' young   *g*
men as other dangerous places were to young children. In my judgment the
gravity of the risk of injury, the frequency with which those using the park came
to be exposed to the risk, the failure of warning signs to curtail the extent to which
the risk was being run, indeed the very fact that the attractiveness of the beach
and the lake acted as a magnet to draw so many into the cooling waters, all that   *h*
leads me to the conclusion that the occupiers were reasonably to be expected to
offer some protection against the risks of entering the water. It follows that in my
judgment the defendants were under a duty to the claimant.

[30] The standard of care is defined by s 1(4). It is—

> 'to take such care as is reasonable in all the circumstances of the case to see   *j*
> that he does not suffer injury on the premises by reason of the danger
> concerned.'

By now the focus has to be on the duty owed to the individual claimant whereas
at the earlier stages of the inquiry it was probably more accurate to think of the
duty owed to the claimant as a member of a class of persons, young or old,

a nefariously on the premises or using them to the occupier's knowledge, if not with his permission. The Law Commission rejected the invitation to give guidelines for determining what may reasonably be expected of an occupier. I should do likewise. Whilst, therefore, this does not pretend to be a checklist, it is obvious that among the facts and circumstances which inevitably will have to be taken into account—and this is not an exhaustive list by any means—the court

b will have regard to the age and character of the claimant, the nature and purpose of the trespassory entry on the premises, the extent to which any protective steps which were taken had proved to have been inadequate, the difficulty or ease with which steps could be taken to reduce or eliminate the danger and the question of the cost of taking those precautions balanced against the gravity of the risks of injury. Once again the key words are 'reasonable in all the circumstances of the

c case'.

[**31**] Before looking at the matter generally, the question under s 1(5) arises first. Is this an appropriate case where the duty can be said to have been discharged by the warnings given of the danger concerned and the discouragement to persons from incurring the risk of injury from that danger? Subsection (5)

d expressly recognises that the giving of a warning '*may*, in an appropriate case' discharge the duty. It follows that a warning does not necessarily or inevitably discharge the duty. In the time-honoured phrase, it must all be a matter of fact and degree. That, in my judgment, is the weakness of the judgment under appeal. The judge found that the risk was obvious, which means no more than that the claimant acknowledged the inevitable, namely that diving into water

e where one cannot see the bottom creates the risk that one will dive too steeply and so suffer injury. That may be a sufficient answer in many cases, perhaps even most cases. But here the history both of the danger and of the exposure to it drove the authorities inevitably, and rightly, to the conclusion that warnings were not working. The authorities were inviting public use of this amenity

f knowing that the water was a siren call strong enough to turn stout men's minds. In my judgment the posting of notices, shown to be ineffective, was not enough to discharge the duty.

[**32**] The next question is whether the claimant willingly accepted as his the risk of his suffering injury from the dangers concerned. There are, in my judgment, two answers to this. The first is that the claimant did not freely and

g voluntarily accept the risk. For the defence to succeed it must be shown that he had full knowledge of the nature and extent of the risk he ran and impliedly agreed to incur it. I accept the submission made on the claimant's behalf that he made an assumption which was erroneous that it was safe to dive. He did not know that the water where he dived was so shallow and the dive he made so

h steep that he would be injured. There were risks in general but he thought that what he did was safe. He did not freely and voluntarily wish the injury on himself. The second point is that if the duty on the defendants was to take reasonable steps to prevent the claimant from diving into the mere, then the defendants concede that they could not seek to argue that in diving into the mere

j the claimant voluntarily assumed the risk of injury attendant upon such act. I have identified the risk of injury to be the risk of entering the water but, in agreement with Turner J (at [15], above), the greater includes the less and consequently upon entering the water there is a risk of diving into it.

[**33**] The crucial question is, therefore, whether there was a breach by the defendants of the duty owed to the claimant. What care was it reasonable in all the circumstances of this case for the authorities to take to see that the claimant

did not suffer injury on the premises by reason of the danger concerned? The
defendants' own documents provide the answer. The recommendation after a
water safety site visit on 11 May 1990 was:

> 'The creation of beach areas is a great encouragement for people to indulge
> in beach-type activities and this includes swimming. Suggest cutting down
> on beach area by increasing reed zones.'

[34] Dealing with water safety in Cheshire, a meeting on 25 May 1990 noted
that precautions against the hazards of swimming included introducing reed beds
in littoral zones and planting shrubs on the littoral zone. It was said that
precautions which could easily be implemented should be undertaken with
immediate effect.

[35] On 7 December 1992 the minutes of the Congleton countryside progress
meeting reveal that the estates department was being asked for a plan and
costings for covering the beach areas.

[36] When the rangers met on 19 January 1994 the borough council's area
service manager stated that a decision had been taken by the council to remove
the beaches; that £10,000 had been allocated for that purpose but that the
proposal had not been activated because of financial restraint. At the same time
Mr Tyler-Jones, the chairman of the Cheshire Water Safety Committee was
reporting that his major recommendation to remove the beaches had not been
carried out. Later in March he recommended a reputable landscape architect to
advise on suitable plant species to reclaim the water margins. The Brereton
Heath Park Management Advisory Group were told in July 1994 that the 1994/95
bid for landscaping the beaches had been rejected but there was the possibility of
money being left at the end of the year to do one beach at a time. The following
month, on 10 August, 'all agreed on the urgency to take action to landscape the
beaches to deter swimming'. In putting forward a recommendation to cover the
beach with soil and planting the margin of the water with reeds and other aquatic
plants at a capital cost of £15,000 it was stated that:

> 'We have on average three or four near drownings every year and it is only
> a matter of time before someone dies. The recommendation from the
> National Water Safety Committee, endorsed by County Councils is that
> something must now be done to reduce the "beach areas" both in size and
> attractiveness. If nothing is done about this and someone dies the borough
> council is likely to be held liable and would have to accept responsibility.'

At a meeting of the community services committee of the borough council on
21 November the general capital programme for 1995/1996 allocated £5,000 for
safety improvements to the Brereton Heath Country Park. The work of covering
the beach with topsoil and planting the beaches began shortly before this
accident.

[37] In my judgment the defendants, prudent and responsible as they showed
themselves to be, came under a duty to the claimant to carry out the landscaping
and planting that was recommended in the minutes I have recited. The carrying
out of the work presented no practical problems and if carried out was likely to
prove to be and in fact did turn out to be an effective deterrent to swimming in
the mere. The expense, be it £5,000 or £15,000, was not excessive, especially
having regard to the serious risk of injury from the accident that was waiting to
happen.

a [**38**] It follows that in my judgment the defendants were in breach of a duty they owed the claimant to take reasonable care to see that he did not suffer injury at the country park by reason of the dangers which awaited those who entered the water for a swim.

[**39**] The final question is the extent to which the court thinks it just and equitable that the damages recoverable be reduced having regard to the

b claimant's share in the responsibility for the damage. The judge would have assessed his contribution at two-thirds, an apportionment Mr Machell supports whereas Mr Braithwaite submits the proportions be reversed: one-third to the claimant, two-thirds to the defendants. The claimant knew he should not enter the water and he took some risk. The defendants knew that someone was bound to do just that sooner or later and that comparatively simple remedial steps

c would absolve them from responsibility. If the matter had been left to my judgment, I would have held that the relative share of blameworthiness and the relative importance of the acts and omissions in causing this damage fell equally on claimant and defendants. However, this court is always loath to interfere with an assessment of contributory negligence even where the judge expressed his

d conclusions from the difficult position that he had already found against the claimant. Since Sedley and Longmore LJJ, whose judgments I have been able to read in draft, would not interfere with the judge's apportionment, I recognise that my views should not be imposed.

[**40**] I do not pretend to have found this case easy. My views have swung one way and the other. That admitted, I am satisfied now that the appeal must be

e allowed and the matter must be remitted to the High Court for the assessment of damages to be reduced by two-thirds for the claimant's contributory negligence.

SEDLEY LJ.

[**41**] I agree with Ward LJ that this appeal should be allowed. But because I

f have read Longmore LJ's judgment in favour of dismissing the appeal, I add some brief reasoning of my own.

[**42**] I do not consider that it is appropriate to reason out a claim like the present one from its consequences. If the logic of our decision is that other public lakes and ponds require similar precautions to those which were lacking at Brereton Heath, so be it. But negligence is fact-specific, and we are able neither

g to determine what the occupiers' duties are in other places nor to predicate our decision on what its effect on those occupiers might be. We are creating no duty and no standard of care which is not already laid down by Parliament. Our task, like that of the trial judge, is simply to apply a general law to specific facts.

[**43**] The other matter to which Longmore LJ draws attention is the

h particularity of the hazard to which the claimant fell prey. It is, I agree, an apparent oddity that a person who is injured by diving into shallow water—a pretty obvious hazard—should be able to claim the benefit of precautions which in reality were needed in order to stop people losing their footing where the lake bed shelved steeply or becoming entangled in thick weeds. But there are two

j separate answers, one relating to the obviousness of the hazard, the other to its nature.

[**44**] As to the nature of the hazard, it was rightly not argued by the defendants that this could make the difference between liability and no liability in the present case. It is well settled by authority that if there is a duty to protect people against foreseeable injury, it does not matter if the accident which happens was not itself foreseeable, so long as it is not in an entirely different league: see *Hughes v Lord*

Advocate [1963] 1 All ER 705, [1963] AC 837 and *Smith v Leech Brain & Co Ltd* [1961] 3 All ER 1159, [1962] 2 QB 405.   *a*

[45] If primary liability is established, the obviousness of the hazard goes to contributory negligence; for it is only where the risk is so obvious that the occupier can safely assume that nobody will take it that there will be no liability. Even so, in a gross case contributory negligence can approach one hundred per cent. This is not such a case, but it is a case in which the claimant did something   *b* which he was old enough to realise was stupid—not so much by entering the mere (everyone was doing that, and the defendants had failed to take reasonable measures to stop it) but by diving steeply from a standing position in a couple of feet of water. I see no reason to differ from Jack J's contingent assessment of the claimant's share of responsibility for his consequent misfortune as two-thirds.

[46] The nub of the defendants' case was that the mere did not present any   *c* unusual or special risks at all. As to this, the logic of Ward LJ's judgment seems to me compelling, and I do not need to add to it. I would accordingly allow the appeal and direct entry of judgment for one-third of the damages to be assessed.

LONGMORE LJ.   *d*

[47] One of the dangers of going for a swim in any stretch of water other than a dedicated swimming pool is that the swimmer may slip and injure himself. He may also quickly find himself out of his depth and be unable to cope; he may get cramp or be assailed by the coldness of the water and be unable to recover. All these are obvious dangers to anyone except a small and unaccompanied child. Another danger is that a swimmer may decide to dive into the water and hit his   *e* head on the bottom, if the water is too shallow; in my judgment that is an equally obvious danger and cannot provide a reason for saying that the owner or occupier of the water should be under any duty to take reasonable steps to prevent people swimming or diving in the relevant stretch of water.

[48] The position would, of course, be different if the occupier knew of some   *f* concealed danger or some danger that was not obvious to people using the water. But in this case Jack J has held in terms that there was nothing about the mere at Brereton Heath which made it any more dangerous than any other ordinary stretch of open water in England. The judge thought (and I agree) that if there was a duty to take reasonable steps to prevent public access for the purpose of swimming at Brereton Heath, similar steps would have to be taken in relation to   *g* other stretches of open water in the country.

[49] Mr John Tomlinson has suffered appalling injuries as a result of his unfortunate dive while enjoying the water on a warm May bank holiday weekend in 1995. Mr Braithwaite QC on his behalf has submitted that the mere at Brereton Heath was a special case different from other stretches of water   *h* because: (1) the heath was a managed site where the defendants encouraged the public to go to spend their leisure time; (2) the defendants knew that accidents were liable to happen (and, indeed, had happened on three previous occasions); and (3) the defendants were in the process of taking steps to eliminate injuries from swimming accidents in that they: (a) put up signs prohibiting swimming;   *j* and (b) when it became clear that the signs were being ignored, they were advised that the beaches on the mere should be fenced off and covered in vegetation but had not got round to doing this by the time of Mr Tomlinson's accident.

[50] I do not consider that these factors either singly or together make the mere at Brereton Heath different from other stretches of open water. The fact that the defendants arranged and even promoted the site for leisure activity does

a   not mean that they should have taken reasonable steps to prevent swimming unless they knew of any particular hazard. Even then it would probably be sufficient to give a warning in relation to that hazard. There was here no allegation or evidence of any particular hazard, beyond the ordinary hazards of swimming in open water.

b   [51] The fact that during the defendants' management of the site three accidents had occurred to people swimming in the mere cannot of itself impose a duty of care since swimming in open stretches of water is often an inherently dangerous activity. It would only be if the number of accidents was significantly above the norm that any duty could arise and that would then be because it would be possible to conclude that there was a particular hazard in relation to the stretch of water (even if the hazard might not at first be easily identifiable).

c   Likewise, the fact that a local authority may responsibly seek to deter or prevent swimming does not to my mind give rise to any duty to an individual member of the public or the public at large to take steps to prevent people swimming, unless there is a particular hazard (over and above the ordinary risks of swimming) about which the public should know.

d   [52] I should add that, for myself, I would have reached the same conclusion even if the claimant had not conceded that he was a trespasser. I find it odd that if there is a general licence to the public to come to a park for leisure activities but there are notices which prohibit swimming, someone who enters the water intending to swim becomes a trespasser. At what point does he become a trespasser? When he starts to paddle, intending thereafter to swim? There was

e   no evidence that Mr Tomlinson in fact swam at all. He dived from a position in which swimming was difficult, if not impossible. I would be troubled if the defendants' duty of care differed depending on the precise moment when a swim could be said to have begun.

[53] For these reasons which are much the same as those given by this court

f   in *Darby v National Trust* [2001] EWCA Civ 189, [2001] PIQR P372 it seems to me that this appeal should fail. It is noteworthy that the Supreme Court of Canada seems to have come to a similar conclusion in relation to a similar stretch of water in British Columbia (see *Vancouver-Fraser Park District v Olmstead* (1974) 51 DLR (3d) 416).

g   [54] On contributory negligence, I would not interfere with the judge's apportionment.

Appeal allowed in part.

                                        Kate O'Hanlon   Barrister.

h

Appeal

The defendants appealed with permission of the Appeal Committee of the House of Lords given on 23 July 2002. The claimant cross-appealed, with permission of

j   the Appeal Committee given on 9 October 2002, as to quantum of contributory negligence.

Raymond Machell QC and *Peter Burns* (instructed by *James Chapman & Co*, Manchester) for the councils.
Bill Braithwaite QC and *Gerard Martin QC* (instructed by *Paul Ross & Co*, Manchester) for the claimant.

31 July 2003. The following opinions were delivered.

a

LORD NICHOLLS OF BIRKENHEAD.

[1] My Lords, I have had the advantage of reading in draft the speech of my noble and learned friend Lord Hoffmann. For the reasons he gives, with which I agree, I would allow this appeal.

b

LORD HOFFMANN.

THE ACCIDENT

[2] My Lords, in rural south-east Cheshire the early May Bank Holiday weekend in 1995 was unseasonably hot. John Tomlinson, aged 18, had to work *c* until midday on Saturday 6 May but then met some of his friends and drove them to Brereton Heath Country Park, between Holmes Chapel and Congleton. The park covers about 80 acres. In about 1980 Congleton Borough Council acquired the land, surrounding what was then a derelict sand quarry, and laid it out as a country park. Paths now run through woods of silver birch and in summer bright *d* yellow brimstone butterflies flutter in grassy meadows. But the attraction of the park for John Tomlinson and his young friends was a 14-acre lake which had been created by flooding the old sand quarry. The sandy banks provided some attractive beaches and in hot weather many people, including families with children, went there to play in the sand, sunbathe and paddle in the water. A *e* beach at the far end of the lake from the car park was where in fine weather groups of teenagers like John Tomlinson would regularly hang out. He had been going there since he was a child.

[3] After sitting in the hot sun for a couple of hours, John Tomlinson decided that he wanted to cool off. So he ran out into the water and dived. He had done the same thing many times before. But this time the dive was badly executed *f* because he struck his head hard on the sandy bottom. So hard that he broke his neck at the fifth vertebra. He is now a tetraplegic and unable to walk.

[4] It is a terrible tragedy to suffer such dreadful injury in consequence of a relatively minor act of carelessness. It came nowhere near the stupidity of Luke Ratcliff, a student who climbed a fence at 2.30 am on a December morning to *g* take a running dive into the shallow end of a swimming pool (*Ratcliff v McConnell* [1999] 1 WLR 670) or John Donoghue, who dived into Folkestone Harbour from a slipway at midnight on 27 December after an evening in the pub (*Donoghue v Folkestone Properties Ltd* [2003] EWCA Civ 231, [2003] 3 All ER 1101, [2003] 2 WLR *h* 1138). John Tomlinson's mind must often recur to that hot day which irretrievably changed his life. He may feel, not unreasonably, that fate has dealt with him unfairly. And so in these proceedings he seeks financial compensation: for the loss of his earning capacity, for the expense of the care he will need, for the loss of the ability to lead an ordinary life. But the law does not provide such *j* compensation simply on the basis that the injury was disproportionately severe in relation to one's own fault or even not one's own fault at all. Perhaps it should, but society might not be able to afford to compensate everyone on that principle, certainly at the level at which such compensation is now paid. The law provides compensation only when the injury was someone else's fault. In order to succeed in his claim, that is what Mr Tomlinson has to prove.

OCCUPIERS' LIABILITY

a

[5] In these proceedings Mr Tomlinson sues the Congleton Borough Council and the Cheshire County Council, claiming that as occupiers of the park they were in breach of their duties under the Occupiers' Liability Acts 1957 and 1984. If one had to decide which of the two councils was the occupier, it might not be easy. Although the park belongs to the borough council, it is managed on their

b behalf by the countryside management service of the county council. The borough council provides the funds to enable the countryside management service to maintain the park. It is the county which employs the rangers who look after it. But the two councils very sensibly agreed that one or other or both was the occupier. Unless it is necessary to distinguish between the county council and the borough council for the purpose of telling the story, I shall call them both

c the council.

VISITOR OR TRESPASSER?

[6] The 1957 Act was passed to amend and codify the common law duties of occupiers to certain persons who came upon their land. The common law had

d distinguished between invitees, in whose visit the occupier had some material interest, and licensees, who came simply by express or implied permission. Different duties were owed to each class. The Act, on the recommendation of the Law Reform Committee (*Third Report: Occupiers' Liability to Invitees, Licensees and Trespassers* (1954) Cmd 9305), amalgamated (without redefining) the two common law categories, designated the combined class 'visitors' (s 1(2)) and

e provided that (subject to contrary agreement) all visitors should be owed a 'common duty of care'. That duty is set out in s 2(2), as refined by sub-ss (3)–(5):

'(2) The common duty of care is a duty to take such care as in all the circumstances of the case is reasonable to see that the visitor will be

f reasonably safe in using the premises for the purposes for which he is invited or permitted by the occupier to be there.

(3) The circumstances relevant for the present purpose include the degree of care, and of want of care, which would ordinarily be looked for in such a visitor, so that (for example) in proper cases—(a) an occupier must be prepared for children to be less careful than adults; and (b) an occupier may

g expect that a person, in the exercise of his calling, will appreciate and guard against any special risks ordinarily incident to it, so far as the occupier leaves him free to do so.

(4) In determining whether the occupier of premises has discharged the common duty of care to a visitor, regard is to be had to all the circumstances,

h so that (for example)—(a) where damage is caused to a visitor by a danger of which he had been warned by the occupier, the warning is not to be treated without more as absolving the occupier from liability, unless in all the circumstances it was enough to enable the visitor to be reasonably safe; and (b) where damage is caused to a visitor by a danger due to the faulty

j execution of any work of construction, maintenance or repair by an independent contractor employed by the occupier, the occupier is not to be treated without more as answerable for the danger if in all the circumstances he had acted reasonably in entrusting the work to an independent contractor and had taken such steps (if any) as he reasonably ought in order to satisfy himself that the contractor was competent and that the work had been properly done.

(5) The common duty of care does not impose on an occupier any
obligation to a visitor in respect of risks willingly accepted as his by the visitor
(the question whether a risk was so accepted to be decided on the same
principles as in other cases in which one person owes a duty of care to
another).'

[7] At first Mr Tomlinson claimed that the council was in breach of its
common duty of care under s 2(2). His complaint was that the premises were not
reasonably safe because diving into the water was dangerous and the council had
not given adequate warning of this fact or taken sufficient steps to prevent or
discourage him from doing it. But then a difficulty emerged. The county council,
as manager of the park, had for many years pursued a policy of prohibiting
swimming or the use of inflatable dinghies or mattresses. Canoeing and
windsurfing were allowed in one area of the lake and angling in another. But not
swimming; except, I suppose, by capsized canoeists or windsurfers. Notices had
been erected at the entrance and elsewhere saying 'DANGEROUS WATER. NO
SWIMMING'. The policy had not been altogether effective because many
people, particularly rowdy teenagers, ignored the notices. They were sometimes
rude to the rangers who tried to get them out of the water. Nevertheless, it was
hard to say that swimming or diving was, in the language of s 2(2), one of the
purposes 'for which [Mr Tomlinson was] invited or permitted by the occupier to
be there'. The council went further and said that once he entered the lake to
swim, he was no longer a 'visitor' at all. He became a trespasser, to whom no
duty under the 1957 Act is owed. The council cited a famous bon mot of
Scrutton LJ in *The Calgarth, The Otarama* [1927] P 93 at 110: 'When you invite a
person into your house to use the staircase, you do not invite him to slide down
the banisters ...' This quip was used by Lord Atkin in *Hillen v ICI (Alkali) Ltd*
[1936] AC 65 at 69, [1935] All ER Rep 555 at 558 to explain why stevedores who
were lawfully on a barge for the purpose of discharging it nevertheless became
trespassers when they went onto an inadequately supported hatch cover in order
to unload some of the cargo. They knew, said Lord Atkin ([1936] AC 65 at 69–70,
[1935] All ER Rep 555 at 558) that they ought not to use the covered hatch for this
purpose 'for them for such a purpose it was out of bounds; they were trespassers'.
So the stevedores could not complain that the barge owners should have warned
them that the hatch cover was not adequately supported. Similarly, says the
council, Mr Tomlinson became a trespasser and took himself outside the 1957
Act when he entered the water to swim.

[8] Mr Tomlinson's advisers, having reflected on the matter, decided to
concede that he was indeed a trespasser when he went into the water. Although
that took him outside the 1957 Act, it did not necessarily mean that the council
owed him no duty. At common law the only duty to trespassers was not to cause
them deliberate or reckless injury, but after an inconclusive attempt by the House
of Lords to modify this rule in *British Railways Board v Herrington* [1972] 1 All ER
749, [1972] AC 877, the Law Commission recommended the creation of a
statutory duty to trespassers (see its *Report on Liability for Damage or Injury to
Trespassers and Related Questions of Occupiers' Liability* (1976) (Law Com no 75)
(Cmnd 6428)). The recommendation was given effect by the Occupiers' Liability
Act 1984. Section 1(1) describes the purpose of that Act:

'(1) The rules enacted by this section shall have effect, in place of the rules
of the common law, to determine—(a) whether any duty is owed by a person
as occupier of premises to persons other than his visitors in respect of any risk

a   of their suffering injury on the premises by reason of any danger due to the
state of the premises or to things done or omitted to be done on them; and
(b) if so, what that duty is.'

[9] The circumstances in which a duty may arise are then defined in sub-s (3)
and the content of the duty is described in sub-ss (4)–(6):

b   '(3) An occupier of premises owes a duty to another (not being his visitor)
in respect of any such risk as is referred to in subsection (1) above if—
(a) he is aware of the danger or has reasonable grounds to believe that it
exists;
(b) he knows or has reasonable grounds to believe that the other is in the
c   vicinity of the danger concerned or that he may come into the vicinity of the
danger (in either case, whether he has lawful authority for being in that
vicinity or not); and
(c) the risk is one against which, in all the circumstances of the case, he
may reasonably be expected to offer the other some protection.
(4) Where, by virtue of this section, an occupier of premises owes a duty
d   to another in respect of such a risk, the duty is to take such care as is
reasonable in all the circumstances of the case to see that he does not suffer
injury on the premises by reason of the danger concerned.
(5) Any duty owed by virtue of this section in respect of a risk may, in an
appropriate case, be discharged by taking such steps as are reasonable in all
e   the circumstances of the case to give warning of the danger concerned or to
discourage persons from incurring the risk.
(6) No duty is owed by virtue of this section to any person in respect of
risks willingly accepted as his by that person (the question whether a risk was
so accepted to be decided on the same principles as in other cases in which
f   one person owes a duty of care to another).'

[10] Mr Tomlinson says that the conditions set out in sub-s (3) were satisfied.
The council was therefore under a duty under sub-s (4) to take reasonable care to
see that he did not suffer injury by reason of the danger from diving.
Subsection (5) shows that although in appropriate circumstances it may be
g   sufficient to warn or discourage, the notices in the present case had been patently
ineffectual and therefore it was necessary to take more drastic measures to
prevent people like himself from going into the water. Such measures, as I shall
later recount in detail, had already been considered by the council.

[11] The case has therefore proceeded upon a concession that the relevant
duty, if any, is that to a trespasser under s 1(4) of the 1984 Act and not to a lawful
h   visitor under s 2(2) of the 1957 Act. On one analysis, this is a rather odd
hypothesis. Mr Tomlinson's complaint is that he should have been prevented or
discouraged from going into the water, that is to say, from turning himself into a
trespasser. Logically, it can be said, that duty must have been owed to him (if at
all) while he was still a lawful visitor. Once he had become a trespasser, it could
j   not have meaningful effect. In the Court of Appeal ([2002] EWCA Civ 309, [2003]
3 All ER 1122, [2003] 2 WLR 1120), Longmore LJ was puzzled by this paradox:

        '[52] … At what point does he become a trespasser? When he starts to
paddle, intending thereafter to swim? There was no evidence that
Mr Tomlinson in fact swam at all. He dived from a position in which
swimming was difficult, if not impossible. I would be troubled if the

defendants' duty of care differed depending on the precise moment when a
swim could be said to have begun.'

a

[12] In the later case of *Donoghue v Folkestone Properties Ltd* [2003] EWCA Civ
231 at [45], [2003] 3 All ER 1101 at [45], [2003] 2 WLR 1138 Lord Phillips of Worth
Matravers MR said that he shared these reservations about the concession:

b

'What was at issue in the case was whether the council should have taken
steps which would have prevented Mr Tomlinson from entering the lake,
that is, whether a duty of care was owed to him before he did the
unauthorised act.'

[13] As a matter of logic, I see the force of these observations. But I have
nevertheless come to the conclusion that the concession was rightly made. The
duty under the 1984 Act was intended to be a lesser duty, as to both incidence and
scope, than the duty to a lawful visitor under the 1957 Act. That was because
Parliament recognised that it would often be unduly burdensome to require
landowners to take steps to protect the safety of people who came upon their land
without invitation or permission. They should not ordinarily be able to force
duties upon unwilling hosts. In the application of that principle, I can see no
difference between a person who comes upon land without permission and one
who, having come with permission, does something which he has not been given
permission to do. In both cases, the entrant would be imposing upon the
landowner a duty of care which he has not expressly or impliedly accepted. The
1984 Act provides that even in such cases a duty may exist, based simply upon
occupation of land and knowledge or foresight that unauthorised persons may
come upon the land or authorised persons may use it for unauthorised purposes.
But that duty is rarer and different in quality from the duty which arises from
express or implied invitation or permission to come upon the land and use it.

c

d

e

f

[14] In addition, I think that the concession is supported by the high authority
of Lord Atkin in *Hillen's* case. There too, it could be said that the stevedores'
complaint was that they should have been warned not to go upon the hatch cover
and that logically this duty was owed to them, if at all, when they were lawfully
on the barge.

g

[15] I would certainly agree with Longmore LJ that the incidence and content
of the duty should not depend on the precise moment at which Mr Tomlinson
crossed the line between the status of lawful visitor and that of trespasser. But
there is no dispute that the act in respect of which Mr Tomlinson says that he was
owed a duty, namely, diving into the water, was to his knowledge prohibited by
the terms upon which he had been admitted to the park. It is, I think, for this
reason that the council owed him no duty under the 1957 Act and that the
incidence and content of any duty they may have owed was governed by the 1984
Act. But I shall later return to the question of whether it would have made any
difference if swimming had not been prohibited and the 1957 Act had applied.

h

j

[16] It is therefore necessary to consider the conditions which s 1(3) of the
1984 Act requires to be satisfied in order that any duty under s 1(4) should exist.
But before looking at the statutory requirements, I must say something more
about the history of the lake, upon which Mr Braithwaite QC, who appeared for
Mr Tomlinson, placed great reliance in support of his submission that the council
owed him a duty with which it failed to comply.

THE HISTORY OF THE LAKE

a   [17] The working of the sand quarry ceased in about 1975 and for some years thereafter the land lay derelict. People went there for barbecues, camp fires, open-air parties and swimming. The borough council bought the land in 1980 and most of the work of landscaping and planting was finished by 1983. The land was reclaimed for municipal recreation. But the traditions established in the previous anarchic state of nature were hard to eradicate. From the beginning, the

b   county council's management plan treated swimming as an 'unacceptable water activity'. The minutes of the county council's advisory group of interested organisations (anglers, windsurfers and so forth) record that on 21 November 1983 the managers proposed to put up more signs to dissuade swimmers: 'The risk of a fatality to swimmers was stressed and agreed by all.' The windsurfers in

c   particular were concerned about swimmers getting in their way; perhaps being injured by a fast-moving board. The chairman summed up by saying that although the lake with its sandy beaches was a great attraction to visitors, it was also a management problem because of misuse and dangerous activities on the water.

d   [18] In the following year, 1984, the management reported that larger notice boards had prevented the swimming problem from getting any worse: 'Every reasonable precaution had now been taken, but it was recognised that some foolhardy persons would continue to put their lives at risk.'

[19] The management report for 1988 stated that a major concern was—

e   'the unauthorised use of the lake and the increasing possibility of an accident; this is swimming and the use of rubber boats. Warnings are ignored by large numbers who see Brereton as easy, free access to open water. On busy days the overwhelming numbers make it impossible to control this use of the lake, and it is difficult to see how the situation can change unless the whole concept of managing the park and the lake is

f   revised.'

[20] In 1990 there was an inspection by Mr Victor Tyler-Jones, the county council's water safety officer. He reported that the swimming problem continued, due to the ease of access, the grassy lakeside picnic areas and the beaches and the long history of swimming in the lake. His recommendation was

g   to reduce the beach areas by planting them with reeds. His guidelines for the entire county said that swimming in lakes, rivers and ponds should be discouraged:

'We do not recommend swimming as a suitable activity for any of our

h   managed sites. Potential swimmers could be dissuaded by noticeboard reference to less pleasant features e.g. soft muddy bottom, danger of contracting Weil's Disease, presence of blue-green algae.'

If this did not have the desired effect, ballast should be dumped on beaches and banks to make them muddy and unattractive and reeds and shrubs should be

j   planted.

[21] The money to implement these recommendations had to be provided by the borough council, which was under some financial pressure. But impetus was provided in the summer of 1992 by a number of incidents. Over Whitsuntide there were three cases of 'near drowning resulting in hospital visits'. The only such incident of which more details are available concerned a man who 'was swimming in lake, after drinking, and got into difficulty'. He was rescued by a

relative, resuscitated by an off-duty paramedic and taken to hospital. Two men
cut their heads by hitting them on something when diving into the lake; there is
no information about where they dived.   Mr Kitching, the county council's
countryside manager, prepared a paper for the borough council at the end of the
first week in June. He said that the park had become very popular:

> '... the total number of visitors now exceeds 160,000 per annum ... The
> lake acts as a magnet to the public and has become heavily used for
> swimming in spite of a no swimming policy due to safety considerations ...
> Advice has been sought from the County Council's water safety officer as to
> how the problem should be addressed and this has been carefully followed.
> Notices are posted warning of the dangers and leaflets are handed to visitors
> to emphasise the situation. Life belts and throwing lines are provided for use
> in emergencies. In spite of these actions the public continue to ignore the
> advice and the requests of the rangers not to swim. The attitude is that they
> will do what they want to do and that rangers should not interfere with their
> enjoyment. There have been several occasions when small children have
> been out in the middle of the lake and their parents have been extremely
> rude to staff when approached about this. As a result of the general flaunting
> of the policy there have been a number of near fatalities in the lake with three
> incidents requiring hospital treatment in the week around Whitsun. Whilst
> the rangers are doing all they can to protect the public it is likely to be only
> a matter of time before someone drowns.'

[22] In July 1992 the borough council's leisure officer visited the park and
concluded that the notices and leaflets were not having the desired effect. On 23
July 1992 he proposed to other officers the preparation of a report to the borough
council recommending the adoption of Mr Tyler-Jones' scheme for making the
beaches less hospitable to visitors:

> '... I want the water's edge to be far less accessible, desirable and inviting
> than it currently is for children's beach/water's edge type of play activities.
> I personally find this course of action a regrettable one but I have to remind
> myself that Council policy was to establish a Country Park and not
> specifically to provide a swimming facility, no matter how popular this may
> have become in consequence. To provide a facility that is open to the public
> and which contains beach and water areas is, in my view, an open invitation
> and temptation to swim and engage in other water's edge activities despite
> the cautionary note that is struck by deterrent notices etc., and in that type
> of situation accidents become inevitable. We must therefore do everything
> that is reasonably possible to deter, discourage and prevent people from
> swimming or paddling in the lake or diving into the lake ... Work should be
> prepared for the report with a view to implementation of a scheme at the
> earliest opportunity, bearing in mind that we shall require a supplementary
> estimate for the exercise ...'

[23] As a result of this proposal, the borough leisure officer was asked to
prepare a feasibility report with costings. £5,000 was provided in the draft
estimates for the borough's amenities and leisure services committee, but it was
one of many items deleted at the committee's meeting on 1 March 1993 to
achieve a total saving of £200,000. In 1994, the officers tried again. It was listed
as a 'desirable' growth bid in the budget (below 'essential' and 'highly desirable').

a But the bid failed. When it came to the 1995 budget round, the officers presented a strongly-worded proposal:

> 'Cheshire Countryside Management Service has now taken all reasonable steps with regard to providing information and attempting to educate the public about the dangers of bathing in the lake. This has had a limited effect
> *b* on the numbers entering the water for short periods but there are still numbers of people, including young children, swimming, paddling and using inflatable rafts and dinghies whenever the weather is warm and sunny. We have on average three or four near drownings every year and it is only a matter of time before someone dies. The recommendation from the
> *c* National Safety Water Committee, endorsed by County Councils is that something must now be done to reduce the "beach areas" both in size and attractiveness. If nothing is done about this and someone dies the Borough Council is likely to be held liable and would have to accept responsibility.'

d [24] The borough council found this persuasive and in 1995 £5,000 was allocated to the scheme. But the work had not yet begun when Mr Tomlinson had his accident. At that time, the beach to which he and his friends had been accustomed to go since childhood was still there. The diggers, graders and planters arrived to destroy it a few months later.

e THE SCOPE OF THE DUTY UNDER THE 1984 ACT

[25] The conditions in s 1(3) of the 1984 Act determine whether or not a duty is owed to 'another' in respect of 'any such risk as is referred to in subsection (1)'. Two conclusions follow from this language. First, the risks in respect of which the Act imposes a duty are limited to those mentioned in sub-s (1)(a)—risks of
f injury 'by reason of any danger due to the state of the premises or to things done or omitted to be done on them'. The Act is not concerned with risks due to anything else. Secondly, the conditions have to be satisfied in respect of the claimant as 'another'; that is to say, in respect of a class of persons which includes him and a description of risk which includes that which caused his injury.

g A DANGER 'DUE TO THE STATE OF THE PREMISES'

[26] The first question, therefore, is whether there was a risk within the scope of the statute; a danger 'due to the state of the premises or to things done or omitted to be done on them'. The judge found that there was 'nothing about the
h mere at Brereton Heath which made it any more dangerous than any other ordinary stretch of open water in England'. There was nothing special about its configuration; there were no hidden dangers. It was shallow in some places and deep in others, but that is the nature of lakes. Nor was the council doing or permitting anything to be done which created a danger to persons who came to the lake. No power boats or jet skis threatened the safety of either lawful
j windsurfers or unlawful swimmers. So the council submits that there was no danger attributable to the state of premises or things done or omitted on them. In *Donoghue v Folkestone Properties Ltd* [2003] 3 All ER 1101 at [53] Lord Phillips MR expressed the same opinion. He said that he had been unable to identify the 'state of the premises' which carried with it the risk of the injury suffered by Mr Tomlinson:

'It seems to me that Mr Tomlinson suffered his injury because he chose to indulge in an activity which had inherent dangers, not because the premises were in a dangerous state.'

[27] In making this comment, Lord Phillips MR was identifying a point which is in my opinion central to this appeal. It is relevant at a number of points in the analysis of the duties under the 1957 and 1984 Acts. Mr Tomlinson was a person of full capacity who voluntarily and without any pressure or inducement engaged in an activity which had inherent risk. The risk was that he might not execute his dive properly and so sustain injury. Likewise, a person who goes mountaineering incurs the risk that he might stumble or misjudge where to put his weight. In neither case can the risk be attributed to the state of the premises. Otherwise any premises can be said to be dangerous to someone who chooses to use them for some dangerous activity. In the present case, Mr Tomlinson knew the lake well and even if he had not, the judge's finding was that it contained no dangers which one would not have expected. So the only risk arose out of what he chose to do and not out of the state of the premises.

[28] Mr Braithwaite was inclined to accept the difficulty of establishing that the risk was due to the state of the premises. He therefore contended that it was due to 'things done or omitted to be done' on the premises. When asked what these might be, he said that they consisted in the attraction of the lake and the council's inadequate attempts to keep people out of the water. The council, he said, were 'luring people into a deathtrap'. Ward LJ ([2003] All ER 1122 at [31]) said that the water was 'a siren call strong enough to turn stout men's minds'. In my opinion this is gross hyperbole. The trouble with the island of the sirens was not the state of the premises. It was that the sirens held mariners spellbound until they died of hunger. The beach, give or take a fringe of human bones, was an ordinary mediterranean beach. If Odysseus had gone ashore and accidentally drowned himself having a swim, Penelope would have had no action against the sirens for luring him there with their songs. Likewise in this case, the water was perfectly safe for all normal activities. In my opinion 'things done or omitted to be done' means activities or the lack of precautions which cause risk, like allowing speedboats among the swimmers. It is a mere circularity to say that a failure to stop people getting into the water was an omission which gave rise to a duty to take steps to stop people from getting into the water.

[29] It follows that in my opinion, there was no risk to Mr Tomlinson due to the state of the premises or anything done or omitted upon the premises. That means that there was no risk of a kind which gave rise to a duty under the 1957 or 1984 Acts. I shall nevertheless go on to consider the matter on the assumption that there was.

THE CONDITIONS FOR THE EXISTENCE OF A DUTY

(i) *Knowledge or foresight of the danger*

[30] Section 1(3) of the 1984 Act has three conditions which must be satisfied. First, under para (a), the occupier must be aware of the danger or have reasonable grounds to believe that it exists. For this purpose, it is necessary to say what the relevant danger was. The judge thought it was the risk of suffering an injury through diving and said that the council was aware of this danger because two men had suffered minor head injuries from diving in May 1992. In the Court of Appeal, Ward LJ described the relevant risk much more broadly. He regarded all the swimming incidents as indicative of the council's knowledge that a danger

a existed. I am inclined to think that this is too wide a description. The risk of injury from diving off the beach was in my opinion different from the risk of drowning in the deep water. For example, the council might have fenced off the deep water or marked it with buoys and left people to paddle in the shallows. That would have reduced the risk of drowning but would not have prevented the injury to Mr Tomlinson. We know very little about the circumstances in which *b* two men suffered minor cuts to their heads in 1992 and I am not sure that they really provide much support for an inference that there was knowledge, or reasonable grounds to believe, that the beach posed a risk of serious diving injury. Dr Penny, a consultant occupational health and safety physician with long experience of advising organisations involved in acquatic sports (and himself a diver) said that the *Code of Safety for Beaches*, published in 1993 by the Royal Life *c* Saving Society and the Royal Society for the Prevention of Accidents, made no mention of diving risks, no doubt assuming that, because there was little possibility of high diving from a beach, the risk of serious diving injuries was very small compared with the risk of drowning. I accept that the council must have known that there was a possibility that some boisterous teenager would injure *d* himself by horseplay in the shallows and I would not disturb the concurrent findings that this was sufficient to satisfy para (a). But the chances of such an accident were small. I shall return later, in connection with para (c), to the relevance of where the risk comes on the scale of probability.

e (ii) *Knowledge or foresight of the presence of the trespasser*

[**31**] Once it is found that the risk of a swimmer injuring himself by diving was something of which the council knew or which they had reasonable grounds to believe to exist, para (b) presents no difficulty. The council plainly knew that swimmers came to the lake and Mr Tomlinson fell within that class.

f (iii) *Reasonable to expect protection*

[**32**] That leaves para (c). Was the risk one against which the council might reasonably be expected to offer Mr Tomlinson some protection? The judge found that 'the danger and risk of injury from diving in the lake where it was shallow were obvious'. In such a case the judge held, both as a matter of common sense and following consistent authority (*Staples v West Dorset DC* (1995) *g* 93 LGR 536, *Ratcliff v McConnell* [1999] 1 WLR 670, *Darby v National Trust* [2001] PIQR P372), that there was no duty to warn against the danger. A warning would not tell a swimmer anything he did not already know. Nor was it necessary to do anything else. 'I do not think', said the judge, 'that the defendants' legal duty to the claimant in the circumstances required them to take the extreme measures *h* which were completed after the accident'. Even if Mr Tomlinson had been owed a duty under the 1957 Act as a lawful visitor, the council would not have been obliged to do more than they did.

[**33**] The Court of Appeal disagreed. Ward LJ said that the council was obliged to do something more. The gravity of the risk, the number of people who *j* regularly incurred it and the attractiveness of the beach created a duty. The prohibition on swimming was obviously ineffectual and therefore it was necessary to take additional steps to prevent or discourage people from getting into the water. Sedley LJ said ([2003] 3 All ER 1122 at [45]): '... it is only where the risk is so obvious that the occupier can safely assume that nobody will take it that there will be no liability.' Longmore LJ dissented. The majority reduced the damages by two-thirds to reflect Mr Tomlinson's contributory negligence,

although Ward LJ said that he would have been inclined to reduce them only by
half. The council appeals against the finding of liability and Mr Tomlinson
appeals against the apportionment, which he says should have been in
accordance with the view of Ward LJ.

THE BALANCE OF RISK, GRAVITY OF INJURY, COST AND SOCIAL VALUE.

[34] My Lords, the majority of the Court of Appeal appear to have proceeded
on the basis that if there was a foreseeable risk of serious injury, the council was
under a duty to do what was necessary to prevent it. But this in my opinion is an
oversimplification. Even in the case of the duty owed to a lawful visitor under
s 2(2) of the 1957 Act and even if the risk had been attributable to the state of the
premises rather than the acts of Mr Tomlinson, the question of what amounts to
'such care as in all the circumstances of the case is reasonable' depends upon
assessing, as in the case of common law negligence, not only the likelihood that
someone may be injured and the seriousness of the injury which may occur, but
also the social value of the activity which gives rise to the risk and the cost of
preventative measures. These factors have to be balanced against each other.

[35] For example, in *Overseas Tankship (UK) Ltd v Miller Steamship Co Pty, The
Wagon Mound (No 2)* [1966] 2 All ER 709, [1967] 1 AC 617, there was no social
value or cost saving in the defendant's activity. Lord Reid said:

> 'In the present case there was no justification whatever for discharging the
> oil into Sydney Harbour. Not only was it an offence to do so, but also it
> involved considerable loss financially. If the ship's engineer had thought
> about the matter there could have been no question of balancing the
> advantages and disadvantages. From every point of view it was both his duty
> and his interest to stop the discharge immediately.' (See [1966] 2 All ER 709
> at 718, [1967] 1 AC 617 at 643.)

[36] So the defendants were held liable for damage which was only a very
remote possibility. Similarly in *Jolley v Sutton London BC* [2000] 3 All ER 409,
[2000] 1 WLR 1082 there was no social value or cost saving to the council in
creating a risk by leaving a derelict boat lying about. It was something which they
ought to have removed whether it created a risk of injury or not. So they were
held liable for an injury which, though foreseeable, was not particularly likely.
On the other hand, in *The Wagon Mound (No 2)* [1966] 2 All ER 709 at 718, [1967]
1 AC 617 at 642 Lord Reid drew a contrast with *Bolton v Stone* [1951] 1 All ER 1078,
[1951] AC 850 in which the House of Lords held that it was not negligent for a
cricket club to do nothing about the risk of someone being injured by a cricket
ball hit out of the ground. The difference was that the cricket club were carrying
on a lawful and socially useful activity and would have had to stop playing cricket
at that ground.

[37] This is the kind of balance which has to be struck even in a situation in
which it is clearly fair, just and reasonable that there should in principle be a duty
of care or in which Parliament, as in the 1957 Act, has decreed that there should
be. And it may lead to the conclusion that even though injury is foreseeable, as
it was in *Bolton v Stone*, it is still in all the circumstances reasonable to do nothing
about it.

THE 1957 AND 1984 ACTS CONTRASTED

[38] In the case of the 1984 Act, there is the additional consideration that
unless in all the circumstances it is reasonable to expect the occupier to do

a   something, that is to say, to 'offer the other some protection', there is no duty at
all. One may ask what difference there is between the case in which the claimant
is a lawful visitor and there is in principle a duty under the 1957 Act but on the
particular facts no duty to do anything, and the case in which he is a trespasser
and there is on the particular facts no duty under the 1984 Act. Of course in such
a case the result is the same. But Parliament has made it clear that in the case of
b   a lawful visitor, one starts from the assumption that there is a duty whereas in the
case of a trespasser one starts from the assumption that there is none.

THE BALANCE UNDER THE 1957 ACT

[39] My Lords, it will in the circumstances be convenient to consider first the
question of what the position would have been if Mr Tomlinson had been a
c   lawful visitor owed a duty under s 2(2) of the 1957 Act. Assume, therefore, that
there had been no prohibition on swimming. What was the risk of serious injury?
To some extent this depends upon what one regards as the relevant risk. As I
have mentioned, the judge thought it was the risk of injury through diving while
the Court of Appeal thought it was any kind of injury which could happen to
d   people in the water. Although, as I have said, I am inclined to agree with the
judge, I do not want to put the basis of my decision too narrowly. So I accept that
we are concerned with the steps, if any, which should have been taken to prevent
any kind of water accident. According to the Royal Society for the Prevention of
Accidents, about 450 people drown while swimming in the United Kingdom
every year (see *Darby v National Trust* [2001] PIQR P372 at 374). About 25–35
e   break their necks diving and no doubt others sustain less serious injuries. So there
is obviously some degree of risk in swimming and diving, as there is in climbing,
cycling, fell walking and many other such activities.

[40] I turn then to the cost of taking preventative measures. Ward LJ
described it (£5,000) as 'not excessive'. Perhaps it was not, although the outlay
f   has to be seen in the context of the other items (rated 'essential' and 'highly
desirable') in the borough council budget which had taken precedence over the
destruction of the beaches for the previous two years.

[41] I do not however regard the financial cost as a significant item in the
balancing exercise which the court has to undertake. There are two other related
considerations which are far more important. The first is the social value of the
g   activities which would have to be prohibited in order to reduce or eliminate the
risk from swimming. And the second is the question of whether the council
should be entitled to allow people of full capacity to decide for themselves
whether to take the risk.

[42] The Court of Appeal made no reference at all to the social value of the
h   activities which were to be prohibited. The majority of people who went to the
beaches to sunbathe, paddle and play with their children were enjoying
themselves in a way which gave them pleasure and caused no risk to themselves
or anyone else. This must be something to be taken into account in deciding
whether it was reasonable to expect the council to destroy the beaches.

j   [43] I have the impression that the Court of Appeal felt able to brush these
matters aside because the council had already decided to do the work. But they
were held liable for having failed to do so before Mr Tomlinson's accident and the
question is therefore whether they were under a legal duty to do so. Ward LJ
placed much emphasis upon the fact that the council had decided to destroy the
beaches and that its officers thought that this was necessary to avoid being held
liable for an accident to a swimmer. But the fact that the council's safety officers

thought that the work was necessary does not show that there was a legal duty to do it. In *Darby*'s case the claimant's husband was tragically drowned while swimming in a pond on the National Trust estate at Hardwick Hall. Miss Rebecca Kirkwood, the water and leisure safety consultant to the Royal Society for the Prevention of Accidents, gave uncontradicted evidence, which the judge accepted, that the pond was unsuitable for swimming because it was deep in the middle and the edges were uneven. The National Trust should have made it clear that swimming in the pond was not allowed and taken steps to enforce the prohibition. But May LJ said robustly that it was for the court, not Miss Kirkwood, to decide whether the Trust was under a legal duty to take such steps. There was no duty because the risks from swimming in the pond were perfectly obvious.

FREE WILL

[44] The second consideration, namely the question of whether people should accept responsibility for the risks they choose to run, is the point made by Lord Phillips MR in *Donoghue v Folkestone Properties Ltd* [2003] 3 All ER 1101 at [53] and which I said was central to this appeal. Mr Tomlinson was freely and voluntarily undertaking an activity which inherently involved some risk. By contrast, Miss Bessie Stone, to whom the House of Lords held that no duty was owed, was innocently standing on the pavement outside her garden gate at 10 Beckenham Road, Cheetham when she was struck by a ball hit for six out of the Cheetham Cricket Club ground. She was certainly not engaging in any activity which involved an inherent risk of such injury. So compared with *Bolton v Stone*, this is an a fortiori case.

[45] I think it will be extremely rare for an occupier of land to be under a duty to prevent people from taking risks which are inherent in the activities they freely choose to undertake upon the land. If people want to climb mountains, go hang gliding or swim or dive in ponds or lakes, that is their affair. Of course the landowner may for his own reasons wish to prohibit such activities. He may be think that they are a danger or inconvenience to himself or others. Or he may take a paternalist view and prefer people not to undertake risky activities on his land. He is entitled to impose such conditions, as the council did by prohibiting swimming. But the law does not require him to do so.

[46] My Lords, as will be clear from what I have just said, I think that there is an important question of freedom at stake. It is unjust that the harmless recreation of responsible parents and children with buckets and spades on the beaches should be prohibited in order to comply with what is thought to be a legal duty to safeguard irresponsible visitors against dangers which are perfectly obvious. The fact that such people take no notice of warnings cannot create a duty to take other steps to protect them. I find it difficult to express with appropriate moderation my disagreement with the proposition of Sedley LJ ([2003] 3 All ER 1122 at [45]) that it is 'only where the risk is so obvious that the occupier can safely assume that nobody will take it that there will be no liability'. A duty to protect against obvious risks or self-inflicted harm exists only in cases in which there is no genuine and informed choice, or in the case of employees, or some lack of capacity, such as the inability of children to recognise danger (see *British Railways Board v Herrington* [1972] 1 All ER 749, [1972] AC 877) or the despair of prisoners which may lead them to inflict injury on themselves (see *Reeves v Metropolitan Police Comr* [1999] 3 All ER 897, [2000] 1 AC 360).

a   [47] It is of course understandable that organisations like the Royal Society for the Prevention of Accidents should favour policies which require people to be prevented from taking risks. Their function is to prevent accidents and that is one way of doing so. But they do not have to consider the cost, not only in money but also in deprivation of liberty, which such restrictions entail. The courts will naturally respect the technical expertise of such organisations in drawing

b   attention to what can be done to prevent accidents. But the balance between risk on the one hand and individual autonomy on the other is not a matter of expert opinion. It is a judgment which the courts must make and which in England reflects the individualist values of the common law.

   [48] As for the council officers, they were obviously motivated by the view that it was necessary to take defensive measures to prevent the council from

c   being held liable to pay compensation. The borough leisure officer said that he regretted the need to destroy the beaches but saw no alternative if the council was not to be held liable for an accident to a swimmer. So this appeal gives your Lordships the opportunity to say clearly that local authorities and other occupiers of land are ordinarily under no duty to incur such social and financial costs to

d   protect a minority (or even a majority) against obvious dangers. On the other hand, if the decision of the Court of Appeal were left standing, every such occupier would feel obliged to take similar defensive measures. Sedley LJ was able to say that if the logic of the Court of Appeal's decision was that other public lakes and ponds required similar precautions, 'so be it'. But I cannot view this prospect with the same equanimity. In my opinion it would damage the quality

e   of many people's lives.

   [49] In the particular case of diving injuries, there is little evidence that such defensive measures have had much effect. Dr Penny, the council's expert, said that over the past decade there had been little change in the rate of serious diving accidents. Each year, as I have mentioned, there are about 25–35 fracture-

f   dislocations of the neck. Almost all those affected are males and their average age is consistently around 25 years. In spite of greatly increased safety measures, particularly in swimming pools, the numbers (when Dr Penny gave evidence) had remained the same for a decade:

> 'This is probably because of the sudden, unpredictable nature of these
g   > dangerous dives, undertaken mostly by boisterous young men … hence the
> common description the "Macho Male Diving Syndrome".'

   [50] My Lords, for these reasons I consider that even if swimming had not been prohibited and the council had owed a duty under s 2(2) of the 1957 Act, that duty would not have required them to take any steps to prevent Mr Tomlinson

h   from diving or warning him against dangers which were perfectly obvious. If that is the case, then plainly there can have been no duty under the 1984 Act. The risk was not one against which he was entitled under s 1(3)(c) to protection. I would therefore allow the appeal and restore the decision of Jack J. It follows that the cross-appeal against the apportionment of damages must be dismissed.

j

LORD HUTTON.

   [51] My Lords, I have had the advantage of reading in draft the speech of my noble and learned friend Lord Hoffmann and I gratefully adopt his account of the background facts to the tragic injury which Mr Tomlinson suffered in the lake in Brereton Heath Country Park in Cheshire. I agree with your Lordships that the appeal brought by Congleton Borough Council and Cheshire County Council

(together the council) should be allowed, but as I was attracted for a considerable
time during the hearing of the appeal by Mr Tomlinson's argument supporting
the reasoning of Ward LJ in the Court of Appeal (with which Sedley LJ agreed)
([2002] EWCA Civ 309, [2003] 3 All ER 1122, [2003] 2 WLR 1120) that
Mr Tomlinson was entitled to recover damages, I wish to add some observations
of my own.

[**52**] I approach the case on the basis that Mr Tomlinson was, in strict law, a
trespasser at the time he dived and struck his head on the bottom of the lake. It
is clear that he was invited by the council to come to the country park but it is
also clear that swimming in the lake was expressly prohibited by the council and,
as the trial judge found, Mr Tomlinson was fully aware of this prohibition.
Therefore when he began to dive he became a trespasser because, as Lord Atkin
stated in *Hillen v ICI (Alkali) Ltd* [1936] AC 65 at 69, [1935] All ER Rep 555 at 558:

> 'So far as he sets foot on so much of the premises as lie outside the invitation
> or uses them for purposes which are alien to the invitation he is not an invitee
> but a trespasser, and his rights must be determined accordingly.'

However I agree with Lord Hoffmann that even if Mr Tomlinson had not been a
trespasser at the time of his dive but had been a visitor within the meaning of the
Occupiers' Liability Act 1957, he would still not have been entitled to recover
damages.

[**53**] In relation to s 1(1)(a) of the Occupiers' Liability Act 1984 I recognise that
there is force in the argument that the injury was not due to the state of the
premises but was due to Mr Tomlinson's own lack of care in diving into shallow
water. But the trial judge found that Mr Tomlinson could not see the bottom of
the lake and, on balance, I incline to the view that dark and murky water which
prevents a person seeing the bottom of the lake where he is diving can be viewed
as 'the state of the premises' and that if he sustains injury through striking his
head on the bottom which he cannot see this can be viewed as a danger 'due to
the state of the premises'. If water were allowed to become dark and murky in
an indoor swimming pool provided by a local authority and a diver struck his
head on the bottom I consider that the danger could be regarded as 'due to the
state of the premises', and whilst there is an obvious difference between such
water and water in a lake which in its natural state is dark and murky, I think that
the term 'the state of the premises' can be applied both to the swimming pool and
to the lake.

[**54**] Section 1(3) and (4) of the 1984 Act provide:

> '(3) An occupier of premises owes a duty to another (not being his visitor)
> in respect of any such risk as is referred to in subsection (1) above if—
>
> (a) he is aware of the danger or has reasonable grounds to believe that it
> exists;
>
> (b) he knows or has reasonable grounds to believe that the other is in the
> vicinity of the danger concerned or that he may come into the vicinity of the
> danger (in either case, whether the other has lawful authority for being in
> that vicinity or not); and
>
> (c) the risk is one against which, in all the circumstances of the case, he
> may reasonably be expected to offer the other some protection.
>
> (4) Where, by virtue of this section, an occupier of premises owes a duty
> to another in respect of such a risk, the duty is to take such care as is

a   reasonable in all the circumstances of the case to see that he does not suffer injury on the premises by reason of the danger concerned.'

[55] There is no doubt from the reports and proposals of the council's officials to the borough's amenities and leisure services committee and to the borough council which Lord Hoffmann has described that paras (a), (b) of s 1(3) are
b   satisfied. If s 1(3) were satisfied and the risk was one against which, in all the circumstances of the case, the council might reasonably be expected to offer Mr Tomlinson some protection, I consider that there would be an argument of some force that they were in breach of the duty specified in s 1(4), because the minutes of the meetings showed that they knew that there were dangers to persons swimming or diving in the lake (there had been two cases of swimmers
c   sustaining head injuries) and they knew that the dangers might lead to death or serious injury, but they had decided not to take the recommended steps such as planting reeds on the beach, which would probably have stopped swimming, because of financial constraints, although the cost of these precautionary measures would have been only in the region of £15,000.

d   [56] Therefore I think the crucial question is whether Mr Tomlinson has established that the risk was one to which s 1(3)(c) applies. On this point the reasoning of Ward LJ was contained in [2003] 3 All ER 1122 at [29]:

'Here the authorities employed rangers whose duty it was to give oral warnings against swimming albeit that this met with mixed success and
e   sometimes attracted abuse for their troubles. In addition to the oral warnings, the rangers would hand out safety leaflets which warned of the variable depth in the pond, the cold, the weeds, the absence of rescue services, waterborne diseases and the risk of accidents occurring. It seems to me that the rangers' patrols and advice and the handing out of these leaflets reinforced the ineffective message on the sign and constituted "some
f   protection" in fact given and reasonably expected to be offered in the circumstances of this case.'

[57] I thought for a time that this reasoning was persuasive, but I have concluded that it should not be accepted because I consider that it is contrary to a principle stated in the older authorities which is still good law. In *Stevenson v*
g   *Corp of Glasgow* 1908 SC 1034 at 1039 Lord M'Laren stated:

'... in a town, as well as in the country, there are physical features which may be productive of injury to careless persons or to young children against which it is impossible to guard by protective measures. The situation of a town on the banks of a river is a familiar feature; and whether the stream be
h   sluggish like the Clyde at Glasgow, or swift and variable like the Ness at Inverness, or the Tay at Perth, there is always danger to the individual who may be so unfortunate as to fall into the stream. But in none of these places has it been found necessary to fence the river to prevent children or careless persons from falling into the water. Now, as the common law is just the
j   formal statement of the results and conclusions of the common sense of mankind, I come without difficulty to the conclusion that precautions which have been rejected by common sense as unnecessary and inconvenient are not required by the law.'

[58] In *Corp of the City of Glasgow v Taylor* [1922] 1 AC 44 at 61 Lord Shaw of Dunfermline stated:

'Grounds thrown open by a municipality to the public may contain objects of natural beauty, say precipitous cliffs or the banks of streams, the dangers of the resort to which are plain.'

Lord Shaw then cited with approval the words of Lord M'Laren in *Stevenson's* case that 'in a town, as well as in the country, there are physical features which may be productive of injury to careless persons or to young children against which it is impossible to guard by protective measures'. I think that when Lord M'Laren referred to physical features against which 'it is impossible to guard by protective measures' he was not referring to protective measures which it is physically impossible to put in place; rather he had in mind measures which the common sense of mankind indicates as being unnecessary to take. This statement echoed the observation of the Lord President (Lord Dunedin) in *Hastie v Magistrates of Edinburgh* 1907 SC 1102 at 1106 that there are certain risks against which the law, in accordance with the dictates of common sense, does not give protection—such risks are 'just one of the results of the world as we find it'.

[59] *Stevenson's* and *Hastie's* cases (which were not concerned with trespassers) were decided almost a century ago and the judgments are couched in old-fashioned language, but I consider that they express a principle which is still valid today, namely, that it is contrary to common sense, and therefore not sound law, to expect an occupier to provide protection against an obvious danger on his land arising from a natural feature such as a lake or a cliff and to impose a duty on him to do so. In my opinion this principle, although not always explicitly stated, underlies the cases relied on by the council where it has been held that the occupier is not liable where a person has injured himself or drowned in an inland lake or pool or in the sea or on some natural feature.

[60] In *Cotton v Derbyshire Dales DC* [1994] CA Transcript 753 the Court of Appeal upheld the decision of the trial judge dismissing the plaintiff's claim for damages for serious injuries sustained from falling off a cliff. Applying the judgment of Lord Shaw in *Taylor's* case the Court of Appeal held that the occupiers were under no duty to provide protection against dangers which are themselves obvious.

[61] In *Whyte v Redland Aggregates Ltd* [1997] CA Transcript 2034 the appellant dived into a disused gravel pit and alleged that he had struck his head on an obstruction on the floor of the pit. The Court of Appeal dismissed his appeal against the judgment of the trial judge who held that he was not entitled to damages. Henry LJ stated:

'In my judgment, the occupier of land containing or bordered by the river, the seashore, the pond or the gravel pit, does not have to warn of uneven surfaces below the water. Such surfaces are by their nature quite likely to be uneven. Diving where you cannot see the bottom clearly enough to know that it is safe to dive is dangerous unless you have made sure, by reconnaissance or otherwise, that the diving is safe ie that there is adequate depth at the place where you choose to dive. In those circumstances, the dangers of there being an uneven surface in an area where you cannot plainly see the bottom are too plain to require a specific warning and, accordingly, there is no such duty to warn (see Lord Shaw in *Corp of the City of Glasgow v Taylor* [1922] 1 AC 44 at 60). There was no trap here on the judge's finding. There was just an uneven surface, as one would expect to find in a disused gravel pit.'

a

[62] In *Bartrum v Hepworth Minerals and Chemicals Ltd* (29 October 1999, unreported), the claimant dived from a ledge on a cliff. In order to avoid shallow water he knew that he had to dive out into the pool but he failed to do so and fractured his neck. Turner J dismissed his claim for damages and stated:

b

'So far as the Act is concerned, by s 1(3) of the Occupiers' Liability Act 1984 the defendants were under a duty to those whom they had reasonable grounds to believe would be in the vicinity of the danger, that is on the cliff for the purpose of diving, and the risk was one which, in all the circumstances, [they] may be reasonably expected to offer some protection. In my judgment the danger here was so obvious to any adult that it was not reasonably to be expected of the defendants that they would offer any

c   protection.'

[63] In *Darby v National Trust* [2001] EWCA Civ 189, [2001] PIQR P372 the claimant's husband was drowned whilst swimming in a pond on National Trust property. The Court of Appeal allowed an appeal by the National Trust against the trial judge's finding of liability and May LJ stated (at [27]):

d

'It cannot be the duty of the owner of every stretch of coastline to have notices warning of the dangers of swimming in the sea. If it were so, the coast would have to be littered with notices in places other than those where there are known to be special dangers which are not obvious. The same would apply to all inland lakes and reservoirs. In my judgment there was no

e   duty on the National Trust on the facts of this case to warn against swimming in this pond where the dangers of drowning were no other or greater than those which were quite obvious to any adult such as the unfortunate deceased. That, in my view, applies as much to the risk that a swimmer might get into difficulties from the temperature of the water as to

f   the risk that he might get into difficulties from mud or sludge on the bottom of the pond.'

[64] I also think that the principle stated by Lord M'Laren in *Stevenson's* case is implicit in the judgment of Lord Phillips of Worth Matravers MR in *Donoghue v Folkestone Properties Ltd* [2003] EWCA Civ 231 at [34], [2003] 3 All ER 1101 at [34],

g   [2003] 2 WLR 1138. In that case the claimant dived from a slipway into Folkestone harbour after midnight in mid-winter. He struck his head on a grid pile under the water adjacent to the harbour wall and broke his neck. The Court of Appeal allowed an appeal by the defendant against the trial judge's finding of liability. Lord Phillips MR stated:

h

'[33] The obvious situation where a duty under the 1984 Act is likely to arise is where the occupier knows that a trespasser may come upon a danger that is latent. In such a case the trespasser may be exposed to the risk of injury without realising that the danger exists. Where the state of the premises constitutes a danger that is perfectly obvious, and there is no reason

j   for a trespasser observing it to go near it, a duty under the 1984 Act is unlikely to arise for at least two reasons. The first is that because the danger can readily be avoided, it is unlikely to pose a risk of injuring the trespasser whose presence on the premises is envisaged.

[34] There are, however, circumstances in which it may be foreseeable that a trespasser will appreciate that a dangerous feature of premises poses a risk of injury, but will nevertheless deliberately court the danger and risk the

injury. It seems to me that, at least where the individual is an adult, it will be rare that those circumstances will be such that the occupier can reasonably be expected to offer some protection to the trespasser against the risk.'

a

Lord Phillips MR then went on to state that where a person was tempted by some natural feature of the occupier's land to engage in some activity such as mountaineering which carried a risk of injury, he could not ascribe to 'the state of the premises' an injury sustained in carrying on that activity. However in the present case, as I have stated, I incline to the view that the dark and murky water can be viewed as 'the state of the premises'.

b

[65] Therefore I consider that the risk of Mr Tomlinson striking his head on the bottom of the lake was not one against which the council might reasonably have been expected to offer him some protection, and accordingly they are not liable to him because they owed him no duty. I would add that there might be exceptional cases where the principle stated in *Stevenson's* and *Taylor's* case should not apply and where a claimant might be able to establish that the risk arising from some natural feature on the land was such that the occupier might reasonably be expected to offer him some protection against it, for example, where there was a very narrow and slippery path with a camber beside the edge of a cliff from which a number of persons had fallen. But the present is not such a case and, for the reasons which I have given, I consider that the appeal should be allowed.

c

d

LORD HOBHOUSE OF WOODBOROUGH.

e

[66] My Lords, in this case the trial judge after having heard all the evidence made findings of fact which are now accepted by Mr Tomlinson:

'There was nothing about the mere which made it any more dangerous than any other stretch of open water in England. Swimming and diving held their own risks. So if the mere was to be described as a danger, it was only because it attracted swimming and diving, which activities carry a risk. Despite having seen signs stating "DANGEROUS WATER: NO SWIMMING", the claimant ignored them. The danger and risk of injury from diving in the lake where it was shallow was obvious. At the time of the accident, the claimant was 18 years of age and had regularly been going to the park since he was a small child. He knew it well. The accident occurred when he waded into the water until the water was a little above his knees and threw himself forward in a dive or plunge. He knew that he shouldn't. He could not see the bottom. In fact it was a smooth sandy surface without any obstruction or hazard. He dived deeper than he had intended and his head hit the sandy bottom causing his injury. Besides the notices already referred to, visitors were handed leaflets warning them of the dangers of swimming in the mere. Wardens patrolled the park and told people further that they should not swim in the mere. However it was the fact that visitors often took no notice and very many people did bathe in the mere in summer.'

f

g

h

j

[67] Mr Tomlinson has made his claim for personal injuries under the Occupiers' Liability Act 1984 on the basis that at the time that he suffered his injury he was a trespasser in that he was swimming in the mere and swimming was, as he was aware, forbidden. This seems to me to be a somewhat artificial approach to the case; since paddling was apparently allowed but not swimming and Mr Tomlinson was at the material time in water which only came a little

a above his knees. However, under the Occupiers' Liability Act 1957 (and at common law) when an invitee or licensee breaches the conditions upon which he has entered the premises, he ceases to be a visitor and becomes a trespasser (s 2(2)). Mr Tomlinson was permitted to enter the park on the condition that (inter alia) he did not swim in the mere. If he should swim in the mere, he broke this condition and as a result ceased to be a visitor. However, like all of your

b Lordships, I consider that whether he makes his claim under the 1984 Act or the 1957 Act, he does not succeed.

[68] The two Acts apply the same general policy and the 1984 Act is a supplement to the 1957 Act. The earlier Act was the result of a re-examination of the common law relating to occupiers' liability. Its primary purpose was to

c simplify the law. It had previously been based upon placing those coming on another's land into various different categories and then stipulating different standards of care from the occupier in respect of each category. This was the historical approach of the common law to the question of negligence and found its inspiration in Roman law concepts (as was the case in the law of bailment (see *Coggs v Bernard* (1703) 2 Ld Raym 909, [1558–1774] All ER Rep 1)). By 1957, the

d dominant approach had become the 'good neighbour' principle enunciated in *Donoghue v Stevenson* [1932] AC 562, [1932] All ER Rep 1. But special rules still applied to relationships which were not merely neighbourly. One such was occupiers' liability. The relevant, indeed, principal simplification introduced in the 1957 Act was to introduce the 'common duty of care' as a single standard covering both invitees and licensees (see s 2(2)). The 1957 Act applied only to

e visitors, ie persons coming onto the land with the occupier's express or implied consent. It did not apply to persons who were not visitors including trespassers. The 1984 Act made provision for when a duty of care should be owed to persons who were not visitors (I will for the sake of convenience call such persons 'trespassers') and what the duty should then be, that is, a duty of care in the terms

f of s 1(3), more narrow than that imposed by the 1957 Act. Thus the duty owed to visitors and the lesser duty which may be owed to trespassers was defined in appropriate terms. But, in each Act, there are further provisions which define the content of the duty and, depending upon the particular circumstances, its scope and extent.

g [69] The first and fundamental definition is to be found in both Acts. The duty is owed 'in respect of dangers due to the state of the premises or to things done or omitted to be done on them'. In the 1957 Act it is s 1(1). In the 1984 Act it is in s 1(1)(a) which forms the starting point for determining whether any duty is owed to the trespasser (see also s 1(3)) and provides the subject matter of any duty

h which may be owed. It is this phrase which provides the basic definition of 'danger' as used elsewhere in the Acts. There are two alternatives. The first is that it must be due to the state of the premises. The state of the premises is the physical features of the premises as they exist at the relevant time. It can include footpaths covered in ice and open mine shafts. It will not normally include parts

j of the landscape, say, steep slopes or difficult terrain in mountainous areas or cliffs close to cliff paths. There will certainly be dangers requiring care and experience from the visitor but it normally would be a misuse of language to describe such features as 'the state of the premises'. The same could be said about trees and, at any rate, natural lakes and rivers. The second alternative is dangers due to things done or omitted to be done on the premises. Thus if shooting is taking place on the premises, a danger to visitors may arise from that fact. If speed boats are

allowed to go into an area where swimmers are, the safety of the swimmers may
be endangered.   *a*

[70] In the present case, the mere was used for a number of
activities—angling, board-sailing, sub-aqua, canoeing and sailing model
yachts—but none of these was suggested to have given rise to any danger to
Mr Tomlinson or others. Therefore Mr Tomlinson has to found his case upon a
danger due to the 'state of the premises'. His difficulty is that the judge has found   *b*
that there was none and he has accepted that finding. Therefore his case fails in
limine. If there was no such danger the remainder of the provisions of the Acts
all of which depend upon the existence of such a danger cannot assist him.
Mr Tomlinson clearly appreciated this when he brought his claim since his
statement of claim specifically pleaded that there had been 'an obstruction under
the surface of the water' on which he struck his head. The judge found that there   *c*
was no such obstruction.

[71] Section 2 of the 1957 Act deals with the content of the duty (if any). Thus
s 2(2) defines the common duty of care as one—

> 'to take such care as in all the circumstances of the case is reasonable to see
> that the visitor will be reasonably safe in using the premises for the purposes   *d*
> for which he is invited or permitted by the occupier to be there.'

If swimming is not one of those purposes, the duty of care does not extend to him
while he is swimming. Section 2(3) deals with what circumstances are relevant
to assessing any duty owed. They include 'the degree of care, and of want of care,
which would ordinarily be looked for in such a visitor'. Examples are given: '(a)   *e*
an occupier must be prepared for children to be less careful than adults ...' A
skilled visitor can be expected to appreciate and guard against risks ordinarily
incident to his skilled activities (see s 2(2)(b)). An obvious instance of the second
example is a steeple jack brought in to repair a spire or an electrician to deal with
faulty wiring. Here, Mr Tomlinson was an 18-year-old youth who ought to be   *f*
well able to appreciate and cope with the character of an ordinary lake. He can
take care of himself; he does not need to be looked after in the same way as a
child.

[72] Turning to the 1984 Act, one can observe the same features. The basic
requirement of a 'danger due to the state of the premises' is there. Section 1(2)
contains a cross-reference to s 2(2) of the earlier Act. Section 1(3) depends upon   *g*
the existence, and knowledge, of a danger coming within s 1(1). The risk of
personal injury arising from that danger must further be one against which, in all
the circumstances, it is reasonable to expect the occupier 'to offer the [trespasser]
some protection'. The equivalent phrase 'reasonable in all the circumstances' is
used in sub-ss (4), (5). Subsection (5) specifically permits the use of warnings and   *h*
discouragements against incurring the relevant risk.

[73] It is an irony of the present case that Mr Tomlinson has found it easier to
put his case under the 1984 Act than under the 1957 Act and argue, in effect, that
the occupier owed a higher duty to a trespasser than to a visitor. This is because
the inclusion of the words in s 2(4), duty 'to see that he does not suffer injury on   *j*
the premises by reason of the danger concerned'. Mr Tomlinson did suffer injury
whilst on the premises; the councils failed to see that he did not. Whilst this
argument in any event fails on account of the fundamental point that the state of
the premises did not give rise to any danger, it would be perverse to construe
these two Acts of Parliament so as to give the 1984 Act the effect which
Mr Tomlinson contends for. (See also the quotation from the Law Commission

a report by Brooke LJ in his judgment in *Donoghue v Folkestone Properties Ltd* [2003] EWCA Civ 231 at [72], [2003] 3 All ER 1101 at [72], [2003] 2 WLR 1138.) The key is in the circumstances and what it is reasonable to expect of the occupier. The reference to warnings and discouragements in sub-s (5) and the use of the words 'some protection' in sub-s (3)(c) both demonstrate that the duty is not as onerous as Mr Tomlinson argues. Warnings can be disregarded (as was the case here);

b discouragements can be evaded; the trespasser may still be injured (or injure himself) while on the premises. There is no guarantee of safety any more than there is under the 1957 Act. The question remains what is it reasonable to expect the occupier to do for unauthorised trespassers on his land. The trespasser by avoiding getting the consent of the occupier, avoids having conditions or restrictions imposed upon his entry or behaviour once on the premises. By

c definition, the occupier cannot control the trespasser in the same way as he can control a visitor. The Acts both lay stress upon what is reasonable in all the circumstances. Such circumstances must be relevant to the relative duties owed under the two Acts.

d [74] Returning to the facts of this case, what more was it reasonable to expect of the councils beyond putting up the notices and issuing warnings and prohibitions? It will not have escaped your Lordships that the putting up of the notices prohibiting swimming is the peg which Mr Tomlinson uses to acquire the status of trespasser and the benefit of the suggested more favourable duty of care under the 1984 Act. But this is a case where, as held by the judge, all the relevant characteristics of this mere were already obvious to Mr Tomlinson. In these

e circumstances, no purpose was in fact served by the warning. It told Mr Tomlinson nothing he did not already know. (See *Staples v West Dorset DC* (1995) 93 LGR 536, *Whyte v Redland Aggregates Ltd* [1997] CA Transcript 2034, *Ratcliff v McConnell* [1999] 1 WLR 670, *Darby v National Trust* [2001] EWCA Civ 189, [2001] PIQR P372.) The location was not one from which one could dive into water from a height. There was a shallow gradually sloping sandy beach.

f The bather had to wade in and Mr Tomlinson knew exactly how deep the water was where he was standing with the water coming up to a little above his knees. Mr Tomlinson's case is so far from giving a cause of action under the statute that it is hard to discuss coherently the hypotheses upon which it depends. There was no danger; any danger did not arise from the state of the premises; any risk of

g striking the bottom from diving in such shallow water was obvious; Mr Tomlinson did not need to be warned against running that risk; it was not reasonable to expect the occupier to offer the claimant (or any other trespasser) any protection against that obvious risk.

h [75] Faced with these insuperable difficulties and with the fact that they had failed to prove the pleaded case, counsel for Mr Tomlinson put the argument in a different way. They pointed to the internal reports and minutes disclosed by the defendant councils. Passing over a minute of 22 November 1984 which under the heading 'Swimming' accurately stated:

j 'Probably as a result of the larger notice boards the problems of swimming were no worse than in previous years and perhaps marginally better. Every reasonable precaution had now been taken, but it was recognised that some foolhardy persons would continue to put their lives at risk.'

They referred to an undated report of some time in 1992 concerning swimming in the mere. It reported many instances of swimming during hot spells with up to 2,000 people present and as many as 100 in the water. It referred to the popularity of the extensive beach areas with families where children paddled and made sandcastles and groups picnicked, adding 'not unnaturally many [people] will venture into the water for a swim'. The 'hazards' pointing to the likelihood of future problems were stated to include 'lakeside grassy picnic area'. The recommendations were directed at the beach areas: 'Suggest cutting down on beach area by increasing reed zones'. 'Signs should indicate the nature of the hazard e g "Danger—Water 5m deep".' It is clear that accidents such as that suffered by Mr Tomlinson were not in the writer's mind. Other similar reports are referred to in the opinion of my noble and learned friend Lord Hoffmann and it is otiose to quote from them again.

[76] In July of the same year a departmental memorandum referred to the council's policy to stop all swimming. It therefore called upon the council to engage on a scheme of landscaping to make 'the water's edge to be far less accessible, desirable and inviting than it currently is for children's beach/water's edge type of play activities'. The solution called for was to remove or cover over the beaches and replace them by muddy reed beds. Part of the reasoning was that with attractive beaches 'accidents become inevitable' and 'we must therefore do everything that is reasonably possible to deter, discourage and prevent people from swimming or paddling in the lake or diving into the lake'. An estimate of cost was asked for.

[77] Funds were short but in 1994 a request for finance was presented. It was based upon the public's disregard of the embargo on bathing in the lake despite having 'taken all reasonable steps' to educate the public. The request states that 'we have on average three or four near drownings every year and it is only a matter of time before someone dies'. 'If nothing is done about [the landscaping] and someone dies the Borough Council is to be held liable and would have to accept responsibility.' This was the nub of Mr Tomlinson's case. The situation was dangerous. The councils realised that they should do something about it—remove the beaches and make the water's edge unattractive and not so easily accessible. They recognised that they would be liable if they did not do so. This reasoning needs to be examined.

[78] The first point to be made is that the councils were always at liberty, subject to the Local Government Acts, to have and enforce a no swimming policy. Indeed this had all along been one of the factors which had driven their management of this park. Likewise, subject to the same important qualification, they were at liberty to take moral responsibility for and pay compensation for any accident that might occur in the park. It is to be doubted that this was ever, so stated, their view. But neither of these factors create any legal liability which is what is in question in the present case. If they mistakenly misunderstood what the law required of them or what their legal liabilities were, that does not make them legally liable.

[79] The second point is the mistreatment of the concept of risk. To suffer a broken neck and paralysis for life could hardly be a more serious injury; any loss of life is a consequence of the greatest seriousness. There was undoubtedly a risk of drowning for inexperienced, incompetent or drunken swimmers in the deeper parts of the mere or in patches of weed when they were out of their depth although no lives had actually been lost. But there was no evidence of any incident where anyone before Mr Tomlinson had broken his neck by plunging from a standing position and striking his head on the smooth sandy bottom on which he was standing. Indeed, at the trial it was not his case that this was what had happened; he had alleged that there must have been some obstruction.

a   There had been some evidence of two other incidents where someone suffered a minor injury (a cut or a graze) to their head whilst diving but there was no evidence that these two incidents were in any way comparable with that involving Mr Tomlinson. It is then necessary to put these few incidents in context. The park had been open to the public since about 1982. Some 160,000 people used to visit the park in a year. Up to 200 would be bathing in the mere

b   on a fine summer's day. Yet the number of incidents involving the mere were so few. It is a fallacy to say that because drowning is a serious matter that there is therefore a serious risk of drowning. In truth the risk of a drowning was very low indeed and there had never actually been one and the accident suffered by Mr Tomlinson was unique. Whilst broken necks can result from incautious or reckless diving, the probability of one being suffered in the circumstances of

c   Mr Tomlinson were so remote that the risk was minimal. The internal reports before his accident make the common but elementary error of confusing the seriousness of the outcome with the degree of risk that it will occur.

[80] The third point is that this confusion leads to the erroneous conclusion that there was a significant risk of injury presented to Mr Tomlinson when he

d   went into the shallow water on the day in question. One cannot say that there was no risk of injury because we know now what happened. But, in my view, it was objectively so small a risk as not to trigger s 1(1) of the 1984 Act, otherwise every injury would suffice because it must imply the existence of some risk. However, and probably more importantly, the degree of risk is central to the

e   assessment of what reasonably should be expected of the occupier and what would be a reasonable response to the existence of that degree of risk. The response should be appropriate and proportionate to both the degree of risk and the seriousness of the outcome at risk. If the risk of serious injury is so slight and remote that it is highly unlikely ever to materialise, it may well be that it is not reasonable to expect the occupier to take any steps to protect anyone against it.

f   The law does not require disproportionate or unreasonable responses.

[81] The fourth point, one to which I know that your Lordships attach importance, is the fact that it is not, and should never be, the policy of the law to require the protection of the foolhardy or reckless few to deprive, or interfere with, the enjoyment by the remainder of society of the liberties and amenities to

g   which they are rightly entitled. Does the law require that all trees be cut down because some youths may climb them and fall? Does the law require the coastline and other beauty spots to be lined with warning notices? Does the law require that attractive water-side picnic spots be destroyed because of a few foolhardy individuals who choose to ignore warning notices and indulge in

h   activities dangerous only to themselves? The answer to all these questions is, of course, No. But this is the road down which your Lordships, like other courts before, have been invited to travel and which the councils in the present case found so inviting. In truth, the arguments for Mr Tomlinson have involved an attack upon the liberties of the citizen which should not be countenanced. They

j   attack the liberty of the individual to engage in dangerous, but otherwise harmless, pastimes at his own risk and the liberty of citizens as a whole fully to enjoy the variety and quality of the landscape of this country. The pursuit of an unrestrained culture of blame and compensation has many evil consequences and one is certainly the interference with the liberty of the citizen. The discussion of social utility in the Illinois Supreme Court is to the same effect (see *Bucheleres v Chicago Park District* (1996) 171 Ill 2d 435 at 457–458).

[82] I cannot leave this case without expressing my complete agreement with
the reasoning of the judgment of Lord Phillips MR in *Donoghue v Folkestone
Properties Ltd* [2003] 3 All ER 1101.

[83] For these reasons and those given by my noble and learned friend Lord
Hoffmann, and in agreement with the judgment of Longmore LJ, I too would
allow this appeal.

LORD SCOTT OF FOSCOTE.

[84] My Lords, I have had the advantage of reading in draft the opinion of my
noble and learned friend Lord Hoffmann. Subject to one reservation I am in
complete agreement with the reasons he gives for allowing this appeal. But I find
myself in such fundamental disagreement with the approach to this case by the
majority in the Court of Appeal ([2002] EWCA Civ 309, [2003] 3 All ER 1122,
[2003] 2 WLR 1120) that I want to add, also, a few comments of my own.

[85] My reservation is that the Act which must be applied to the facts of this
case in order to decide whether the council is under any liability to Mr Tomlinson
is, in my opinion, the Occupiers' Liability Act 1957, not the Occupiers' Liability
Act 1984.

[86] The 1957 Act regulates the duty of care which an occupier of premises
owes to visitors to the premises (see s 1(1)). 'Visitors' are persons who would, at
common law, be invitees or licensees (see s 1(2)). The 1984 Act, on the other
hand, applies to persons on the premises who are not visitors but are trespassers.
It lays down the criteria for deciding whether the occupier of the premises owes
any duty of care at all to the trespasser in question in relation to the type of injury
he has suffered (see s 1(3)). If a duty of care is owed, the Act describes the duty
(see s 1(4)).

[87] Mr Tomlinson's case against the council is based on an alleged breach of
the duty of care they owed him. There is no doubt at all that he was a visitor at
the park. The park was open to the public and he was entitled to be there.
Wearing the shoes of a visitor, he was owed the duty of care prescribed by the
1957 Act.

[88] The notices prominently displayed at various places in the park forbade
swimming in the lake. But entry into the water was not forbidden. Visitors to
the park were entitled to paddle and splash in the shallows of the lake. Many did
so, particularly children. They were entitled to run into the water and splash one
another. They were entitled to lie in the shallows and let the cool water lap over
them. In doing these things they were visitors and were owed the 1957 Act duty
of care. All they were forbidden to do was to swim. If they had started
swimming, using the lake for a purpose which was forbidden, they would have
lost their status as visitors and become trespassers. The 1984 Act would then
have applied.

[89] Mr Tomlinson did not suffer his tragic accident while swimming in the
lake. He ran into the water and, when the depth of the water was at mid thigh
level, executed the disastrous 'dive' and suffered the accident. At no stage did he
swim. It may be that his 'dive' was preparatory to swimming. But swimming in
water not much above knee level, say 2 feet 6 inches deep, is difficult. There
might be some element of flotation but I do not think the activity would normally
justify the use of the verb 'swim'. In any event, Mr Tomlinson's injury was not
caused while he was swimming and cannot be attributed in any way to the
dangers of swimming. His complaint against the council is that the council did
not take reasonable care to discourage him while in the shallows of the lake from

a executing a 'dive'. If the 'dive' was, which I regard as doubtful for the reasons given, a preliminary to an attempt to swim, the complaint may be regarded as a complaint that the council failed to prevent him from becoming a trespasser. But this must necessarily, in my view, have been a duty owed to him while he was a visitor.

[90] An analogous situation might arise in relation to the trees in the park.
b Suppose there were notices forbidding the climbing of trees. None the less a visitor to the park climbs a tree, falls from it, injures himself and sues the council. He would have been a trespasser vis-à-vis the tree. But a claim under the 1984 Act would be hopeless. The proposition that the council owed him a duty to make the tree easier or safer to climb would be ridiculous. But the injured climber might contend that the presence of the tree posed an enticing, exciting
c and irresistible challenge to those visitors to the park who, like himself, were addicted to the adrenalin surge caused by climbing high trees and that, consequently, the council owed a duty to make it impossible for him, and others like him, to succumb to the temptation, to prevent him from becoming a trespasser vis-à-vis the tree. This duty, if it were owed at all, would be a duty
d owed to him, a visitor, under the 1957 Act. The contention would, of course, be rejected. The council's 1957 Act duty of care to its visitors would not require the trees to be cut down or the trunks and lower branches to be festooned with barbed wire in order to prevent visitors to the park from disobeying the notices and turning themselves into trespassers by climbing the trees. For present purposes, however, the point I want to make is that the climber's contention
e would engage the 1957 Act, not the 1984 Act.

[91] In the present case it seems to me unreal to regard Mr Tomlinson's injury as having been caused while he was a trespasser. His complaint, rejected by the trial judge but accepted by the majority in the Court of Appeal, was that the council ought to have taken effective steps to discourage entry by visitors into the
f waters of the lake. The notices were held to be inadequate discouragement. But, if there was this duty, it was a duty owed to visitors. The people who read the notices, or who could have read them but failed to do so, would have been visitors. These were the people to be discouraged. The alleged duty was a 1957 Act duty.

[92] The council's duty under the 1957 Act to its visitors was a duty 'to take
g such care as in all the circumstances of the case is reasonable to see that the visitor will be reasonably safe in using the premises for the purposes for which he is invited or permitted ... to be there' (see s 2(2)). The purpose for which visitors were invited or permitted to be in the park was general recreation. This included paddling and playing about in the water. The proposition that in order to
h discharge their 1957 Act duty to visitors the council had to discourage them from any entry into the water and, in effect, to prevent the paddling and playing about that so many had for so long enjoyed is, in my opinion, for the reasons so cogently expressed by Lord Hoffmann, wholly unacceptable. There was no breach by the council of its 1957 Act duty. The question whether it owed any 1984 Act duty did
j not, in my opinion, arise. If, wrongly in my opinion, the 1984 Act were to be regarded as applicable, the case would be a fortiori.

[93] There are two respects, in my opinion, in which the approach of the courts below to the facts of this case have been somewhat unreal. First, the action of Mr Tomlinson that brought about his tragic injury has been described as a 'dive'. I think it is misdescribed. A dive into water, as normally understood, involves a hands-arms-head-first movement from a standpoint above the water

136 Reading Cases and Statutes

down into the water. A dive is dangerous if the depth of the water is unknown
for the obvious reason that if the depth is inadequate the head may strike the
bottom of the pool or the lake before the diver is able to check his downwards
trajectory and curve out of the dive. There had, apparently, been two previous
occasions over the past five years or so on which a person diving into the lake had
suffered head injuries. The evidence did not disclose the details but it seems
reasonable to assume that these occasions had involved dives properly so-called.
Mr Tomlinson did not execute a dive in the ordinary sense. He ran into the lake
and, when he thought he was far enough in to do so, he threw himself forward.
His forward plunge may, for want of a better word, be called a 'dive' but it should
not be confused with the normal and usual dive. Mr Tomlinson was not diving
from a standpoint above the lake down into water of uncertain depth. His feet
were on the bottom of the lake immediately before he executed his forward
plunge. He knew how deep the water was when he began the plunge. He must
have expected the downward shelving of the bottom of the lake to continue and
there is no evidence that it did not. The accident happened because the trajectory
of his forward plunge was not sufficiently shallow. This was not a diving accident
in the ordinary sense and there was no evidence that an accident caused in the
manner in which Mr Tomlinson's was caused had ever previously occurred at the
lake.

[94] Second, much was made of the trial judge's finding that the dangers of
diving or swimming in the lake were obvious, at least to adults. No one has
contested that finding of fact. But I think its importance has been overstated.
Mr Tomlinson was not diving in the normal sense, nor was he swimming. He
simply ran into the water and when he could not run any further, because the
water was above his knees and the galloping action that we all adopt when
running into water on a shelving beach had become too difficult, he plunged
forward. This is something that happens on every beach in every country in the
world, temperature and conditions permitting. Mr Tomlinson would not have
stopped to think about the dangers of swimming or diving in the lake. He was
not taking a pre-meditated risk. It would not have occurred to him, if he had
thought about it, that he was taking a risk at all. He was a high-spirited young
man enjoying himself with his friends in a pleasant park with a pleasant water
facility. If he had set out to swim across the lake, it might have been relevant to
speak of his taking an obvious risk. If he had climbed a tree with branches
overhanging the lake and had dived from a branch into the water he would have
been courting an obvious danger. But he was not doing any such thing. He was
simply sporting about in the water with his friends, giving free rein to his
exuberance. And why not? And why should the council be discouraged by the
law of tort from providing facilities for young men and young women to enjoy
themselves in this way? Of course there is some risk of accidents arising out of
the joie de vivre of the young. But that is no reason for imposing a grey and dull
safety regime on everyone. This appeal must be allowed.

Appeal allowed. Cross-appeal dismissed.

Kate O'Hanlon   Barrister.

The following questions relate to the law reports reproduced above for the case of *Tomlinson v Congleton Borough Council and another*. When noting your answers to the questions, you should include reference(s) to the appropriate points in the judgment(s) from which you have drawn your information.

SECTION A

1.   (a) Set out a list of all of the courts before which this case came.
        (b) Indicate what was the outcome of the hearing at each instance.

2. Where in the law reports can we discover who was the dissenting judge in this case?

3. What were the respective arguments put by the barristers for each of the parties before the Court of Appeal?

4. What, according to Lord Justice Sedley, was the task of the Court of Appeal in this case?

SECTION B

5.   (a) In what respect(s) does the judgment of Lord Justice Longmore in the Court of Appeal decision in this case differ from the judgments of Ward and Sedley LL.J.?
        (b) What value or significance does the decision of the Supreme Court of Canada, referred to by Lord Justice Longmore at p. 1139j, have for the British Court of Appeal and the House of Lords?

6.   (a) What is the "one reservation" entertained by Lord Scott [see at p. 1164b]?
        (b) What leads Lord Scott [at p. 1165j] to describe the approach taken by the courts below to the facts of the case as "somewhat unreal"?

7. Since Lord Nicholls merely agreed with and adopted the reasons given by Lord Hoffmann, what purpose, if any, was served by him sitting on the case?

8. Find alternative references to the law reports reproduced here in the case of *Tomlinson v Congleton Borough Council and another*.

9. Has *Tomlinson v Congleton Borough Council and another* been cited in any subsequent case?

11. Write a short statement giving the ratio of the case in relation to *Tomlinson v Congleton Borough Council and another*.

6 Reading research materials

Chapter 4 explained that one of the ways of answering questions about law was the use of the research methods of the social scientist. Because this kind of research is the only way in which some questions about law can be answered, it is important that those interested in law can understand it.

In order to understand research into law you have to understand how and why it is written in the particular way that it is. Once you can understand the structure of the material, you will be able to see whether or not it helps to answer the questions in which you are interested.

Haphazard approaches to research are likely to be unsuccessful, the information gathered being too unrepresentative of the world at large and, therefore, too inaccurate for any conclusions to be drawn safely. Good research is done systematically. Research methods are highly developed. There are three sources of information about how and why the law operates: records, people and activities. There are also three principal methods used in socio-legal research. The researcher may read records, interview people (or send questionnaires), or observe activities.

Record reading

The researcher reads the records and collects the required information which is then either written down or noted on a prepared recording sheet. The researchers must ensure that the information collected from each record is as accurate and as complete as possible. This may involve searching through disordered files of letters and notes or simply copying the details from a form, such as a divorce petition.

Interviews and questionnaires

Interviews are conducted in person; questionnaires are given, or sent, to the respondents to complete. It is important, in so far as is possible, to ask the same questions in the same way each time so as to get comparable information. Questions may be "open-ended," allowing the respondent to reply in his or her own words, or be "closed," requiring selection of the answer from a choice given by the interviewer. The style and wording of the question is selected to fit the data sought. Whatever the questions, the interview must be recorded. This may be done by using a tape recorder or by the interviewer noting the replies. Interviews are most useful for finding out what reasons people have for what they have done and for exploiting their feelings. If questions are asked about the future, the answers can only indicate what respondents currently think they would do. It has also been established that recollection of past events may be inaccurate, particularly about dates, times and the exact sequence of events. Interview and questionnaire design requires considerable skill, as does interviewing itself if it is to reflect the respondent's views rather than those of the researcher.

Observation

The observer attends the event and records what occurs there. The observer may be an outsider; for example, a person watching court proceedings from the public gallery. Alternatively, the observer may be a person actually taking part in the events being described; for example, a police officer researching into the police force. Observation needs to be done systematically and accurately in order to avoid bias. Observers cannot record everything that they see. They must be careful that they do not record only what they want to see and neglect that which is unexpected and, perhaps, thereby unwelcome. One great difficulty in noting observations lies in deciding what to note down and what to omit. What seems unimportant at the time the notes were taken may take on a greater significance when a later analysis is made. It is important that the observer's record is contemporaneous, otherwise the data is weakened by what has been forgotten.

For any particular piece of research, one method may be more suitable than another, because of the nature of the data sources or the approach that the researcher wishes to take. If, for example, you want to research into the reasons magistrates have for their decisions, there is little point in reading records of what those decisions were. Here, the best place to start would be to interview magistrates. No single method can be said to provide the truth about every situation; some would argue that no method can provide the truth about any situation, for no one truth exists. Each method provides information based on the perceptions of the people who provide it, the record keepers, the interviewers or the observers.

Choice of research method depends not only what information is sought but also on practicalities. The researcher may not be given access to records or permitted to carry out interviews. Professional bodies and employers are not always willing to let their members of staff participate in research. This may be because they consider the research unethical (perhaps requiring them to divulge information given in confidence), because they are too busy, because they do not see the value of the research or because they wish to conceal the very information in which the researcher is interested. Thus, for example, it is unusual for researchers to be able to interview judges about cases, although there is nothing to prevent them sitting in the public gallery and watching cases from there.

For many research studies more than one method is used to obtain a complete picture. However, practical matters, including budget and time limits, may mean that not every avenue of enquiry is pursued. What is important is that the methods chosen are appropriate to the subject of study, the approach of the researcher and the conclusions drawn.

Sampling

Looking at every case is not normally practical in detailed social research. Instead, the researcher takes a sample of cases. Thus, one may interview some lawyers or some defendants or observe, or read records at some courts. If a completely random sample is taken, then it should have the characteristics of the population as a whole. A sample of judges should, for example, include judges of the different ages, backgrounds and experience to be found amongst the judiciary. However, if a characteristic is very rare a sample may not contain any example of having that characteristic. Thus, a 10 per cent sample of judges, (*i.e.* contacting every tenth judge) might well fail to include any women judges since there are very few of them. The size of sample and method of sampling must be chosen to fit with the study. In a study of attitudes of clients to lawyers there is clearly no point in interviewing only successful clients. The number of people refusing to take part in a study is also important. Researchers will try to obtain a high response rate (over 75 per cent) and also attempt to find out if those who refuse are likely to be different in any material way from those who agree to participate in the study.

Research findings

The account of any research will usually include some background information about the subject, the purpose of the study (the questions to be answered) and the methods used. Findings presented in words should cause no difficulty to the reader, but numbers may be quite confusing. Where comparisons are made, it is usually thought better to use either *proportions* or *percentages* rather than actual numbers. It is then important to be clear what the percentage represents: for example, was it 20 per cent of all plaintiffs or 20 per cent of successful plaintiffs. Some researchers do not give the actual figures, but prefer to use words such as "some", "most" or "the majority". This is not very helpful, since a word like "majority" can mean anything from 51 per cent to 99 per cent. There is a variety of ways of presenting figures so as to make them clearer. Tables (lists of figures) are commonly used because they make it easier to compare two or more categories or questions. Graphic presentation, using bar charts (histograms), pie charts or graphs, can create a clear overall impression of a complex set of figures.

Figure 1 below is a bar chart. It shows clearly the different numbers of the three offences where guns were used. It also shows for each the relative proportion in which particular types

Figure 1. Notifiable offences in which firearms were reported to have been used, by type of offence and type of weapon.

England and Wales 1982

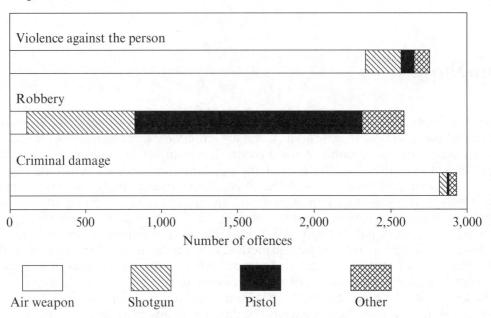

of gun were used. As can be seen from this example, the greatest advantage of a bar chart is the way in which it makes a quick visual comparison of information easy.

Figure 2 is a pie chart. The whole circle represents 100 per cent of the particular group. The segments represent different percentages. In this example, the exact percentages represented in the different segments have been printed on to the chart. This is not always done. Different circles represent both different types of original sentence and different courts in which that sentence was imposed. The segments themselves indicate what happened to people who breached their original sentence: for example, by committing a further crime whilst on probation.

Figure 3 is a graph. This is probably the best way of showing a trend over time. The graph is designed to show the rise in the number of females found guilty of indictable (basically, serious offences). There are two major problems in doing this. One is that an increase in numbers caused by an increase in the size of the population as a whole is not very interesting. Thus, rather than counting the absolute number of offenders, the graph shows the number of offenders per 100,000 in the population. Secondly, the law relating to who is guilty of an indictable offence was changed in the course of the period which the graph records. Thus, some of the increase in the number of offenders may be due to the fact that the categories of indictable crime have become different. The graph indicates this by showing a dotted vertical line through 1977 (the year in which the change took effect).

Figure 2. Person breaching their original sentence or order by type of sentence or order imposed for the breach.

England and Wales 1982

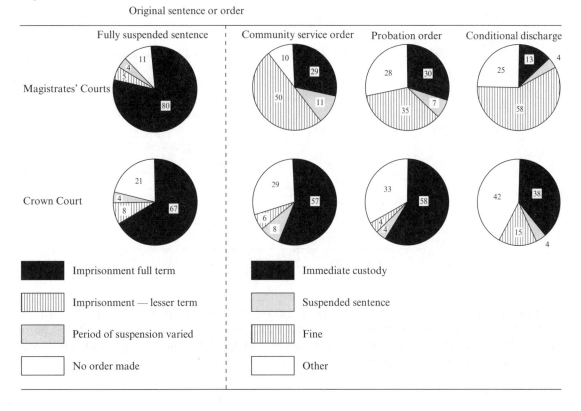

Original sentence or order

Imprisonment full term

Imprisonment — lesser term

Period of suspension varied

No order made

Immediate custody

Suspended sentence

Fine

Other

As well as graphs and tables, most researchers will state the conclusions that they have drawn from the material and summarise the main findings of the study. It is crucial that the data should establish no more and no less than is stated in the conclusions. Some researchers make great claims for their data, whilst others do not draw out all the answers that it could provide. To avoid being persuaded by poor reasoning, look at the data and see what conclusions seem appropriate, then read the explanation given, and compare it with what you originally thought. A critical approach to any empirical research should always consider the following three questions. First, are the methods chosen appropriate? This includes both, "have the right questions been asked" and "have the right people (people who should know about the topic) been asked?" There may have been better sources of information available to the researcher, but were the ones used good enough for this study? Secondly, is the sample big enough and has it been properly drawn? Thirdly, does the data justify the conclusions that have been drawn? If it does not, can you see any other conclusions that it would justify?

Figure 3. Females found guilty of, or cautioned for, indictable offences[1] per 100,000 population in the age group by age.

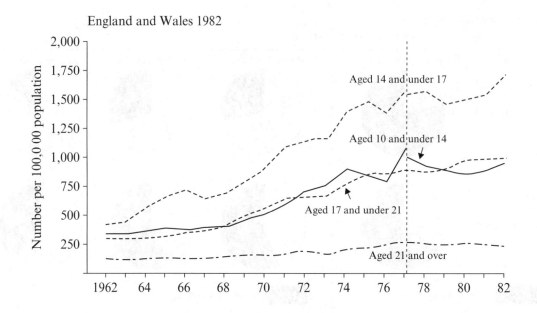

England and Wales 1982

Research often leaves as many questions raised as answered provided. Further studies may be indicated, interesting new areas that need to be explored. Studying this type of material will, hopefully, increase your interest and insight into the operation of law. It will not provide you with all the answers.

Exercise 5

Reading research materials

Reading and understanding research materials does not just involve seeing what conclusion the author has reached. Understanding the evidence the author has for the conclusion drawn is as important as understanding the conclusion itself. This section is intended to improve your critical awareness of the materials that you are reading. Reading something critically means reading it to see what weaknesses there are in it. The fewer the weaknesses the stronger will be the conclusion. When reading something, remember that there are flaws in all articles and books. As a reader your task is to assess the merit of a particular argument by being aware of its weaknesses as well as its strengths. With practice critical reading will become an unconscious habit that you will bring to all your reading. Start by reading "Doctors as Good Samaritans: Some Empirical Evidence Concerning Emergency Medical treatment in Britain" by Kevin Williams, the article reprinted below. When you have read the article once go back and read it again making detailed notes. When doing this, concentrate on trying to identify the strand of argument Williams is trying to develop, paying close attention to the evidence that he presents for the various points that they make. Your notes should tell you both what the author has written and what you think the possible objections to the various details his argument is. When you think you understand the article, and have made your notes, try to answer the questions set out in Section A below. Refer to the original article when your notes give you insufficient information to answer the question. After you have finished the questions in Section A compare your answers with those that we have given at the back of this book. If your answers differ from ours you may need to go back and reread the article in order to get a better understanding of it. Once you are sure you understand the answers to Section A go on and complete the questions in Section B.

Section A

1. What issue do you think the author is intending to discuss?
2. What do you understand Good Samaritan behaviour to be?
3. What method is used to gather the empirical data that is used in the study? Can you suggest any problems or queries that you have with relation to this method?
4. How knowledgeable about the law are doctors according to this study?

5. Williams observes:

> "[f]or a minority of respondents their limited training and experience of emergency medicine is a concern and deterrent to volunteering, which suggests that the scope of medical education might profitably be reviewed." (page 280)

What implicit premise underlies this remark?

Section B

1. Is there any difference between doctors' legal responsibilities to give assistance to a stranger in distress and their professional responsibilities with respect to the same thing?
2. Why is there a discrepancy between the figure given for the number of doctors who doubted that they would help and old lady who had collapsed in the street and that given or the number of doctors who had helped in a Good Samaritan type situation? How might that discrepancy be explained?
3. Williams' article contains a discussion of the common law relating to "medical rescue". Why might this discussion now be wrong? How would you find out if it is right?
4. What is the relationship between respondents to the survey in this study having been the subject of claims with respect to alleged malpractice or negligence and their willingness to engage in Good Samaritan behaviour?
5. What potential disadvantages are there, either to doctors or to society at large, in doctors engaging in Good Samaritan behaviour?

JOURNAL OF LAW AND SOCIETY
VOLUME 30, NUMBER 2, JUNE 2003
ISSN: 0263-323X, pp. 258–82

Doctors as Good Samaritans: Some Empirical Evidence Concerning Emergency Medical Treatment in Britain

KEVIN WILLIAMS*

This paper reports the results of the first survey of British doctors' attitudes towards the provision of emergency treatment outside the usual confines of a surgery or hospital. The experience and perceptions of NHS doctors practising in Sheffield concerning Good Samaritan behaviour are discussed against the background of the rather uncertain common law of medical rescue. The implications of the survey's findings for the direction of legal policy and the promotion of medical altruism are also considered. Despite the alleged deterioration in standards of social responsibility, the potentially fraught nature of such interventions, and the theoretical possibility of legal liability should any rescue attempt go badly, it seems that the overwhelming majority of doctors (in this survey, at least) are willing Samaritans.

INTRODUCTION

From time to time the media highlight some shocking incident said to illustrate the callous indifference (or worse) of modern society. In the immediate aftermath of the death of 10-year-old Damilola Taylor in November 2000, questions were asked about the alleged failure of passers-by to go to his aid as he lay bleeding helplessly in a south London street. The then Home Secretary took the opportunity to condemn what he called "the walk on by culture"[1] — a culture the common law appears to endorse.

It is commonplace for tort texts to instruct readers that, whatever moral decency may require, there is no legal duty to act as a Good Samaritan by going to the aid of a stranger in distress, and that this is so no matter how grave the emergency or how easy it would be to render effective assistance.[2] Unsurprisingly, critics have doubted the social desirability of this "no duty" rule,[3] which in England apparently now goes so far as to excuse certain failures by the emergency services to undertake properly (or at all) the duties they are paid from public funds to perform.[4]

*Law Division, Sheffield Hallam University, 51–53 Broomgrove Road, Sheffield S10 2BP, England

Thanks are due to the *Journal's* anonymous referees for their helpful comments. The usual disclaimer applies.

[1] Jack Straw, quoted in the *Guardian*, 30 November 2000.

[2] See, for example, W.V.H. Rogers (ed.), *Winfield and Jolowicz on Tort* (16th edn., 2002) 134, citing Lord Diplock in *Dorset Yacht Co Ltd* v. *Home Office* [1970] A.C. 1004, 1060: "the priest and the Levite would have incurred no civil liability in English law".

[3] See, for example, A.L. Linden, "Rescuers and Good Samaritans" (1971) 34 *Modern Law Rev.* 241.

[4] See, for example, *Capital and Counties plc* v. *Hampshire CC* [1997] Q.B. 1004 (limited duty on fire brigade once it has elected to fight a fire), *OLL* v. *Secretary of State for Transport* [1997] 3 All E.R. 897 (no duty on coastguard co-ordinating air-sea rescue), *Alexandrou* v. *Oxford* [1993] 4 All E.R. 328 (no duty on police to respond to 999 call).

In contrast, doctors have at least a *professional* responsibility to go to the aid of anyone in nearby need of emergency medical care, regardless of whether the casualty is an existing patient or a stranger. All registered practitioners are bound by the General Medical Council's (GMC) ethical code which declares that "In an emergency, wherever it may arise, you must offer anyone at risk the assistance you could reasonably be expected to provide".[5] In this latest version, the nature of the duty has been redefined (and, arguably, expanded) by substituting the word "assistance" for "treatment".[6] The phrase "wherever it may arise" has also been added in order to make it clear that the obligation is not restricted to emergencies arising in this country or to those occurring on professional premises, such as a surgery or hospital. Failure to comply with the code renders the doctor liable to a charge of serious professional misconduct.[7] In this sense, it may be said that doctors are not fully volunteers and that altruism is a compulsory core value.

Whether doctors additionally have a legal duty to help a needful stranger is a question the answer to which, it will be suggested later, is less clear-cut than was once assumed to be the case. Meanwhile, we should note that the contractual position of General Practitioners (GPs) and hospital doctors working in the NHS is not identical. The statutory terms of service of GPs require them to treat anyone in their practice area who is in immediate need owing to an accident or other emergency, so long as they have been asked to attend.[8] Where treatment has been provided in this way to a person not on their list, GPs are entitled to be paid a prescribed fee by their Health Authority.[9] The regulations allow for a GP who unreasonably fails to treat to be disciplined, though they provide no remedy to the untreated casualty. NHS hospital doctors have no similar obligation towards strangers. If they do volunteer assistance, it is unclear whether they are entitled to claim to be paid by the casualty.[10] More significantly, because the provision of Good Samaritan treatment ordinarily forms no part of the employment duties of hospital doctors, the NHS indemnity scheme appears to accept no responsibility should there be negligence on the part of a rescuing doctor.[11] However, both medical

---

[5] General Medical Council, *Good Medical Practice* (3rd edn. 2001) para. 9. Similar ethical declarations can be found in the medical codes of other common law jurisdictions, including Australia, Canada, Ireland, and the United States of America.

[6] The earlier version of *Good Medical Practice* (2nd edn., 1998) para. 4, reads "In an emergency, you must offer anyone at risk the treatment you could reasonably be expected to provide". Presumably "assistance" extends beyond treatment to include other help, such as calling the emergency services.

[7] See Medical Act 1983, s. 35. R.G. Smith, *Medical Discipline* (1994), provides a detailed analysis of the professional conduct jurisdiction of the GMC up to 1990 but cites no examples of neglect charges other than in relation to existing patients. My own search of the minutes of the Professional Conduct Committee for the years 1990–2001 identified only one charge grounded on a failure to provide emergency treatment to a non-patient. In 1997, a locum GP was "admonished" for refusing to attend an elderly man who had collapsed in the street outside the surgery.

[8] See para. 4(1)(h), Sch. 2, National Health Service (General Medical Services) Regulations 1992, S.I. 1992/635, deeming such persons to be patients of the GP. GPs are also required to attend those outside their practice area provided no other doctor is available, they have agreed to give treatment, and the person in need is in the locality of the GP's Health Authority (now Primary Care Trust).

[9] See para. 33, *Statement of Fees and Allowances for General Medical Practitioners in England and Wales* (the "Red Book"). In October 2002, this responsibility transferred from Health Authorities to Primary Care Trusts.

[10] The issue of restitutionary recovery is considered later, see n. 83 below and text.

[11] See Department of Health, *Health Circular (89) 34*, Annex A, para. 13. However, the NHS Litigation Authority (which administers the Clinical Negligence Scheme for Trusts) has confirmed, in correspondence with the author, that where a hospital trust expects or authorizes Good Samaritan treatment (as some ambulance services do in relation to off-duty paramedics) any claim to indemnity submitted by the employing trust would be covered by the Scheme.

protection societies provide worldwide indemnity cover for Good Samaritan acts by members, whether hospital doctors or GPs.[12]

In an attempt to establish how doctors themselves see their ethical and legal responsibilities, GPs and hospital doctors working in the NHS in Sheffield, England's fourth largest city, were asked about their experience of, and attitudes towards Good Samaritan emergency treatment. So far as is known no previous work of this sort has been undertaken in Britain, though the willingness of doctors in Canada and the United States was surveyed some thirty years ago.[13] The North American results showed wide variations. Whereas some 90 per cent of Canadian respondents said they would stop and assist at a roadside accident, only half of United States physicians said they would do likewise, citing fear of a possible malpractice claim as their principal reason. If doctors here are similarly afflicted by a litigation-induced reluctance to help or by Jack Straw's "bystander apathy" that would be much more socially significant than the absence of any legal duty on passers-by to go to the aid of babies drowning in shallow pools.[14] Medical researchers have recently pointed out that traffic accidents are now so common (causing over 3,400 deaths and 40,000 serious injuries every year) that many doctors will find themselves faced with giving roadside treatment at some point in their careers.[15]

THE SHEFFIELD GOOD SAMARITAN SURVEY[16]

1. Sample and response rate

In the autumn of 2001, questionnaires were sent to all 331 Sheffield Health Authority GPs and 940 hospital doctors working in the Sheffield Teaching Hospitals NHS Trust. The surveyed population of 1271 thus comprised 26 per cent GPs and 74 per cent hospital doctors. A total of 459 questionnaires were completed, an overall response rate of 36 per cent. The return rate for the two groups was substantially identical so that respondents were, in this regard, representative of the survey population — 26 per cent identified themselves as GPs with the balance being hospital doctors (of whom 52 per cent were consultants).

---

[12] The Medical Defence Union and the Medical Protection Society first introduced this discretionary cover in 1999. Seemingly, it is available whether a claimant alleges incompetent treatment or a failure to assist at all. The GMC's code, n. 5, para. 33, advises doctors "In your own interests, and those of your patients, you must obtain adequate insurance or professional indemnity cover for any part of your practice not covered by your employer's indemnity scheme".

[13] See R.J. Gray and G.S. Sharpe, "Doctors, Samaritans and the Accident Victim" (1973) 11 *Osgoode Hall Law J.* 1.

[14] A commonly cited exemplar of the "no duty" rule. See, for example, Lord Nicholls in *Stovin* v. *Wise* [1996] A.C. 923, 931.

[15] See T.J. Coats and G. Davies, "Prehospital care for road traffic casualties" (2002) 324 *Brit. Medical J.* 1135.

[16] I am indebted to Maria Smith of the Survey and Statistical Research Centre at Sheffield Hallam University for help with the design of the survey and for the statistical analysis of the questionnaire returns. The University's Human Rights Research Centre kindly provided the funding. My thanks are also due to Sheffield Health Authority and to Professor Chris Welsh, Medical Director, Sheffield Teaching Hospitals NHS Trust, for facilitating distribution of the questionnaires, as well as to the 459 doctors who took the time to participate in the survey.

2. Scope and purpose of the survey

The survey investigates both the practical experience of doctors and their opinions. In particular, it was designed to elicit information about four aspects of Good Samaritan behaviour. First, the extent to which doctors have been called on in the past to act as a medical Samaritan and their response. Second, regardless of their actual experience, how they anticipate they would react to a medical emergency. Third, how doctors perceive their legal and professional responsibilities. Finally, the questionnaire tried to establish what (other) factors might encourage altruistic behaviour. The survey defined a Good Samaritan act as "examining or providing treatment in an emergency to a sick or injured person who is not an existing patient of the doctor in question and which was done outside the normal confines of a surgery or hospital".

3. Doctors' actual experience of Good Samaritan calls

Overall, 72 per cent of respondents (329 of 459) stated that they had been called on to act as a medical Samaritan at some point in their career. Asked "How often?", over half of the 318 replying to this question said that they had done so on more than two occasions. Intuitively, this seems a very high proportion, the unpredictable nature of accidents and sudden illness notwithstanding. It is possible that the returns overstate the incidence of helping in medical emergencies since doctors who *have* acted as Good Samaritans may be more inclined to complete the questionnaire seeing the survey as of greater interest or relevance. The experience of non-respondents may not be substantially similar. Even so, the results strongly suggest that doctors do not generally succumb to "bystander apathy" when faced with a call for help. Table 1 summarizes their responses.

Only one doctor in the survey admitted having declined to treat. No explanation was offered. The great majority (88 per cent) said they had provided "treatment" (which the questionnaire left undefined) with the remainder assisting in some other way, commonly by summoning an ambulance, occasionally by simply providing reassurance. There were no statistically significant differences in the inclination of GPs and hospital doctors to provide assistance. However, GPs were more likely to report that they had acted as a Good Samaritan (80 per cent compared to 69 per cent: $p = 0.028$), and to have done so on more than one occasion (83 per cent compared to 74 per cent: $p = 0.005$).[17]

Many respondents took the opportunity to say something of their experiences.

> Patient had fainted on aeroplane, recovered and was OK. No treatment needed. Young insulin-dependent diabetic, stayed, and went to hospital in ambulance. Attended an elderly lady who had fallen in the street, diagnosed hip fracture and arranged ambulance.
> Assessed patient, arranged paramedic/ambulance and monitored while awaiting ambulance.
> Put "fitting" patient into recovery.

---

[17] The symbol "p" denotes statistical significance or probability value derived from the application of the Pearson chi-square test. It is a means of expressing the degree of likelihood that an observed or reported pattern of frequencies could have been produced by chance. The smaller the number, the greater the likelihood that the result is not due merely to chance. Thus, if $p = 0.0001$ the odds are a thousand to one (one tenth of 1 per cent) against the difference being random. For this purpose, a difference is regarded as significant if it is less than 0.05 (a one in 20 chance or greater).

Table 1. Number of Times Acted As a Good Samaritan

	Whole Sample (%)	GPs (%)	Hospital Doctors (%)
Once	23	17	26
Twice	20	12	23
More Than Twice	57	71	51
Sample Size	318	90	225

On about six occasions over 30 years — simply stayed with the person until the ambulance arrived, pressed on wound or took lady home.
Immediate roadside assistance — child RTA.
Provided first aid prior to arrival of emergency services. Confirmed death in one case.

4. Doctors' willingness to assist

Anticipating (wrongly, as it turned out) that doctor's experience of medical rescue might be limited, the survey also sought to establish their general willingness to undertake Good Samaritan responsibility. Respondents were asked to imagine that while at work they were reliably informed that an elderly woman had collapsed in the street nearby and, on the assumption that they were not already busy with a patient of their own, to say whether they would go with a view to providing any necessary treatment. Of the 458 who responded to this question, 81 per cent (372) said they would, 12 per cent (56) answered "maybe", while only 7 per cent (30) said "no". There were no statistically significant differences between the responses of males and females or differences linked to how long doctors had been qualified. Nor was there any correlation between doctors' responses to this question and whether or not they had actual experience of providing Good Samaritan treatment. GPs were, however, more likely than hospital doctors to say that they would offer assistance.[18]

When faced with a hypothetical question, it is possible that respondents may tend to overestimate their willingness to assist. Nonetheless, these figures are a convincing vote in favour of altruism, and may mark doctors out from the general population. Psychological research indicates that whether bystanders are prepared to intervene in an emergency depends on how they perceive the situation. In particular, where it appears that other potential rescuers are nearby, feelings of personal responsibility are likely to be diffused so that, ironically, offers of assistance may be less forthcoming from any of those present. Additionally, limited experience of acting decisively in a crisis, feelings of incompetence, and fear of making a fool of oneself may inhibit individual bystanders from attempting rescue.[19] In contrast, research also indicates that those with first-aid training are more likely to come forward when faced with an apparently bleeding casualty, regardless of the presence of others, their training having equipped them to recognize the need for immediate action and made them

[18] 91 per cent of GPs said they would help, 3 per cent said they would not and 6 per cent said maybe. By comparison, 78 per cent of hospital doctors said yes, 8 per cent said no and 14 per cent said maybe (p = 0.004).
[19] See B. Latané and J.M. Darley, *The Unresponsive Bystander: Why doesn't he help?* (1970) and J.P. Rushton and R.M. Sorrentino, *Altruism and Helping Behaviour: Social, Personality, and Developmental Perspectives* (1981).

less fearful of doing the wrong thing.[20] It may be surmised that the extended training of doctors means that they are less likely than first-aiders to be deterred or to believe that others are somehow better qualified to help a casualty. This supposition gains support from a further finding in the survey (discussed in the next section) showing that the minority of doctors who doubted that they would help the collapsed elderly woman commonly attributed this reluctance to anxieties about their competence to provide effective treatment.

Those respondents who said that they would go and assist the elderly woman were asked to say why. Their replies are given in Table 2.

Table 2. Reasons for Offering Assistance

	Percentage	Sample size
It is a professional ethical responsibility	95	352
It is a moral responsibility	99	359
It is a legal responsibility	22	309
Other	28	61

As can be seen, overwhelmingly the answer was that it was a moral or professional responsibility or both, though about one in five believed that it was also a legal responsibility.[21] Those doctors who said they would have "other" than the specified reasons for offering help also turned out to be driven largely by moral or ethical concerns. Some examples of the reasons this group gave are listed below.

> It is a question of personal values and compassion for others in need.
> Christian duty.
> It is a human response. I would go to see if my knowledge could add anything in the circumstances.
> I would want the same for myself and my family.

These returns almost certainly provide only a partial explanation of doctors' motivations.[22] Identifying fully the reasons for what psychologists call "agentic helping" is a difficult and complex task and is beyond the capacity of this sort of survey. The precise significance of the diverse personal, cultural, physical, and other factors likely to influence those faced with an emergency are the subject of ongoing debate in the behavioural science literature.[23] Amongst other disputed questions is the relative importance of empathetic and altruistic motives compared to egoistic and self-regarding concerns. Perhaps all that can be said here is that these respondents predominantly attributed their attitudes to an ethical understanding of their professional role as doctors, though other complex considerations

---

[20] See R.L. Shotland and W.D. Heinhold, "Bystander response to arterial bleeding" (1985) 49 *J. of Personality and Social Psychology* 347.

[21] In response to a later question, 42 per cent wrongly endorsed the proposition that all doctors are legally obliged to treat anyone in nearby and urgent need, regardless of their status as an existing patient.

[22] Here, as elsewhere in the survey, the checklist of reasons specified in the questionnaire may have constrained the range of responses and so may be a source of potential bias.

[23] For a review of the debate, see R. Gross, *Psychology. The Science of Mind and Behaviour* (3rd edn., 1998) 404–415 and fn. 19.

(such as cost-benefit assessments of helping or not) may also play a part in some decisions.[24] One pragmatic GP wrote "it would be extremely bad publicity for me personally, and the surgery generally, if we responded anything less than 100 per cent".

In an attempt to see whether other features, such as the location of the casualty, might be influential, those doctors who said that they would offer assistance in the paradigmatic case of the "elderly women collapsed in the street" were asked about four alternative scenarios. Here "a person in apparent medical distress" was either on board an aircraft, at a party, injured by the roadside or taken ill in a large shopping center. In each case, doctors were asked whether they would be more or less likely to help. For the great majority it seems that location is irrelevant and would make "no difference."[25] The results are summarized in Table 3.

Though most respondents were not inclined to discriminate between the four hypothetical emergencies, a minority said that they would be "more" or "less" likely to offer assistance in one situation or another. Arguably, the "shopping centre" example is nearest to the initial "elderly woman in the street" scenario and, perhaps for that reason, attracted the

Table 3. Other Scenarios and How Likely To Help

	More Likely	Less Likely	No Difference	Sample Size
The person was on board an aircraft	16%	12%	71%	367
At a party you were attending	16%	8%	76%	364
By the roadside injured in a traffic accident	14%	15%	70%	367
Taken ill in a large shopping centre	5%	12%	82%	362

highest "no difference" score. It also drew the lowest "more likely" rating, seemingly because other sources of help were thought likely to be to hand. The availability of other sources of help was generally the most frequently cited explanation for intervention being "less likely".[26] The fact that they would be "off duty" seems not to be influential.[27] The casualty's

[24] See J. Richardson and J. McKie, *The Rule of Rescue* (2000) Working Paper 112, Centre for Health Program Evaluation for discussion of the potential conflict between ethical and cost-effective approaches to providing life-saving health care generally.

[25] Factors other than location may be important, such as the nature of the emergency, the victim's appearance, the perceived degree of their distress, and its apparent cause. A study of hospital doctors in New York suggested that they would be most likely to give aid where a person was complaining of chest pains in a restaurant and to respond to a call for assistance on an aeroplane. Unsurprisingly, perhaps, they were least likely to help a dishevelled, apparently drunken man lying on the pavement. See C.P. Gross et al., "The Physician as Ambivalent Samaritan" (1998) 13 *J. of General Internal Medicine* 491.

[26] We saw earlier that psychological research suggests that the presence of others nearby may make bystander intervention less likely in some circumstances, see n. 19 above and text.

[27] Doctors usually encounter Good Samaritan emergencies when away from their usual place of work, and so are more likely to be "off duty". Compare *Lowns* v. *Woods* [1996] Aust. Torts Reports 81–376 where an Australian GP was held liable when he refused to leave his surgery to attend a sick child not on his list. I have argued elsewhere that a legal duty to treat strangers should be recognized, but that it should not turn on the precise location of either doctor or casualty, see K. Williams, "Medical Samaritans: Is there a duty to treat?" (2000) 21 *Ox. J. of Legal Studies* 393, 409–10.

status as a stranger was similarly unimportant, except in the "party" situation, though here reservations were commonly expressed about the possibility of having had alcohol to drink.

5. *Doctors' reluctance to assist*

Medical researchers in the United States and elsewhere have suggested that "a medical emergency outside the hospital or medical practice can be one of the most unnerving situations a physician encounters".[28] Given this, it may be thought surprising that fewer than one in five doctors (86 of 458) doubted they would go to help in the imagined case of the old lady collapsed in the street. On the other hand, the "doubters" response is in marked contrast to the replies given to the earlier question about actual experience of Good Samaritan emergencies. There, all but one of the 329 doctors faced with a real life emergency had helped in some way. At first sight this discrepancy appears startling, particularly bearing in mind the GMC's instruction that in an emergency every registered practitioner "must offer anyone at risk the assistance [they] could reasonably be expected to provide".[29] The explanation may be that more doctors are readier to express doubts about a hypothetical case than will fail to respond in fact, and that doubts are likely to be resolved in favour of action when faced with a real casualty in evident medical need.

The "doubters" were asked to provide an explanation. Table 4 shows the range of options the questionnaire made available and the responses selected.

Table 4. Reason for Not Offering Assistance[30]

	Percentage	Sample size
None of my business. My responsibilities are to my own patients	37	49
It is the job of the ambulance or other emergency services	85	61
Limited expertise in emergency medicine	64	59
No legal responsibility to do so	51	49
No ethical responsibility to do so	9	45
I might be sued	44	50
I could not charge for my services	7	44
Other	82	33

The commonest specific explanations selected were that attendance was "the job of the ambulance or other emergency services" and "limited expertise in emergency medicine". These responses are consistent with the evidence from the behavioural sciences, which suggests that failures to help are commonly justified on a similar basis, namely, that others are better placed to act effectively.[31] Hospital doctors constituted the majority here and it may

[28] See Gross et al., op. cit., n. 25, and Coats and Davies, op. cit., n. 15.
[29] See n. 5 above.
[30] Some explanation of Table 4 may be helpful. Despite each reason on the questionnaire having a yes/no box, none of the 86 doctors replying to this question checked every option, instead choosing only some of the listed reasons. For example, 49 doctors in total checked "None of my business." Of these, 18 (37 per cent) said "yes" and 31 (63 per cent) said "no". Thus, almost twice as many considered this not to be an explanatory factor as did.
[31] See nn.19 and 26 above.

be that they feel less confident than GPs about their "first-aid" skills. One respondent, remarking on the subject matter of the survey generally, said "It highlights the lack of emergency medicine of many doctors". Others made the not infrequent claim that "paramedics are probably better than doctors in these situations" and that it is important to "act within the limits of our experience and qualifications". Such caution is understandable. It has been said that even "if well trained in hospital trauma management, a doctor will not be able to perform well at the roadside without considerable extra training".[32] Among the residual "other" explanations offered for refusing or being doubtful about helping were remarks such as "I'm a pathologist" and "there are more appropriate practitioners available for such an occurrence". Many of these might be readily fitted into the specified category "Limited expertise in emergency medicine." Clearly, for this minority of doctors, the quality of on-the-spot care they feel able to provide is a real concern.

Those who checked the "no legal responsibility" option were more or less equally divided about whether or not it was a relevant factor likely to influence their decision. More unexpectedly, given the common (but largely untested) assertion that the threat of liability operates as a powerful disincentive to altruistic behaviour, the "doubters" do not seem to be much affected by this fear. Only fifty doctors considered the "I might be sued" option to be a possible explanation — with the majority (56 per cent) saying that it was not. Moreover, of the total of 86 doctors who might have checked for or against this option, only 22 (26 per cent) actually did so. Doctors' perceptions of the legal position are discussed next.

6. Doctors' knowledge of the law

Respondents were presented with a series of statements about different aspects of the law and asked to say whether they are true or false. The statements and the responses are summarized in Table 5.

Overall, just less than half the respondents (47 per cent) gave the right answer to a majority of the eleven questions. This is worse than random chance. It seems likely that many answers were mere guesswork, as a number of respondents candidly admitted. Indeed, it would be surprising if doctors were more familiar with the law. Not only are many of the propositions really quite technical for a doctor (or even for a lawyer[33]) in a hurry to answer correctly but, as the following section shows, the rescue rules are in a state of flux.

Nonetheless, almost three-quarters of doctors correctly identified the general "no duty" rule, rejecting as false the first proposition that "everyone is obliged to help a stranger in distress provided they can do so without endangering themselves". They were much less sure about the apparent obverse in the following question, with only 42 per cent saying that "no one need help a stranger, whatever the circumstances". Perhaps this was because the statement appears to be counter-intuitive, offending "common-sense". Alternatively, respondents may

---

[32] Coats and Davies, op. cit., n. 15, at p. 1136.
[33] Twenty colleagues in the Law Division at Sheffield Hallam University were kind enough to answer the eleven questions in Table 5 impromptu. Seventeen (85 per cent) got six or more right, compared to 47 per cent of doctors. Even so, none scored more than nine out of eleven.

Table 5. Knowledge of Good Samaritan Law

	True or False	% Who Answered Correctly	Sample Size
1. Everyone is obliged to help a stranger in distress provided they can do so without endangering themselves	False	73	445
2. No one need help a stranger, whatever the circumstances	True	42	441
3. Only "professional rescuers", such as the police or fire brigade, can be liable for failing to respond to a call for help in an emergency	False	62	430
4. Not even "professional rescuers" are legally obliged to help others known to be in distress	True	36	433
5. An ambulance service that unreasonably fails to dispatch an available ambulance promptly in response to an emergency call can be legally liable	True	93	439
6. All doctors must provide emergency treatment to anyone in nearby and urgent need, regardless of whether that person is an existing patient	False	58	442
7. Only GPs in the NHS (but not other doctors) must provide emergency treatment to anyone in the area of their Health Authority, whether or not that person is an existing patient	True	14	437
8. Any registered medical practitioner who, in an emergency, fails to offer anyone at risk (whether or not an existing patient) the treatment they could reasonably be expected to provide may be charged with serious professional misconduct by the General Medical Council	True	54	434
9. The Medical Defence Union and the Medical Protection Society provide worldwide cover to their members in respect of claims arising out of Good Samaritan acts	True	60	435
10. What are sometimes called "Good Samaritan laws" protect doctors who voluntarily go to the aid of a stranger in distress, so long as they act without gross negligence	True	59	421
11. "Good Samaritan laws" protect doctors in the United States but not in this country	True	22	388

have seen it as too stark to be true or to have had understandable doubts about who counts as a "stranger".[34]

The sixth question, which declared that "all doctors must provide emergency treatment to anyone in nearby and urgent need", proved similarly perplexing to a minority. Around two in five respondents (42 per cent) wrongly believing the statement to be true, perhaps confusing the legal position with their professional obligation. In fact, many doctors barely seem to understand the latter obligation. Only just over half of those who attempted question eight correctly identified their professional responsibility to "offer assistance" as set out in the GMC's code *Good Medical Practice*.[35] This level of ignorance seems surprising. On the other hand, it is worth recalling that the near universal explanation for being prepared to act as a medical Samaritan was firmly located in perceptions of "professional ethical" or "moral" responsibility.[36] It is an open question whether the remaining one in five doctors who doubted they would assist would be more inclined to do so if they better understood the GMC rule and the associated risk of being charged with professional misconduct should they unreasonably fail to help. As Levmore observed, in an analogous context, "rewards or penalties will motivate a potential rescuer only if he is aware of these incentives and then only if in a crucial moment he is able to be influenced by this knowledge".[37]

There were no significant differences between GPs' and hospital doctors' overall scores,[38] between men and women, or how long respondents had been qualified. Moreover, the willingness of doctors to volunteer in the hypothetical case of the elderly woman collapsed in the street seems entirely unrelated to their knowledge of the law. Also, as we saw earlier, those who doubted they would go and assist her seem not to have been much influenced in this by the threat of possible legal liability. We may be justified in concluding that doctors' (mis)understanding of their legal position is unlikely to affect their actual behaviour should a stranger require medical assistance.[39] Before considering further doctors' perceptions of the liability climate, we turn to the uncertain state of the common law of medical rescue.

THE COMMON LAW OF "MEDICAL RESCUE"[40]

Despite the apparent clarity of the "no duty to strangers" rule set out at the beginning of the paper, the law of "medical rescue" is less than clear cut. A starting point is *Barnett v.*

---

[34] The "no duty" rule has never been absolute. The difficulty lies in identifying the "non-stranger" cases in which the defendant is obliged to go to the aid of the claimant in his moment of need. E.J. Weinrib "The Case for a Duty to Rescue" (1980) 90 *Yale Law J.* 247, 248, suggests that no single rationale explains "the widening ambit of exceptions", which in the United States of America threaten to consume the rule itself.

[35] GMC, op. cit., n. 5.

[36] See Table 2 above and text.

[37] S. Levmore, "Waiting for Rescue: An Essay on the Evolution and Incentive Structure of the Law of Affirmative Obligations" (1986) 72 *Virginia Law Rev.* 879, 882.

[38] GPs were, however, almost twice as likely as hospital doctors to know that they must provide emergency treatment when summoned to a casualty within their practice area (21 per cent compared with 11 per cent). What is more surprising is that only about one in five GPs seem to understand that they are so obliged by their terms of service, see n. 8 above and text.

[39] This is consistent with the findings of both Gray and Sharpe, op. cit., n. 13, and Gross et al., op. cit., n. 25, who similarly failed to detect any association between doctors' knowledge of the law and their willingness to help.

[40] This section draws on some of the arguments in Williams, op. cit., n. 27.

Chelsea and Kensington HMC[41] in which it was held that an open Accident and Emergency facility was, in principle, duty-bound to provide necessary treatment to a casualty who physically presented in obvious distress.[42] There was a sufficiently "close and direct relationship" to warrant imposing a duty: the fact that the night watchman was not an existing (out) patient of the NHS hospital in question was not critical.

More recently, *Kent* v. *Griffiths*[43] decided that the unexcused failure of an available ambulance to reach a casualty within a reasonable time of an emergency 999 call having been accepted rendered the London Ambulance Service liable to pay compensation for such damage as would have been averted by a timely arrival.[44] In the Sheffield Survey, a remarkable 93 per cent of doctors correctly identified this as the law.[45] While some respondents may have read about *Kent* in the medical press, so high a score more likely reflects doctors' expectations of what the law *should* be. If so, it can be seen as a strong endorsement of the position taken by the court.

The London Ambulance Service having undertaken to respond, it seems clear that the outcome in *Kent* turned on the voluntarily given promise.[46] Accordingly, it is possible to read the decision as being merely concerned with what constitutes breach of the duty owed to a *patient*, rather than being about whether there was an initial duty to rescue a stranger. Having agreed to go to her aid, the question became whether the defendants were required to do so promptly and for what consequences they should be responsible. On this basis, *Kent* may do little more than confirm that there can be liability for unreasonably delayed treatment that results in a deterioration of a patient's condition, in much the same way that there can be liability for timely but incompetent treatment.[47] This outcome is well within mainstream understandings about the law of proper medical care.[48] The more interesting question is whether the ambulance service would have been liable if their controller had wrongly declined to accept the 999 call, mistakenly believing that no ambulance was available. Here there would be no active "assumption of responsibility". Nonetheless, presumably the Court of Appeal would have held that there was a positive duty to respond, at lease in the absence, in fact, of compelling grounds for refusing to go to the aid of a casualty known to be in urgent need. After all, Lord Woolf MR rejected the defendant's primary submission, namely, that the ambulance service is like the fire service — under no liability whether it refuses to respond at all or does so incompetently, so long as no more damage results than if nothing had been done.[49]

---

[41] [1969] Q.B. 428.

[42] Presumably the same is true where a casualty presents at a GP's surgery during consultation hours.

[43] [2001] Q.B. 36.

[44] Performance statistics for English ambulance services are available at <http://tap.ccta.gov.uk/doh/intpress>. Most ambulance services now operate a system of target response times and "call prioritization".

[45] See Table 5 above, question 5.

[46] The decision would have gone against the claimant had there been no ambulance available or if there had been conflicting demands on the service's resources, see *Kent* v. *Griffiths*, op. cit., n. 43, at p. 53.

[47] Arguably, this reading pays too little regard to Lord Woolf's analysis of the "duty to attend", which was a live issue. Initially the duty point had been fully conceded, but following the decision in *Capital and Counties*, op. cit., n. 4, that admission was withdrawn and an unsuccessful application was made to strike out the claim, see *Kent* v. *London Ambulance Service* [1999] P.I.Q.R. P192.

[48] See *Bolitho* v. *City and Hackney HA* [1998] A.C. 232.

[49] *Kent* v. *Griffiths*, op. cit., n. 43, at pp. 52–3.

For that failed submission, the defendants in *Kent* had relied on dicta in *Capital and Counties plc* v. *Hampshire County Council*, which is concerned with the liability of fire brigades.[50] There, Stuart-Smith LJ had said, *obiter*, that mere physical proximity between a doctor and a sick person, of itself, creates no duty to treat. On this view, a doctor who witnesses a road accident is not bound to stop and help. Moreover, if he does stop and volunteers assistance, allegedly "his only duty is not to make the victim's condition worse".[51] Yet, even assuming that a doctor is free to drive by with impunity, is this latter claim true? By stopping and treating, it seems proper to describe the doctor as having assumed responsibility for the injured person, who thereby becomes his *patient*. Patients are legally entitled to expect that an attending doctor will exercise reasonable professional skill and care and not simply that he will refrain from making them "worse".[52] His lordship conceded this principle but effectively denied that it applied, refusing to accept that a doctor who volunteers roadside assistance, thereby, puts himself into a doctor-patient relationship.[53] If these dicta truly represent the law, we are left with a curious situation. While both an assigned ambulance crew and the hospital receiving a traffic casualty must make reasonable efforts to save the casualty, a doctor who happens upon the scene can only be liable once his active intervention results in additional harm. This incongruous possibility seems to have been acknowledged in *Watson* v. *British Boxing Board of Control Ltd*, where Lord Phillips MR laconically observed, also *obiter*, that there can be no duty on a doctor unless there is "acceptance of the patient as a patient".[54]

This denial of patient-status (and the consequent "not making worse" standard) may be designed to forestall the possibility that volunteers who botch rescues might be sued, resulting in what Professor Fleming called "the anomaly of subjecting the incompetent Samaritan to liability while excusing the Levite".[55] Yet this risk seems more theoretical than real. The evidence suggests that few (if any) claims are likely to be brought. As we shall see in the next section, none of the doctors in the Sheffield survey reported having had a Good Samaritan claim made against them, despite almost three-quarters having helped in a medical emergency, the majority on several different occasions.[56] This is entirely in line with what is

---

[50] *Capital and Counties*, op. cit., n. 4 While *Capital and Counties* is often regarded as a "duty" case, it is possible that it too did no more than decide a "breach" question. Having turned up, the real issue was whether a fire brigade, once at the scene, must act carefully and for what consequences it should be responsible.

[51] id., p. 1035. Whether the behaviour of volunteer rescuers (who have no initial duty to act) must inevitably be tested against the "not making worse" standard was accepted in *The Ogopogo* [1970] 1 Lloyd's Rep. 257, but, on appeal to the Canadian Supreme Court, the point was left open, see *Horsley* v. *MacLaren* (1972) 22 D.L.R. (3d) 545.

[52] See *Bolam* v. *Friern HMC* [1954] 1 W.L.R. 582 and *Bolitho* v. *City and Hackney HA*, n. 48.

[53] It may be significant that respondents who had acted as Good Samaritans consistently described themselves as having treated "patients".

[54] [2001] 2 W.L.R. 1256, 1269. Where this leaves NHS GPs is unclear. Unlike other doctors, they may have no choice but to treat local casualties, who are deemed to be patients, See n. 8 above and text.

[55] J.G. Fleming, *The Law of Torts*, (7th edn., 1987) 135. Distaste of anomaly aside, courts may be reluctant to see the rescuee as having been "damaged" or to accept that the costs of his private misfortune ought to be transferred to the public purse or to the Samaritan's indemnifier. Stuart-Smith LJ in *Capital and Counties*, op. cit., n. 4, at p. 1037, said it was unclear why a volunteer should be assuming a duty to be careful merely by attempting a rescue. "It would be strange if such a person were liable to . . . a drowning man who but for his carelessness he would saved, but without the attempt would have drowned anyway".

[56] See Table 1 above.

known about the position nationally. Neither the NHS Litigation Authority nor either of the medical protection organizations know of any claims against Samaritan doctors.[57]

Moreover, as a leading text points out, if an action were to be brought, the court "would be understandably reluctant to find on the facts that the defendant had been careless".[58] Doctors who elect to treat their own patients are, quite rightly, deemed to be holding themselves out as possessing the skills necessary to the particular task so that inexperience or want of expertise ordinarily provide no excuse.[59] However, it is evident that such an assumption may be highly inappropriate in the case of a Samaritan doctor. The law requires only reasonable skill and care in the circumstances. Judges are likely to be sensitive to the treatment having been provided in "battle conditions" and to approach the question of what can be expected accordingly. The fact that a Samaritan doctor will probably have encountered the casualty unexpectedly, that the emergency was not of his making, and that he may have only limited training in first aid (let alone in emergency medicine) are all relevant to the question of breach. Apart from the Samaritan doctor's background and training, other material factors include the likely absence of any clinical history for the casualty, and the limited time and facilities available to enable a full examination and diagnosis to be undertaken and the best treatment provided. Furthermore, faced with a sudden peril, a rescuer is "entitled to be judged in light of the situation as it appeared to him at the time".[60] Accordingly, it would be manifestly unjust (as well as unrealistic) for the law to demand that every medical Samaritan come up to the standards of a specialist trained in pre-hospital care.[61] Whatever the standard of care demanded by the law, we saw earlier that some doctors in the survey are sufficiently anxious about their limited expertise that they may be inhibited from volunteering.[62]

Whether there is a legal (as well as a professional) duty to give emergency treatment to a stranger may be more complicated than the account so far, and the dicta in *Capital and Counties*, allow. In *Lowns* v. *Woods*,[63] the New South Wales Court of Appeal held a GP liable in damages after he refused to attend a fitting 11-year-old who was not his patient. The court rejected Dr. Lowns's denial that he was ever asked to help: he had had the gravity and urgency of the situation sufficiently explained to him by the older sister who had been sent to his nearby surgery by her mother to get help. In the view of the court, though the boy was

---

[57] Confirmed in correspondence with the author. The *only* litigation in Britain against a medical Samaritan appears to be the unreported case of *Cattley* v. *St John's Ambulance Brigade* (first-aider attending a casualty, though no breach on the facts) discussed by G. Griffiths, "The Standard of Care Expected of a First-Aid Volunteer" (1990) 53 *Modern Law Rev.* 255. Even in North America, such litigation "occurs with the frequency of hens' teeth" according to Gray and Sharpe, op. cit., n. 13 at p. 4. More recently, A. Kirkpatrick, "Good Samaritan acts" (2002) 324 *Brit. Medical J.* S29 claims to have located only one case in the United States where a doctor was sued following a Good Samaritan act.

[58] See R.F.V. Heuston and R.A. Buckley (eds.), *Salmond and Heuston on the Law of Torts*, (21st edn., 1996) 224. Published prior to *Capital and Counties*, the learned editors (rightly) assume that a negligence action by a traffic victim against a passing doctor who stops and negligently renders first aid is possible

[59] See *Wilshire* v. *Essex AHA* [1987] Q.B. 730.

[60] See *Baker* v. *T.E. Hopkins & Son Ltd* [1959] 1 W.L.R. 966, 984.

[61] Even in a hospital, a casualty doctor is only judged against the standards of the reasonably competent Accident and Emergency casualty officer, rather than against the standards of a specialist in the particular condition that afflicts the patient, see *Hardaker* v. *Newcastle Health Authority* [2001] Lloyd's Rep. Med. 512. However, courts may be less forgiving where the complaint concerns post-emergency negligent after-care, see *Lanphier* v. *Phipos* (1838) 8 C. & P. 475.

[62] See Table 4 above.

[63] Lowns, op. cit., n. 27.

not on his list, the doctor should have been prepared to travel the 300 metres or so to visit the house. Had he done so, the epileptic seizure would likely have been arrested and the consequent brain damage and quadriplegia averted. Although foreseeability of harm alone was insufficient, what the court described as the "physical", "circumstantial", and "causal" proximity of the parties was held to justify the imposition of a duty to treat in this case. Dr. Lowns was close by, had the competence and capacity to respond, and no prior commitments. There was no inconvenience, much less impediment, in the way of the doctor providing effective treatment in what he should have recognized to be a life-threatening emergency when called on in the "professional context" of his surgery. The failure to attend was causative of the dire consequences for young Patrick Woods. *Lowns* has been described by one Australian commentator as an "extraordinary development" because "it recognizes the tortious duty of a physician, when receiving a call for help, to render assistance to a person in peril notwithstanding the lack of any prior doctor-patient relationship".[64] Whilst the decision may seem radical when judged against the traditional pro-Levite stance of the English common law, it is important to notice, as another local commentator did at the time, that the reaction of the Australian medical profession to the judgment "has not been agitated". This may well be because doctors have for some years accepted "that assistance in such circumstances [is] at least an ethical obligation".[65] That supposition gains strong support from the findings of the Sheffield survey, as well as being enshrined in the GMC's code of professional conduct. Overwhelmingly, Sheffield doctors explained their willingness to help a stranger in medical need as arising from a sense of professional (or moral) responsibility.[66]

Lowns was not cited in either *Kent* or *Capital and Counties* and, of course, is technically not binding in this country in any event. Moreover, it does not purport to create a general duty on medical personnel to act as Samaritans, whatever the circumstances. In both *Lowns* and *Kent* there was a clearly identified individual in urgent medical need, and an explicit call for help that could have been met without inconvenience. There were no competing demands on the services of either defendant, both of whom were professionally "on call". Additionally, in *Kent* there was a voluntarily given undertaking. Accordingly, neither decision mandates that doctors must stop unbidden and assist at roadside accidents. Nevertheless, it is open to the appellate courts in this country to create such a duty. I have argued elsewhere that they should do so.[67]

ENCOURAGING MEDICAL ALTRUISM

The liability profile of the NHS is the subject of widespread, virtually daily publicity. In the Sheffield survey, just over one in five respondents (95 of 450) reported having faced one or

---

[64] See L. Haberfield, *"Lowns v Woods* and the Duty to Rescue" (1998) 6 *Tort Law Rev.* 56, J.L. Powell and R. Stewart (eds.), *Jackson and Powell on Professional Negligence* (5th edn., 2002) 761 offer a circular rationalization of the outcome. Patrick Woods, they say, "presumably became a patient as soon as the defendant . . . came under a duty to attend and treat him".
[65] See K. Day, "Medical Negligence — the Duty to Attend Emergencies and the Standard of Care: *Lowns & Anor v Woods & Ors"* (1996) 18 *Sydney Law Rev.* 386, 394.
[66] See Table 2 above.
[67] See Williams, op. cit., n. 27.

more claims alleging some form of "medical negligence or malpractice", of which 51 per cent were "successful".[68] However, their Good Samaritan behaviour generated no claims, despite almost three-quarters of respondents saying they had provided emergency assistance at some time.[69] Providing Good Samaritan treatment is, comparatively speaking, a rare activity so that the absence of claims should not be too surprising. More than forty years ago, the American Medical Association pointed out that "the risk of legal liability for a physician who gives emergency care to a stranger . . . is infinitesimal in comparison with the legal risks in other phases of medical practice".[70] The Sheffield survey disclosed no significant relationship between doctors having had a claim made against them and their willingness to provide emergency assistance. We saw earlier that fear of being sued was cited as a possible influence on behaviour by only around a quarter of the small minority of doctors who doubted that they would help. Moreover, doctors' knowledge of the law and their willingness to volunteer seem also to be entirely unrelated.

If the possibility of legal liability seems not to deter altruistic behaviour are there, conversely, any factors that might make it more likely? The questionnaire offered three options indemnity insurance, a favourable liability regime, and the possibility of payment. Table 6 summarizes the overall results.[71]

Table 6. What Would Make Good Samaritan Behaviour More Likely?

	Percentage	Sample Size
My medical defence organization provided indemnity against legal liability	78	427
The law protected me from liability, unless the treatment was inappropriate or unreasonable in the circumstances	78	430
The law protected me from liability, unless the treatment was grossly negligent or reckless	80	429
The law protected me from liability, whatever the circumstances	46	414
I was entitled to be paid for my professional services	13	416
Other	19	47

[68] The questionnaire defined claims as "successful" if "some compensation was agreed or paid, even if only to dispose of the nuisance value of the claim". Hospital doctors were almost twice as likely as GPs to report that claims had been successful (60 per cent compared with 33 per cent).

[69] See Table 1 and n. 57 above and text. Interestingly (if inexplicably) those who had acted as a Good Samaritan were more than twice as likely to have faced a negligence claim (although not one arising from their Good Samaritanism, of course), compared with those who had not acted in this way (25 per cent compared with 11 per cent).

[70] Cited in W.J. Curran, "Legal History of Emergency Medicine from Medieval Common Law to the AIDS Epidemic" (1997) 15 *Am. J. of Emergency Medicine* 658, 662.

[71] Women respondents appear more risk-averse that their male colleagues, as to a lesser extent do GPs compared to hospital doctors. Women doctors were more likely than men to say they would be more inclined to act if their medical defence organization provided indemnity (85 per cent compared with 74 per cent), as were GPs (86 per cent compared with 76 per cent of hospital doctors). Similarly, more women than men declared they would be more inclined to volunteer if the law protected them from liability except where the treatment was grossly negligent or reckless (88 per cent compared with 76 per cent).

1. The availability of indemnity insurance

Over three-quarters of respondents said they would be "more inclined" to provide Good Samaritan emergency treatment if their medical defence organization provided indemnity against legal liability. In fact, worldwide cover is available as part of the standard indemnity package provided by both the Medical Defence Union and the Medical Protection Society, though only 60 per cent of respondents correctly spotted this when answering the earlier question designed to test doctors' understanding of the liability rules.[72] This discretionary cover, introduced in 1999, was prompted by members' anxieties about the possibility of litigation arising from the provision of emergency treatment on board an aircraft.[73]

2. The standard of liability

The questionnaire offered three alternative standards. More than three-quarters said they would be encouraged irrespective of whether the law protected treatment that was "grossly negligent or reckless" or merely "unreasonable." It was argued earlier that the usual *Bolam* standard (reasonable professional care in all the circumstances) is sufficiently flexible to pay due regard to the emergency nature of the activity so as to make Good Samaritan liability unlikely. A gross negligence standard would be an unnecessary and unwelcome refinement since it would make the nature of a doctor's duty turn on the patient-status of the casualty. The ordinary obligation on claimants to prove a causative want of reasonable care, as well as the practical realities of financing (speculative) litigation, should give Samaritan doctors adequate protection against unmeritorious claims.

Interestingly, the most protective option — no liability, whatever the circumstances — garnered least support, from only 46 per cent of respondents. Even in the United States and parts of Canada, where local legislatures have been persuaded that medical altruism is best encouraged by giving doctors special protection from claims brought by ungrateful rescuees, there have been no moves to shut out all such claims completely. The protection offered by these North American so-called "Good Samaritan" statutes varies widely but commonly excuses medical (and sometimes other sorts of) volunteer rescuers unless gross negligence can be shown against them.[74] Considerable scepticism surrounds these enactments: first, because there is little or no evidence that they have been effective in the sense of persuading more doctors to render

---

[72] See Table 5, question 9, and n. 12 above.

[73] In the year to April 1999, British Airways reportedly asked "Is there a doctor on board?" on 872 occasions, see *Doctor*, 23 September 1999. It is likely that the airlines' own insurance protects doctors who give medical help, though they appear rather coy about admitting it.

[74] See M. McInnes, "Good Samaritan Statutes: A Summary and Analysis" (1992) 26 *University of British Columbia Law Rev.* 239 for a review of the North American legislation. See, too, the (US Federal) Volunteer Protection Act 1997 and the Aviation Medical Assistance Act 1998. The former immunizes all volunteers in non-profit organizations (such as charity workers, mountain rescue teams, and amateur sports coaches) unless the harm results from wilful, criminal, reckless or grossly negligent behaviour or from the use of a motor vehicle. The latter protects airlines where, during an in-flight medical emergency, they solicit assistance from a person believed to be medically qualified, as well as exempting those individuals who provide assistance, unless guilty of gross negligence or wilful misconduct.

aid willingly,[75] second, because many observers doubt that they were initially necessary, either to shield doctors from gold-digging litigants or to mollify doctors' falsely exaggerated perceptions about the extent of their exposure to liability in a hostile "blame" culture.[76]

Comparable special protection seems unnecessary here and, even if desirable, might well be incompatible with the "right to life" guarantee contained in Article 2 of the European Convention on Human Rights.[77] Nor do Sheffield's doctors seem to want such immunity, rightly believing that they are not at any great risk of such litigation. Nonetheless, there was a tendency to over-estimate their exposure. Asked to estimate how many Good Samaritan claims there had been in the last five years against British doctors, 10 per cent correctly said none, though a further 46 per cent believed the figure was between one and twenty-five. There were no differences in the perceptions of those who said they would help in an emergency and those who would not.

3. The possibility of payment

Earlier we saw that around one in five doctors doubted they would go to assist in the hypothetical circumstance of the "elderly woman collapsed in the street". When asked to explain, only three doctors said that not being able to "charge for my services" was a reason. Table 6 shows that only a small minority (13 per cent of 416 respondents) selected "entitlement to be paid for my professional services" as a would-be material consideration making Good Samaritan behaviour more likely.[78]

In fact, GPs are already entitled to be paid from public funds where they provide emergency treatment to a casualty who, though not on their list, is within their practice area.[79] And it may be that the general law will allow doctors to be paid in other circumstances. In parts of the United States and Canada, doctors have been allowed to recover their expenses and reasonable remuneration (though not a reward) following efforts (even when unavailing) to save life.[80] The absence of English authority on the point is explained by Goff and

---

[75] Gray and Sharpe, op. cit., n. 13, at p. 27, say they have had "no discernible impact". Indeed, the content of these special liability regimes may frequently be unknown to doctors, see Gross et al., op. cit., n. 25, at p. 493. Moreover, to the extent that they offer highly disparate and conditional (rather than absolute) immunities, they present "ambiguous inducements for rendering emergency assistance", see Anon, "Good Samaritans and Liability for Medical Malpractice" (1964) 64 *Columbia Law Rev.* 1301, 1302. The lack of clarity in their drafting is criticized by McInnes, id., at p. 249.

[76] Curran, op. cit., n. 70, amongst others, notes the absence of any evidence to support the common misconception that American Good Samaritans have been successfully sued and attributes the fears of United States doctors to media distortion and confusion. McInnes, id. at pp. 240–1, suggests that the risk of liability was always minimal, noting that three Canadian Provinces declined to enact "Good Samaritan" protection because it would be "otiose".

[77] As to which, see J. Wright, *Tort Law and Human Rights*, (2001) ch. 2.

[78] GPs nominated payment as a potential factor much more commonly than did hospital doctors (28 per cent of GPs compared with 8 per cent of hospital doctors).

[79] See n. 9 above and text. Additionally, *any* qualified medical practitioner who treats or examines a road traffic casualty in an emergency is entitled to claim a fee and expenses from the person using the vehicle at the time the injury arose, see Road Traffic Act 1988, s. 158.

[80] See *Cotman* v. *Wisdom* (1907) 104 SW 164 (Arkansas) and *Matheson* v. *Smiley* [1932] 2 D.L.R. 787 (CA, Manitoba, upholding doctor's claim to remuneration from the estate of defendant suicide he sought to save). For commentary, see H. Dagan, "In Defense of the Good Samaritan" (1999) 97 *Michigan Law Rev.* 1152 and M. McInnes, "Restitution and the Rescue of Life" (1994) 32 *Alberta Law Rev.* 37.

Jones on the practical basis that doctors rendering such services "do not generally intend to charge for them; and if they do, the assisted person may well be willing to pay". The learned authors go on to suggest that since there is a strong public interest in the performance of altruistic acts, which may be encouraged if a doctor is entitled to restitutionary recovery, there is much to be said for allowing such claims.[81] While an argument based on fairness can certainly be made in favour of allowing recovery by an out-of-pocket Samaritan, it seems clear from the Sheffield survey that the prospect of payment is unlikely to have much effect one way or the other on the propensity of doctors to volunteer or on the incidence of attempted medical rescue.

CONCLUSIONS

Almost three-quarters of respondents in the Sheffield survey say they have provided emergency treatment to a stranger, and an even larger proportion claim they would help if the need arose. Seemingly, media-fuelled concerns about the "walk-on-by-society" are out of place in this context. A strong internalized moral and professional compulsion is the professed principal force motivating doctors. The GMC's external obligation, which threatens professional sanctions for unreasonably failing to offer assistance, is only poorly understood and, consequently, must frequently have been honoured in ignorance.

For a minority of respondents their limited training and experience of emergency medicine is a concern and a deterrent to volunteering, which suggests that the scope of medical education might profitably be reviewed. Criticism has recently been levelled at the NHS for failing to establish a general system of immediate pre-hospital care (particularly to deal with the consequences of traffic accidents) and for not doing more to equip individual doctors with the skills necessary to deal effectively with ad hoc Samaritan emergencies. However, Coats and Davies go on to say that "first aid and immediate care and increasingly part of the undergraduate curricula, so that future doctors may be able to be better Good Samaritans".[82]

The Sheffield survey provides little evidence of self-regarding attitudes or conduct that might be characterized as "defensive medicine".[83] Indeed, the actual or predicted Samaritan behaviour of doctors appears to be largely unaffected by their knowledge of the law (which is understandably patchy) or by fear of potential legal liability. Nor do many help because they know that their medical protection organization will back them should they be sued. One fairly typical response said "I have always helped and have never seen the law as relevant. It is a moral issue". Another reply doubted whether "most people would consider the legal implications at the time of need".

These findings may surprise those politicians, media, and other commentators who see British society as increasingly afflicted by a decline in social responsibility brought on (or at

---

[81] See Lord Goff of Chieveley and G. Jones, *The Law of Restitution* (5th edn., 1998) 473–4.

[82] Coats and Davies, op. cit., n. 15 at p. 1138. There are postgraduate courses in London, Edinburgh, and elsewhere providing training for doctors working in specialist scene-of-accident emergency teams. There are also courses that cater for paramedics and fire service personnel.

[83] One doctor's defensive medicine may be another's good practice. See the discussion in M.A. Jones, *Medical Negligence* (2nd edn., 1996) 5–7 and N. Summerton, "Positive and negative factors in defensive medicine" (1995) 310 *Brit. Medical J.* 27. For a North American perspective see D. Dewees et al., *Exploring the Domain of Accident Law* (1996) ch. 5.

least hastened) by a "blame-and-sue" culture.[84] Although some doctors in the survey did express anxiety about "ambulance-chasing" lawyers and the possibility of ungrateful rescuees suing, the majority feels no very strong need of any special legal immunity (such as operates in North America to relieve incompetent rescuers from the cost of getting it wrong). That intuition seems sound. Providing pre-hospital emergency care is extremely unlikely to result in litigation, let alone liability. So far as is known, no British doctor has faced such a claim. Thus, while we should do all that we sensibly can to encourage medical altruism because, as one respondent said "immediate attention can save lives and is a public expectation', it is suggested that no special protection (such as a recklessness standard) is needed to shield doctors. The ordinary liability rules for deciding what constitutes culpable and causative fault already provide a sufficient safeguard against unmeritorious claims and require no radical alteration. It is, anyway, a mistake to believe that malpractice suits are more likely to arise from medical rescues, which are comparatively rare events, than from the regular day-to-day treatment encounters between doctors and their own patients, which despite generating significant numbers of claims attract no special protection. However, more could be done by the medical press and the medical defence societies to reassure doctors that the risks of being sued are remote and that indemnity cover is ordinarily available to them. Further, the legal rights and responsibilities of doctors might profitably feature in any revised version of the medical curriculum. The President of the Medico-Legal Society has recently advocated this.[85]

One matter does require re-consideration by the courts, however. Samaritan doctors who voluntarily intervene assume responsibility and so ought to be regarded as putting themselves into a doctor-patient relationship with the casualty. It follows from this that the standard test for professional negligence should apply, whether the treatment-provider is a doctor, paramedic or first-aider. Dicta otherwise in *Capital and Counties* are contrary to principle, potentially productive of anomaly, and should be rejected. So too the associated suggestion that responsibility accrues only where the rescuee has been "made worse" since this also is dependant on there being no doctor-patient duty relationship. If the implicit rationale behind these dicta is the need to promote as well as protect Samaritan medical intervention, the available evidence shows that this belief has little or no basis in fact. In any event, arguably the only certain inducement would be the creation of a complete immunity from suit. That would be unprecedented, and would be likely to be condemned as contrary to human rights legislation. Moreover, it is unwanted by a majority of doctors in this survey.

Finally, there remains the question, addressed only indirectly in this paper, whether doctors *should* be legally obliged to act as Good Samaritans. The present position is fairly summarized by Winfield and Jolowicz. They say that "in England the common understanding is (though there appears to be no case precisely in point) that refusal by a doctor

---

[84] See *Guardian*, op. cit., n. 1, and, for example, F. Furedi, *Courting Mistrust. The hidden growth of a culture of litigation in Britain* (1999). Compare a report by the Institute of Actuaries, *The Cost of Compensation Culture* (2002) estimating the annual value of compensation claims in the United Kingdom at some £10bn or 1 per cent of GDP.

[85] See R. Palmer, "Black Sheep, Scapegoats and Lambs to the Slaughter — Some Reflections on the Work of a Medical Protection Organisation" (2001) 68 *Medico-Legal J.* 130, 133 decrying "the woeful lack of teaching of legal aspects of medical practice to medical students and doctors". A number of respondents in the survey commented similarly, one saying "These (Good Samaritan) issues should be explored in medical school and have a higher profile in the journals".

in an emergency to go to the aid of a person who is not his patient would not be actionable".[86] Two brief observations may be in order. First, to the extent that the Sheffield survey shows that a large majority of doctors already behave as if they are so bound, it might be concluded that legal compulsion is unnecessary. An alternative (and preferable) assessment is that the law should buttress the existing altruistic impulses of doctors and reinforce the GMC's professional conduct rules by formally demanding what is already common practice. It is strongly arguable that this would be, as the currently conventional test for novel negligence duties demands, "fair, just and reasonable".[87] Recognizing such a duty may be expected to have some beneficial effects at the margins by encouraging doubtful Samaritans as well as providing a means of compensating those (rare) victims of truly egregious "bad Samaritan" behaviour.

---

[86] Winfield and Jolowicz, op. cit., n.2, at p. 134.
[87] See *Caparo Industries plc* v. *Dickman* [1990] 2 A.C. 605.

7 Study skills

Studying effectively

Most students want their time at university to be successful and enjoyable; they want to get a good degree, as well as making friends and having a good social life. These are some very basic goals; many students have others, such as developing new skills, participating in sports activities or earning some money. The purpose of this chapter of *How to Study Law* is to help you achieve the goal of fulfilling your academic potential. It suggests some strategies that are intended to help you study law more effectively, not only so that you can improve your academic performance, but also so that studying law may become a more enjoyable and satisfying experience.

Successful study does not simply involve spending a lot of time working. Students who spend a lot of time on their work do not necessarily receive high marks (although clearly there is some correlation between the effort you put in to your academic work and the results you can expect to achieve). The purpose of this chapter is to suggest some techniques which you can apply to the tasks which law students are asked to carry out, such as writing essays and answers to problem questions, reading cases and statutes, participating in seminars and sitting examinations. These techniques are intended to enable you to study effectively, so that you do not needlessly waste time and effort. If you are able to study effectively, you should be able not only to be successful in your academic work, but also to have sufficient time for the other things that you want to do.

Independent learning

As a student in a college or university, you will be expected to take responsibility for your own learning. Your tutors will assume that you can work on your own without supervision, develop your research skills, complete assessment tasks and hand them in on time. You are likely to spend a much smaller proportion of your time on timetabled activities than you did at school. You will be responsible for ensuring that you know what lectures and small group sessions you need to attend, where they are held and at what time. You will also be responsible for meeting any deadlines set for coursework or assessment tasks. The freedom to learn in your own way is very rewarding, but some people find this approach extremely different to the one they were used to at school, and that it is much more challenging.

It is up to you to organise your time and plan it so that you can get everything done which you need to do, both in terms of your academic work and your social life, as well as any paid employment you might be engaged in. The next section of this chapter is devoted to time management, because it is one of the most useful skills you can learn. It will not just be useful whilst you are a student; it is one of the skills that are commonly called "transferable", because they can be used not just while you are a student, but also throughout the rest of your life.

Managing your time

As a law student, you will be expected to do a number of different things: attend classes or lectures, prepare work for discussion in tutorials, seminars or classes, write essays. Often you will be given several of these tasks at once. Clearly you cannot do them all at the same time. You will have to plan carefully, working out how much time is available in total, identifying what you need to do, how long it will take you and when you are going to do it, so that you can complete all the tasks before the relevant deadline.

● Buy a diary and use it

You can use your diary to plan your time. To be effective, your diary needs to contain a complete record of what you have to do. You need to carry it with you and add new appointments as you make them. You could start by putting in all your academic commitments — lectures, tutorials/seminars, deadlines for coursework and so on. Then you can add other commitments as they come up.

● Make lists to help you prioritise what you have to do

Make a list of all the things you want to do. There will probably be more things on your list than you have time to do, so you will have to prioritise your list, deciding what you need to do very soon, and what can wait till later. Think about the best order in which to do things. Make a list of those things that you must do, like attending compulsory classes and other tasks which have to be completed by a particular deadline, such as preparation for essays or tutorials. Next make a list of other tasks that are important, such as getting a repair kit for your bike. The next list can be for the things you would like to do fairly soon, such as going round to see friends. Finally, there are a number of things that you would like to do at some point when you have time, such as writing to your brother; these can go on your last list. Use the lists you make to keep track of your progress, crossing out things that you have completed, and highlighting things you still need to do.

● Find out if there are hidden institutional time constraints

Your time management can be upset by the arrangements made by your institution. It is all very well planning to do lots of research for an essay during the vacation, but not if the library is going to be closed for three weeks. Equally, you may come across the problem of "bunched deadlines", where several of the courses you are doing require assessed work to be handed in on the same day. You can alleviate these problems by finding out about the library, computers, and other support services well in advance and by asking tutors to give you assignments in good time, but you may not be able to overcome such difficulties completely. If you are used to planning your time, however, you will be able to deal with the resulting pressure on your time much better than someone who has given no thought to such problems.

● Organise your time and space for study

Create a physical space where you can be undisturbed, where you can have all the things you need conveniently to hand and where you can read and take notes comfortably. Organise your notes and course materials for each course that you study — use different coloured folders or ring-binders for each one. Think about the best times for you to work — in the mornings? In the evenings?

● Be realistic when planning your time

Although you will often be working to deadlines imposed by your tutors, it will be up to you to organise your time around those deadlines. Be realistic about how much time you need to set aside in order to complete your essays or tutorial preparation. It is counterproductive to set yourself a deadline that you cannot possibly hope to meet. Many activities will take longer than you think; for instance, some law students are surprised how long it takes them to do the research for an essay!

When you are planning your time, you need to be realistic about your own strengths and weaknesses, too. If you are the sort of person who can stay in and write your essay on a Saturday afternoon when all your friends are going out together, that's fine. On the other hand, if you are the sort of person who cannot wake up before midday, it is unrealistic to plan to write your essay at 8.30 in the morning. If you do not allow yourself sufficient time to do something, you may start to feel depressed and frustrated. If your schedule is realistic, you will gain satisfaction from knowing that you have achieved what you set out to do. Of course, everyone underestimates the time they need sometimes, but you should try to avoid this happening to you too often.

● Don't leave things until the last minute

This especially applies to preparation for tutorials and seminars, and the research you will need to do for assignments. If you leave things to the last minute, you may well find that most of the books and articles you need to use have already been borrowed by other students. You can sometimes rescue the situation by finding the information you need elsewhere, but it takes a lot of thought, time and energy to discover alternative sources of information.

● Keep a sense of proportion

Don't try to study for long periods of time without a break. You will find that making a coffee, going for a brief stroll or reading a newspaper for ten minutes in between periods of study helps to relax you and enables you to extend your total period of study. Similarly, plan to have some time off each week. The aim of organising your time is to allow you to do your academic work to the best of your ability, but also to have some time left over to do all the other things you want to do, including to enjoy yourself and to relax.

Lectures — listening and notetaking

Lectures are generally seen as a cost-effective way of imparting the main ideas in an area to a large number of people. They also give the lecturer the opportunity to tell students about the latest developments in an area, and to explain any particularly complex parts of a subject. In addition, the content of lectures, and the handouts that often accompany them, form the basis for further independent study. Lectures are often regarded as forming the backbone of a course and it is usually assumed that most students will attend them.

Lecturing style is closely related to the personality of an individual lecturer, so you are likely to come across a wide variety of lectures delivered in many different styles. Some will be excellent, some less so. As a student, you will need to develop a good technique for dealing with lectures, which you can then adapt to cope with the different lecturing styles you come across. Don't forget that while most lecturers want to be good at what they do, and deliver lectures of a very high standard, you are ultimately responsible for your own education. You must make lectures work for you.

● Arrive in reasonably good time

Handouts and important announcements are often given out at the beginning of lectures; you may be very confused if you miss them. Equally, the first few minutes of the lecture itself are important, as the lecturer will often summarise the main points of the lecture, or remind you where they have got up to in their coverage of a topic.

● Listen actively

Listening to a lecture can be a very passive experience. Students are not generally expected to interrupt a lecture by asking questions or making comments, although some lecturers will include interactive elements in their lectures. In a standard lecture, it is very easy to "switch off" and lose the thread of the lecture. In order to get the most out of lectures, you need to listen effectively and take good notes. Doing both of these things helps to make the experience less passive and also helps you to record the lecture in a way that will prove useful for future reference.

Listening effectively does not mean merely that you hear the lecture. It means that you listen actively. Taking notes will help you listen actively, because it provides the listening activity with a purpose. You should also listen reflectively; in other words, you should try to relate what you are hearing to your existing knowledge of the subject and think how the new information fits into it. A lecture can be very boring if the lecturer has a monotonous delivery, but as an effective listener, you need to train yourself to ignore poor delivery, and concentrate on the content of what is being said.

● Eliminate distractions

In order to help you concentrate in lectures, you need to eliminate as many distractions as possible. Make sure you are comfortable; use a clipboard if there is no desk. Use a convenient size of paper, which gives you enough space to set out your notes clearly. Decide whether you prefer lined or unlined paper. If you have a series of consecutive lectures you may become uncomfortable because you are sitting for long periods; try to move your limbs slightly during the lecture and use any brief gaps between the lectures to get out of your seat and move around a bit.

● Take notes

Taking notes in lectures not only helps you to concentrate; it also means that you have a record of the content of the lecture that you can refer to in the future. Since one of the main purposes of taking notes is to use them in the future, it is important to devise a system of note-taking which produces a clear set of notes which you will understand when you come to look at them again, weeks or months after the original lecture.

● Establish your style of note-taking

There is no single "best" way of taking notes. Some people will take quite detailed notes; others will take down the key points in a diagrammatic form. The most important factor here is to establish a style of note-taking which results in a useful set of notes for you to refer to after the lecture has finished. Since law degrees generally rely on lectures as the main source of information, you may feel you need to write down quite a lot in order to be sure that you have everything you need. However, don't attempt to write down everything the lecturer says, as you won't be able to do this, and you will lose the sense of what they are saying. When you have taken some notes in some lectures, it is worth stopping to ask yourself if they will be useful to you in the future. If they are too messy, too short or too confusing, you can take steps to improve your note-taking technique. If you are unsure about the best way in which to take notes, you should consult one of the study guides that are listed in the "Further Reading" section at the end of this chapter.

● How do you know what to write down?

Handouts that support the lecture make the task of note-taking easier; they will show you the broad structure of the lecturer and the main topics which will be covered. The lecturer may help you by summarizing their main points; they may also try to aid your understanding by including examples or illustrations; these are good to include in your notes, as they will help to remind you of the workings of the arguments. Note the names of cases, statutes and academic writers who are mentioned; if there is a lecture handout, this should help you as it will contain names of cases and statutes and other technical legal terms, so you don't need to get all these perfectly during the lecture; you can insert them when you review your lecture notes.

● Evolve your own form of shorthand

This is a very simple but important technique. If you have a good system of abbreviating words, it will enable you to take much more effective notes.

● Good presentation is important

Use headings and sub-headings to emphasise the main points made, and to indicate changes in topics. Numbered points can provide a quick way of noting a large quantity of information. Underlining and the use of different coloured pens can direct your attention to particular points.

● Review your notes as soon as possible

It is important to review your notes while the lecture is still fresh in your mind. You may need to expand what you have written, or add headings, or do a little research on a point which you have not understood. Some people like to summarise their notes in diagrammatic form at this stage.

Tutorials and seminars

Tutorials involve small groups of students who meet regularly with an academic tutor to discuss questions that have generally been set in advance by the tutor. Seminars are similar, but usually involve larger groups of students; sometimes seminars may be led by one or more of the students. These names for small group work are often interchangeable, so you may find something labelled "tutorial" which is attended by 30 students. The title is not important; it merely indicates a "teaching event" which is usually smaller scale and more interactive than a lecture. In both tutorials and seminars, all the students are generally expected to have prepared the topic under discussion in advance and tutors usually expect that all the students involved in the group will participate, by joining in the discussion. The following points will help you get the most benefit from these sessions:

● Ensure you know what is expected of you

Many tutors set specific work for tutorials and seminars. Ensure that you obtain this in good time, so that you can prepare the topic properly. If you are unprepared, and unfamiliar with the subject matter, participating in the discussion is more difficult. Different tutors will run these groups in very different ways. You will need to be adaptable, to fit in with different teaching styles. Some tutors will make this easy for you, by having explicit "ground rules"; with others you will have to work it out for yourself.

● Try to participate

Often, you will attend tutorials and seminars with the same group of people for a whole academic year. Clearly, the experience will be more pleasant if the members of the group get on with each other, but this is essentially a learning experience, so you have to balance your desire to be friendly with your learning needs. No one wants to make a fool of themselves in front of a group of other people, but if you do not try out ideas in discussion, you are not going to develop your thinking, so a little bravery is called for. Try not to be so worried about what the others will think that you do not participate at all. Everyone is in the same situation, so people are generally sympathetic to contributions made by others.

● Consider making a contribution early in the discussion

If you make a contribution to the discussion at a fairly early stage, it is likelier to be easier than if you delay participating, for a number of reasons. In the early stages of discussion, it is less likely that other people will have made the point you have thought of. Tutors who are keen to involve the whole group may single out people who have not said anything and ask them direct questions; this is much less likely to happen to you if you have already made a contribution. If you are less confident about talking in front of other people, the longer you wait to say something, the more difficult you may find it to join in.

● Think about the art of polite disagreement

The aim of academic discussion is to try to develop the ideas you are considering. Often, this involves members of the group disagreeing with one another's ideas. Remember that you are challenging the argument which is put forward, not the person who is advancing it. It is also important to remember this when your ideas are challenged.

● Expect to be challenged

During group discussions, tutors will try to teach you not to make assumptions. Their aim is to help you to think critically and precisely. They will therefore challenge many of the things you say. Most people are not used to being challenged in this way, and the ability of tutors to question almost everything you say can seem unduly negative. However, if you are going to succeed in thinking rigorously, you need to be able to question your own ideas and those of other people, and tutors whose sessions are the most challenging may turn out to be the best ones you have.

● Do not expect to take notes all the time

If you take notes of everything that goes on in a tutorial or seminar, you will be so busy writing that you will not be able to participate in the discussion. Not only will you not be able to say anything, but note-taking also detracts from your ability to think about the points that are being made. Try to limit your note-taking to jotting down the main issues raised and the outline of any answer given. You can then read over your notes later and follow up any points of particular interest.

● Learn to take advantage of small group learning situations

It is much easier to learn in small groups than in large lectures, because small groups should give you the opportunity to ask questions about aspects of the subject under discussion that you do not understand so well. Clearly, you do not want to dominate the discussion, or interrupt with too many questions, but small group situations do give you an opportunity to raise issues that are of particular concern to you.

Researching a topic for an essay/problem, tutorial or seminar

When you are preparing for a tutorial or seminar, or preparing to write an essay or problem answer, you will need to carry out some research in order to find the information you need. In the case of tutorials and seminars, you will often be given specific reading lists, so some of the research has been done for you, but you will still need to use the information to the best advantage, in much the same way as you need to do when you are writing an essay or problem answer.

When you are gathering and using written materials, remember that you must *always* find out things for yourself. The insertion of a footnote in a piece of academic writing that has been published in a journal or book does not necessarily mean that the footnote is accurate. Sometimes, when you find the article or case report that is referred to, you discover that it cannot possibly be used as justification for the proposition which you have just read. In order to find out whether a footnote is accurate, you will need to look up the reference for yourself. You should *never* merely replicate a reference without looking it up for yourself.

● Read the question carefully

Before you start gathering materials, you need to be clear about what you are being asked to do. Titles that invite you to "discuss" or "critically analyse" mean that you are expected to engage in reasoned argument about the topic; you are not being invited merely to describe something. One of the easiest traps to fall into is to fail to answer the question which is set because you are concentrating on conveying as much information as possible about the general area of law, rather than focusing on the specific aspect which is the subject of the question you are answering. Keep the question in mind the whole time; write it out and keep it in front of you while you are researching.

● Identify your key words

First, define the area you are interested in. Think of the key words which you can use to identify relevant materials. You may need to re-define your key words if, for instance, you find that the first few words you think of bring up too many references. In that case, try to think of much more specific terms which you can search.

● Use the references in the text

Academic writing contains a lot of references and footnotes. At first, this can be confusing, and you may tend to ignore them. However, when you are researching a topic, footnotes and references are an important source of further information. If you look up the material referred to in parts of an article or book that are directly relevant to your work, you will find that footnotes serve some important purposes.

(a)   They give full references to articles or books that are just mentioned or summarised in the text. This is useful if the material referred to is relevant to your work, because you can then read the full text.
(b)   They give references to other books or articles on the same topic, which put forward a similar argument (or the opposite one often indicated by the word "contra" in front of the reference). Again, you can extend your knowledge by following up the references.
(c)   They give further explanation about points made in the text.

● Use a variety of sources

Searching the library catalogue will generally direct you to books with titles that include your key words. But library catalogues will not generally direct you to articles in journals. To find these, you will have to use a different research strategy. One good way to start finding articles is to look in the footnotes of any textbooks or specialist books that you have found. Footnotes in academic books often contain references to journal articles, and once you have found the title of a relevant journal article, you can return to your library catalogue and find out whether your library keeps copies of that journal. In addition, once you get an idea of the journals which are the most important in a particular area of law which you are interested in, you can locate them in the library and look through the contents pages of the latest issues to find the most up-to-date articles.

You can also locate books and articles by using any relevant electronic databases that your library subscribes to. Your library should have instructions about how these work; if it doesn't, you can ask one of the librarians to explain them.

You can use specialist law databases, such as Lexis and Westlaw, to locate both cases and statutes on a particular topic; they also contain references to some journal articles. If you are researching a statute, you may also find it helpful to consult the website of the Government department which is responsible for the area of law covered by the statute, since Government websites often contain copies of consultation papers and other official documents which can provide useful background information and help you to understand the statute more easily.

There are a number of publications that give details of all British books in print, arranged by subject, as well as by author and title. The Index to Legal Periodicals will help you to find articles in legal journals and there are similar publications relating to social science literature, often called "Abstracts". Using these sources will help you find a wider range of materials than those referred to on your reading lists. You may then be able to use these as alternatives to the ones that everyone else is using or which are unavailable when you wish to consult them.

● Be time-sensitive

Start with the most recent literature on your chosen topic, *i.e.* the latest books and the most recent issues of relevant journals. These items may not appear on reading lists, so may have been missed by others.

If you are using a legal textbook (usually at the beginning of the research process), remember that new editions are produced quite frequently, so you need to be sure that you are using the latest edition. You can usually check this by looking on the publisher's website. Even if you have the latest edition, do not rely on it as your sole source of information; there may have been a lot of recent developments in that particular area of law, which are not referred to in the textbook, because they have occurred since it was written. Similarly with articles in journals: remember that the law changes frequently; check that any legal points made by the author are still valid.

● Make the best use of your library

You need to ensure that you are using your library as effectively as possible. There may be leaflets designed to help readers find their way around the different catalogues, or there may be a resource page for law on the internet homepage of your law department or the homepage of the library; see if any of these can help your research. Some libraries have specialist librarians who are immensely knowledgeable and helpful. Try to help yourself first, but do not ignore the experts whose job it is to help you.

● Use the internet appropriately

Many students find the internet a very convenient source of information. However, you need to use it *appropriately*. A lot of material on the internet is journalism, which is interesting, but not authoritative enough to be used in an academic essay. The internet can allow you to find a range of official publications, published by government departments, or by official bodies such as the Law Commission, and such documents can be cited as evidence for the arguments you put forward. However, only occasionally can you use a newspaper article, or the opinion of a pressure group as evidence. It is also unlikely that you can rely on the internet as your *only* research tool. You need to read chapters of books and journal articles as well.

● Researching for different approaches to law

Bear in mind the perspective you need to adopt in order to answer the essay or problem question you are working on. Problem questions focus on a "black-letter" or "doctrinal" approach to law; they demand that you use decided cases and statutory materials to justify the points you make. In general, it is not appropriate to include references to other materials, such as academic articles, when writing a problem answer.

When you are answering an essay question, you may have the opportunity to introduce a wider range of materials; in addition to any relevant cases and statutes, you may be expected to discuss Law Commission materials, consultation papers and reports from relevant government departments, academic articles and books, and materials from other disciplines, such as criminology, sociology, economics or politics. You need to find out from your lecturers and tutors which approach you will be expected to adopt when you are writing your essay.

● Search other nearby libraries

Many libraries now have the facility to allow you to search the catalogues of other libraries. Think of other libraries in the area that you could use and have a look in their catalogues to see if it would be worthwhile visiting them. Perhaps their students are not all doing the essay on offences against the person that your year has been set.

Reading for research

It is important to develop a strategy for dealing with the large amount of reading you will have to do. All students have to face this problem, but if you are studying law, you have a particular problem, because although by this stage you are an expert reader, you are unlikely to have had much experience, if any, of reading legal materials, such as case reports and statutes, so in this respect you are a novice again. The chapters in this book which deal with reading cases and statutes will help you develop an effective method of reading these new types of text, and once you have practised, you will find that you can process them as quickly as other types of text, such as articles or textbooks, with which you are already familiar. There are many different ways of reading; for example, you can skim quickly through something, or you can read it slowly and carefully. In order to decide what kind of reading you should be doing at any particular time, you need to think about the purpose of your reading. You also need to be aware of the different techniques of reading and be able to use each type as it becomes relevant.

● Titles are there to help you

When looking at a book, the title and contents pages will give you a broad outline of the information you will find. Sub-headings within an article perform the same function. You can use these headings to decide whether or not to read a piece of text in more detail.

● Scan the text first

To check the relevance of a text, skim through it, looking for the key words and phrases that will give you the general sense of the material and enable you to decide whether it is relevant for your purposes.

● Approach the text gradually

Even when you have decided that a particular chapter of a book or an article is relevant, check it out before you begin to take notes; you may not need to take notes on the whole chapter, but only a part of it; similarly, with an article. It is often suggested that you should read the first sentence of each paragraph to find out more precisely what the text is about.

● Reading statutes

As you have discovered in Chapter 5 of this book, statutes must be read carefully and precisely. At first, they can seem very complicated to read, because they are so detailed. When you read a section of a statute, try to establish the main idea first, then you can re-read it and fill in the details on the second reading. You might find it helpful to photocopy the parts of the statute that you have to read, so that you can use a pen or highlighter to mark the main idea. There is an example below:

Sale of Goods Act 1979 Section 11 (3)
   Whether a stipulation in a contract is a condition, the breach of which may give rise to a right to treat the contract as repudiated, **or a warranty**, the breach of which may give rise to a claim for damages but not to a right to reject the goods and treat the contract as repudiated, **depends in each case on the construction of the contract**; and a stipulation may be a condition, though called a warranty in the contract.
   The main point that is being made is quite simple, and can be identified by reading the phrases in bold type "Whether a stipulation in a contract is a condition or a warranty depends in each case on the construction of the contract". Having established what the section is basically about, you can now go back and find out what the section says about the effect of a stipulation in a contract being classified as either a condition or a warranty.

● Reading cases

Although reading a reported case might seem more straightforward than reading a statute, it is important to remember that reading the judgments in a case and extracting from them both the facts and the decision requires practice.
   Sometimes you will be able to get an indication of the important aspects of a decision

from a textbook or from a lecture. However, if you are faced with a decision about which you know very little, you can read the head-note first, which will summarise both facts and judgments for you. Many students are tempted to regard reading the head-note as sufficient, but this is not a good strategy; you need to read the whole of the leading judgment to understand the *ratio* of the case properly. (You will be able to tell which is the leading judgment by noticing from which judgment most of the points in the head-note are taken.)

Reading dissenting judgments is also helpful. It is a good way to understand the complexities of a legal argument. Often, your tutors will ask you to think critically about decisions; reading dissenting judgments are a good source of ideas about the strengths and weaknesses of a decision.

Recording your research

Research is very enjoyable and interesting, and it helps you discover the subject of law for yourself, but if you don't write down accurately the sources you find when you are researching, you can waste a lot of time looking for that wonderful quotation that you know you read somewhere. When you are researching, you also need to be able to read quickly through the material you locate, so you can decide whether it is sufficiently relevant to look at in more detail, and perhaps make some notes from it. Once you have started taking notes, you will want to ensure that you have a good note-taking technique.

● Always write down a full reference

Whenever you read something which you think might be useful, you should write down its full reference; this not only means you will be able to find it again quickly, it also means you have all the information you will need if you want to refer to it in a footnote and/or bibliography.

For a book, you will need the author, title, edition (if it is not the first edition), publisher, place of publication and date of publication. You may also like to make a note of the catalogue reference so that you can retrieve the item from the library easily; this will usually be a Dewey decimal reference number. Your reference should look something like this:

Bradney *et al. How to Study Law* (3rd edition) Sweet & Maxwell, London, 1995. (340.07 HOW)

If you are recording a journal article, your reference will be something like this:

Addison & Cownie "Overseas Law Students: Language Support and Responsible Recruitment" (1992) 19 JLS p.467 (PER340 J6088)

It is important to write down references in such a way that you can easily distinguish between references to books, and references to articles. The system that has been used here is to underline the titles of books, but put titles of articles inside inverted commas.

● Make concise notes

Always begin by asking yourself why you are taking notes. Refresh your memory as to the question you are trying to answer. Remember that you can take different types of notes on different parts of a text — detailed notes on the directly relevant parts, outline notes on other parts, while sometimes you will be able to read through without taking any notes at all.

● Make clear notes

Your notes will be more use to you if they are reasonably neat. Try to develop a standard way of recording the source you are taking the notes from, perhaps always putting it at the top right-hand corner of the page, or in the margin. You can use this reference for your bibliography, or for footnotes, or for your own use if you need to clarify a point at some later stage. In order to make it even easier to find your way around the original text, you might like to make a note of the actual page you have read, either in the margin, or in brackets as you go along. Here is an example of some notes on the first few pages of a chapter of a book:

> H. Genn (1987)
> *Hard Bargaining*
> Oxford Uni. Press, Oxford.
> (344.6 GEN)

Chapter 3 "Starting Positions"
Structural imbalance between the parties (p.34).
One-shotter pl. v Repeat-player def. See Galanter 1974.
Repeat players — advance intelligence, expertise, access to specialists, economies of
     scale. See Ross 1980.
Distribution of personal injury work (p.35)
Pls huge variety of firms.
Defs-insurance co/specialist firm
Defs solicitors allowed few mistakes (p.36 top)
Defs solicitors nurture relationship w insurance co.
Contrast position of general practitioner.

● Do you need to photocopy the bibliography?

When you are taking notes, you will often note down references to other articles or books referred to in the text you are reading. You will have to decide later whether you need to look these up, but many people find that it disturbs their train of thought to look up the full reference for each of these as they occur in the text. If that is the case, it is important to photocopy the bibliography of your source, so that you have a copy of the full reference in case you need to refer to it later. In the example above, the student would need to photocopy the bibliography of "Hard Bargaining", otherwise they wouldn't know what they meant by references to "Galanter, 1974" or "Ross 1980".

● Keep notes and comments separate

It is a good idea to think critically about the content of what you are reading. However, if you want to make comments, keep these separate in some way, preferably on a different sheet of paper. Otherwise, when you come back to the notes, you might find it impossible to distinguish your great thoughts from those of the original author.

● Good presentation is important

Remember that clear presentation of your notes is just as important when you are taking notes for an essay or seminar as it is when you are taking lecture notes. Use headings and sub-headings, and remember that underlining and the use of different-coloured pens can direct your attention to particular points.

● Consider using a different technique for noting cases

Many tutors recommend that you help yourself to take brief notes of cases by using file-cards, one card for each case. You can note the citation, the facts and the main points of the judgment using two sides of a card and then your notes of cases are in a very flexible form, so you can arrange them alphabetically, or by topic, or by date, depending on your particular needs.

Writing assignments (essays and problem answers)

During your law course, you will be set various types of assignment to submit to your tutor. The most common of these are essays and problem questions, and it is with these types of assessment on which this section of *How to Study Law* is focused. Writing an assignment is a challenge, but it is also one of the most rewarding aspects of studying law. When you focus on a particular area of law for the purposes of writing an assignment, you bring together a lot of the skills you are developing; you need to research, organise the material, reflect on the question and engage in some critical thinking.

● Clarify the task

Before you do anything else, read the question carefully. Identify which area of law it is asking you about. This may not be immediately apparent, particularly in a problem question. Read the whole question through carefully to help you understand which area(s) of law are involved. Then make sure you understand exactly what the question is asking you about the area of law involved. It is highly unlikely that it will just ask you to write down all you know about, for example, the tort of negligence. It is much more likely to ask you to criticise a particular part of the law of negligence, or explain the strengths and weaknesses of an aspect of the law of negligence.

● Make a plan

The next stage of the writing process is to make a plan. A plan provides a structure for your argument and allows you to organise your arguments into a coherent whole. It is a vital stage of the research process and you need to produce one as soon as possible. You may want to do a bit of basic reading first, but generally, the plan should be one of your first tasks. Plans for problem answers are easier to produce than those for essays, because the events that make up the problem give you a structure for your plan. In all cases, jot down the main points of your answer; later, you can refine your plan and fit in subsidiary points in the most logical places.

Example

"Discrimination in the legal profession is a thing of the past" Discuss.
    Introduction — much discrimination on grounds of both race and sex in the past- refer to numbers of women / members of ethnic minorities qualifying as solicitors and barristers, also women not able to qualify as solicitors till well into the twentieth century — see Bebb v The Law Society.
    Currently, still a lot of discrimination on grounds of sex — refer to small numbers of women partners in solicitors' firms, small numbers of female Q.C.s and small numbers of female judges. Also refer to research reports on women in the legal profession.
    Equally, still a lot of discrimination on grounds of race — refer to small numbers of solicitors, barristers and judges drawn from ethnic minority communities, also research reports on racial discrimination at the Bar and in the solicitors' profession.
    Conclusion — although it appears there is still a lot of discrimination on grounds of race and sex in the legal profession, it is arguable that the situation is improving — use statistics to show increased participation in the legal profession by women and by members of ethnic minority groups.
    Your plan is there to help you; you do not have to stick with your original structure too rigidly. If you can see a better way of organising your argument once you have done a bit of reading, then adjust the plan. The plan in the example above is just a first draft. It provides a basic framework, but it does not contain enough ideas at this stage. In order to add more ideas, the student needs to go and do some more research and reading before amending the plan in the light of the additional information. However, this is a good start.

● Reflect and evaluate

When you have gathered the basic information, it is time to review your plan in the light of what you have discovered. Read through your notes, bearing in mind all the time the question you have been asked. Have you changed your mind about any of the points you want to make? Have you discovered additional information that you want to include in your answer? Where does it fit in to your argument? Now you will be able to make a new plan, indicating not only the main points you are going to make, but also any arguments or pieces of information drawn from your research that you wish to include.

● Write a first draft

Once you are satisfied with your revised plan, you can embark on the first draft of your essay. Before you start, read through the plan and make sure that all your points are relevant. To do this, look at the question again, and then look at your plan. Every argument you make should relate to the question you have been asked. This is what makes it relevant.

  Here is an example of a first plan for an essay whose title is "Settlement of major litigation is a necessary evil." Discuss.

- Settlement definition.
- Settlement is necessary because a) saves court time b) saves expense c) saves litigants' time.
- But settlement is an "evil" because a) litigants are not equally experienced and do not have equal resources b) inexperienced litigants often go to lawyers who are not specialists in the relevant field & are not well advised c) inexperienced litigants can easily be put under pressure, *e.g.* by payment into court, delays (often manufactured by the other side), worries about cost, risk-aversion.
- Conclusion settlement is a necessary evil, but currently is so evil it is immoral and unacceptable.

Every point that is made relates directly to the quotation that is under discussion. This is an initial plan. After some research, you would be able to expand some points, and to insert the names of books or articles that you could use to justify the points being made. But you would still ensure that everything related to the quotation that you had been asked to discuss.

● Remember the audience you are writing for

When you write an academic essay in law, you can assume that you are writing for a reasonably intelligent reader who knows almost nothing about your subject. That means you have to explain clearly every step of your argument. At first, many students are ignorant of this convention. They know their essay is going to be marked by an expert, so they do not bother to include all the information about a topic, only to be told by their tutor "I cannot give you credit for anything, unless it is down in your essay. It's no use keeping things in your head".

● Do not make assertions

In academic writing, you must always be able to justify what you say. You cannot make assertions (an assertion is when someone says "X is the case", but provides no reference to prove that X is the case). You must always be able to provide reasons for your statements; in an essay, this is done by providing a reference or footnote. In a problem question, all the points of law you make need to be substantiated by a reference to some legal authority — usually the ration of a case, or a section of a statute.

Example

If someone writes "Small claims are proceedings involving £5,000 or less" that is an assertion. There is no evidence that the statement is true, the author is just expecting us to take their word for it. After a little research, it is possible to rewrite the sentence so as to include the evidence which proves the statement: "Under Part 27.1 of the Civil Procedure Rules, small claims are proceedings involving £5,000 or less."

● What kind of introduction?

The beginning of your essay is very important. Unless you have been instructed that you must have an introduction in a particular form, your essay might have more impact if you start straight away with a comment on the central point. Try to interest your reader by indicating the main issue, so that your tutor knows straight away that you understand the question that has been set. This gives your answer an immediate air of authority. Unless you have been told to do so, do not rehearse all your arguments in the first sentence or two. Openings such as "This essay discusses . . . " can be very boring. They can also give hostages to fortune. If you tell your reader that you are going to discuss X, Y and Z, they will expect you to do exactly that, and penalise you if you don't — but it is very easy to forget to cover one or two of the points you listed in your introduction.

● Consider the style of your writing

An academic essay is a formal piece of writing, so the style in which you write should not be too colloquial. Shortened forms of phrases, such as isn't and mustn't, are inappropriate. However, pomposity is equally inappropriate. Phrases such as "I submit that

. . . " are out of place. Advocates make submissions in court, but you do not make submissions in an academic essay, even in law!

Aim for a clear, direct style, which conveys your arguments in a way which can be readily understood. Use paragraphs to indicate a change of subject, and keep sentences reasonably short. In general, academic writing is written in an impersonal style, so writers do not use phrases such as "I think that . . . ". They use alternative, less personal, phrases, such as "This indicates that . . . "

● Be prepared to write several drafts

Before you arrive at the final version of your essay, you should have produced several drafts. You should read each draft carefully, making additions and alterations that you then incorporate into the next draft. Although it is important to correct the spelling and the grammar in each draft, the primary reason for having several drafts is to give yourself the opportunity to examine your argument and make sure that it is as clear and convincing as possible. Think about what you are saying. Have you justified all the points you have made? Does the argument flow logically from one point to another? Is the material relevant?

● Do not describe too much

In general, the object of writing academic essays is to engage in critical analysis, *i.e.* thought and argument. Your tutors are not looking for detailed descriptions of subjects that they could, after all, read in any competent textbook. A certain amount of description is necessary, to explain what you are talking about, but the main emphasis in any academic piece of work will be on analysing. You are interpreting for the reader the significance of what you have described, and it is this process that is most important.

● Acknowledge your sources

During the course of your writing, you will often put forward arguments and ideas that you have discovered in books or articles. If you do this, you must acknowledge that the idea is not an original one. You can do this expressly in the text by saying something like "As Bradney argues in 'How to Study Law'. Or you can use a footnote to indicate the source of the idea. What you must not do is to pass off someone else's idea as if it were something you had thought of for yourself. That is stealing their idea, and it is a practice known as plagiarism. In academic life, where people's ideas are of the utmost importance, plagiarism is regarded as a form of cheating. Ideally, you will use other people's ideas as a base from which to develop thoughts of your own, acknowledging their idea, and then going on to say something original about them. This is the kind of critical thinking which you are trying to develop.

● A few points about problem answers

It is often said that it is easier to answer a problem than to write an essay, but this is largely a matter of personal preference. Problem answers are certainly easier in one sense, because they provide a framework for your answer by posing certain issues that you must cover. The research and planning process described above will help you when you are answering a problem question, just as much as an essay.

Problem answers do not need lengthy introductions. The convention is that you need to introduce a problem answer by identifying the main issue in the problem, but you do not need a lengthy introduction. Whenever you make a statement about the law, you must give the relevant legal authority; for example, "When X wrote to Y saying that if he did not hear from Y, he would assume that Y agreed to the contract, this has no legal effect, because silence does not imply consent (*Felthouse v Bindley* (1862) 11 C.B. 869)."

Remember that socio-legal information is not relevant in a problem answer. Strictly speaking, problem questions are just asking you to identify the relevant legal rules relating to the issues raised. There may be very interesting research studies on a topic, but these are not relevant to a problem answer.

Exams and assessment

It is likely that you will experience a number of different forms of assessment, including continuous assessment, based on written work submitted during the course of the academic year, and the traditional three-hour unseen examination. The strategies discussed above will help you to cope with the various forms of continuous assessment which you are likely to meet. This section will therefore concentrate on strategies designed to help you cope with the traditional unseen examination.

● Make a revision timetable in good time

It is important to make a realistic revision timetable well in advance of the examinations, allocating a certain amount of time for each subject you have to prepare. Most people find it best to study all their subjects concurrently, doing a bit of each one in turn, rather than finishing one before going on to the next one, which brings the danger that you might never get round to the last subject.

● Reduce your notes to a manageable size

At the beginning of the revision period, you are likely to find that you have a large amount of notes. It is a good idea to reduce the size of these, by taking even briefer notes from your original notes, so that you end up with a manageable quantity of material to work with. As the examinations approach, most people reduce their notes again, perhaps several times, so that a whole topic can be covered comprehensively, but speedily.

● Question-spotting is a risky strategy

It is sensible to consider what sort of subjects might come up in the examination. Consulting old examination papers is a useful way of finding out what is expected of you in the exam. However, it is unwise to "question spot" *too* precisely. It is unlikely that you will be able to revise the whole course; indeed, this would often be a waste of effort, but you need to cover several subjects in addition to the three or four which you hope will come up, so that you have plenty of choice when it comes to deciding which questions you will answer in the examination. Being familiar with a range of subjects is a sensible strategy because:

(a) Your favourite topics might not come up at all.
(b) Some topics might come up, but in a way which is unfamiliar to you.
(c) Your favourite topic might be mixed up with another topic which you have not revised.

● Consider practising timed answers

If you find it difficult to write answers quickly, it is a good idea to practice writing some answers in the same time that you will have in the examination. Use questions from old examination papers.

● Make sure you get enough rest

Studying hard for examinations is a very tiring experience. Try to ensure that you get sufficient sleep and exercise, so that you remain as fresh as possible. Burning the midnight oil is not necessarily a sensible strategy.

● Feel as comfortable as possible during the exam

Before you enter the examination room, make sure you have all the pens, pencils and so on that you need. Wear something comfortable, preferably several layers of clothing so you can discard some if the room is hot, or add additional layers if you are cold. Check whether you are allowed to take drinks or food into the examination room. If you are allowed to do so, it is a matter of personal choice whether you take advantage of this facility or not; some people find it helps to have a can of drink, others find it a distraction. Check that you know where you have to sit, and whether there are any attendance slips or other forms that you have to fill in. Ensure that you know whether or not you will be told when you can start the examination; you do not want to sit there, waiting for an instruction that never comes.

● Read the rubric carefully

Make sure that you read the instructions at the top of the examination paper very carefully. The paper may be divided into different sections and frequently candidates must answer a certain number of questions from each section. Sometimes you will be asked to write certain questions in certain answer books. Always make sure that you comply with any instructions of this kind; the examiner may not give you any marks for material you have written in contravention of such instructions.

● Develop good examination technique

In the examination, plan your time carefully. Provided that all the questions carry an equal number of marks, you should allow an equal amount of time for answering each question. Sub-divide your time into reading the question, planning the answer, writing the answer and checking it. Planning is a very important part of good examination technique. If you spend a few minutes setting out a good plan, it will allow you to write a much fuller answer than if you are thinking out your answer as you go along, because all the basic thinking will be done at the planning stage, and you will be able to concentrate on writing a relevant answer.

● Keep to the timing you have worked out

Do not spend more than the time that you have allocated for each question. If you run out of time, leave that question and go on to the next one, returning to the unfinished question if you have some spare time later.

● Answer the question

Read the question carefully. To gain the maximum number of marks, your answer must be relevant to the question you have been asked. If you are familiar with a topic on which a question is set, it is tempting to write down a version of your notes, which includes all you know about that topic, in the hope that you will get a reasonable number of marks. However, if you merely write all you happen to know about a topic, it is unlikely that you will be answering the question. You need to slant your information to the question, showing how the things you know relate to the precise question that you have been asked.

● Answer the correct number of questions

Under pressure of time, some people fail to answer the whole examination paper by missing out a question. Examiners can only award marks for what is written on the examination paper. By not answering a question, you have forfeited all the marks allocated to that question. However, it is often said that the easiest marks to gain are the ones awarded for the beginning of an answer, so if you do run out of time, it is much better to use those final minutes to start the final question, rather than perfecting answers you have already finished.

● Remember that examiners are human, too

When you are writing an examination paper, you often feel as if the examiner is the enemy "out there", determined to catch you out. In fact, examiners do not want candidates to fail. They generally expect students who have done a reasonable amount of work to pass examinations.

International students

The study skills discussed in this chapter are required by all law students. However, if English is not your first language you may feel that you would like some extra assistance with studying in the United Kingdom. Most institutions which welcome students from around the world have a support service which offers different classes covering a range of English Language and study skills, and you should try and find out about these at an early stage in your course. Many institutions also offer self-access materials, which you can go and use at a time that is convenient for you. The support service will also be able to help you familiarise yourself with the particular types of teaching and learning situations which you will find in British educational institutions, what might be termed the "hidden culture" of learning, such as particular ways of writing essays or behaving in seminars, which might be different to those with which you are familiar at home. This sort of information can be very useful, as it is impossible to discover beforehand, however good your English is.

Further reading

If you would like to find out more about any of the topics covered in this chapter, you will find that there are many books on study skills available. The following brief list includes books that cover a wide range of study skills.

R. Barrass *Study! A guide to effective learning, revision and examination techniques* (2nd edition, 2002) Routledge, London.

S. Cottrell *The Study Skills Handbook* (2nd edition, 2003)Palgrave Macmillan, London.

L. Marshall & F. Rowland, *A Guide to Learning Independently* (3rd ed., 1998) Open University Press, Buckingham.

Exercise 6

Study skills

These exercises have a different format to those that have preceded them.

1. Take brief notes of the first two pages of the case report of *R v Jackson* which you will find in Chapter 5 of this book. Before you start, re-read the suggestions about taking notes in the section of Chapter 7 entitled "Lectures — listening and notetaking". When you have finished take a break of one hour. After your break assess your notes against the following criteria.

   Presentation-
   Use of paragraphs, headings, underlining.

   Clarity-
   How easy are they to read? Can you remember what your abbreviations mean? Are there any words you are likely to come across frequently, for which you could make up your own standard abbreviation?

   Content-
   Have you included all the important information? Do you have a full reference, so that you could consult the original text at a later date if necessary?
      You can do this by yourself, or you can work with another student and compare each other's work.

2. In this exercise, you are asked to evaluate written work. In each case, you are given the plan for an essay, and then the essay that was written, using the plan. In each case you are asked to carry out a number of tasks. Again, you can do this on your own, or with another student.

   (a) Read the plans below. Write down any comments you have on good or bad features of each plan.
   (b) Now read the two essays as if you were the tutor. Decide which one is better, and why. In each case, write down a list of the reasons for your decision.
   (c) Draw up a list of criteria for judging the essays; use your answer to question b) to help you. Read the two answers again, and decide whether the two students have performed well or badly on each item in your list. If you wish, you can award each essay a mark, in the same way as a tutor would.
   (d) Imagine you are the tutor handing back the essays to the students who wrote the essays. What was good about the answers? How are you going to tell them about

the less good points? Make sure you are able to explain clearly how the students might improve their weaker points.

(e) Is there any similarity between these answers and your own, in terms of approach, style, strengths and weaknesses? Imagine you are the student who has written the answer. How would you feel about the comments of the tutor? What are you going to do about them?

Essay evaluation

Essay title:

"Tribunals provide a cheap, effective means of allowing ordinary people to settle disputes without having to use lawyers." Discuss.

Essay Plan 1

Franks Report — purpose of Tribunals

Tribunals — no lawyers, so cheap

Tribunals informal — so good for ordinary people

??Are they effective — better than nothing, but not really effective without lawyers (see Genn research) and for I.T.s especially, lawyers are vital (see Genn research, also Blankenburg and Dickens); this means not really cheap — because lawyers needed, but no legal aid (see Access to Justice Act 1999).

Essay 1

The Franks Report stated that Tribunals should be readily accessible to ordinary people. This attitude is currently reflected in the way in which litigants can bring proceedings in tribunals. Often, it is only necessary to write a letter, or fill in a very simple form.

Currently, it is not compulsory for litigants at tribunals to be represented by lawyers. This means that people do not have to pay the costs of employing lawyers, which can be very expensive.

Also, the rules of procedure of most tribunals make it clear that the proceedings must be informal, so the lawyers do not wear formal court dress, the hearing room is not set out like a court room, and evidence is not taken on oath. This makes tribunals accessible to ordinary members of the public who are not trained as lawyers, because otherwise they might be easily intimidated by lawyers using legal jargon and wearing formal clothes. Also, it removes the inbuilt advantage which lawyers have in a formal court setting with which they are very familiar, but which other people find intimidating.

Tribunals are also made more informal because the panel is not made up of judges, but of two laypeople and one lawyer. The presence of the laypeople (who have expertise in the area over which the tribunal has jurisdiction) is another factor in increasing informality and making the whole atmosphere less awe-inspiring.

Tribunals do appear on the face of it to be effective in providing ordinary people with a means of settling their disputes without going to a court, but research carried out by Genn and Genn (Genn and Genn, 1989) found that applicants had a much greater chance of success if they were represented, particularly if they were represented by a barrister. This means that if ordinary people want to win their cases, tribunals are not really cheap, because a lawyer is needed to increase chances of success and since there is no legal aid available to assist with the cost of employing lawyers for tribunal representation, the cost of lawyers must be met by the litigants themselves.

Another reason why tribunals are not as effective in giving ordinary people access to justice as they might seem to be at first is that some tribunals are in fact very formal in nature and this introduces all the disadvantages of a conventional court hearing. The best example of such a tribunal is the Industrial Tribunal, which deals with all kinds of employer/employee disputes and also with cases of discrimination due to sex or race. Research has established that Industrial Tribunals are very formal and that they are adversarial in nature, just like traditional courts (Blankenburg and Rogowski, 1986). Also, many of the legal rules in this area are very complex, and it is unrealistic to expect that an ordinary person will be able to use and understand them as well as a trained lawyer (Dickens *et al.*, 1985). Dickens *et al.* also found that many litigants did not even understand that they could call witnesses, and many of those who did realise that this was possible did not realise that it would be helpful to do so.

Essay Plan 2
Tribunals intended for ordinary people
Lawyers not necessary
Lots of different kinds of Tribunal
Lawyers always desirable
Tribunals give access to justice but of what quality?

Essay 2
Discussion of the purpose of tribunals often begins with The Franks Committee, which was set up in 1957 to examine "Administrative Tribunals and Enquiries" (Franks, 1957). When it brought out its Report, the Franks Committee said that tribunals should be characterised by " . . . openness, fairness and impartiality . . . ", clearly implying that the objective of tribunals should certainly be to provide a cheap and effective means for ordinary people to settle their disputes (Franks, 1957).

There are some characteristics of tribunals which make it more likely that they will be accessible to ordinary people who wish to settle disputes. For instance, Tribunals are not staffed solely by judges; the decision-making body is a panel of three people (hence the name "tribunal"). The Chair of the panel is legally qualified, but the two "wing people" are not; they are lay people who are selected because of their expertise in the area over which the tribunal in question exercises jurisdiction (see, for example, Special Educational Needs Tribunal Regulations, 1995). The absence of judges, and the presence of lay people on the decision-making body, helps to make tribunals more accessible to ordinary people, as does the fact that tribunals are informal in nature. This means that they do not have to follow the same strict rules of procedure as a court does, nor do they have to take evidence on oath (see, for example, Special Educational Needs Tribunal Regulations, 1995).

However, one of the most important points to be made about tribunals is that it is very difficult to make generalisations about them, because there are many different tribunals, set up at different times, mainly during the twentieth century, to deal with specific areas of law; as government action has impinged more and more on society, so the number of tribunals has increased (Wade, 1963). Tribunals tend to have quite specific jurisdictions, and they can operate in quite different ways. For instance, the Special Educational Needs Tribunal makes efforts to be as accessible as possible to litigants in person, and to ensure that it does not have procedures which ordinary people are likely to find intimidating (Aldridge, 1994). On the other hand, research has repeatedly shown that the Industrial Tribunal is so formal that it is virtually indistinguishable from a court (Dickens *et al.* 1985, Blankenburg and Rogowski 1986).

There is convincing research which suggests that tribunals are not in fact as accessible to litigants in person as they might at first appear. Genn and Genn (1989) found that litigants' chances of winning a case or making an advantageous settlement were greatly increased if they had a representative, rather than going to the tribunal on their own. This means that although tribunals are *supposed* to be places where ordinary people can go to settle their disputes, in fact they are not wholly meeting that objective, since they are places where ordinary people gain a much more satisfactory outcome if they have a representative, particularly a barrister (Genn and Genn, 1989).

Overall, it is possible to conclude that some tribunals (such as the Special Educational Needs Tribunal) meet the objective of providing somewhere for litigants in person to resolve their disputes without having to use lawyers, but other tribunals, such as the Industrial Tribunal, fail to meet this objective; if ordinary people go to the latter type of tribunal without representation, they are likely to be significantly disadvantaged.

Part 3

8 Where next?

This chapter introduces students to questions they should consider when applying to read law as a degree subject and outlines the career options open to students wishing to qualify as lawyers.

Law courses

Law may be studied at degree level at a range of universities and colleges. Law may be studied as a single subject, or in combination with another discipline, such as economics, politics, a foreign language and others. Thus, a student wishing to study law has two different decisions to make, "Do I want to study law on its own?" and "Where do I want to study?" There are currently about eighty institutions offering law degree courses on either a full or part-time basis.

Many institutions offer modular or joint honours degrees that have a substantial element of law study. Such degrees may or may not lead to a qualifying law degree depending on the choice of subjects.

Before making these decisions, it is wise to obtain a wide selection of law prospectuses from universities and colleges. After looking at these, it will quickly become clear that law courses differ radically from institution to institution. There are a wide variety of legal subjects that can be studied, different balances of optional to compulsory subjects, and varying views about the purpose of studying for a law degree.

Begin by asking:

- Why do I want to study law? Is it my intention to qualify as a lawyer or am I studying law for other reasons? Am I mainly interested in obtaining a good professional training or am I mainly interested in studying law as an academic subject or am I trying to combine both interests?
- Do I want to combine the study of law with the study of some other subject? What other subjects am I interested in? Which combination would suit my interests?
- If I want to qualify as a solicitor or barrister does the degree course I am interested in cover the foundations of legal knowledge laid down by the Law Society or Bar Council?

- If I am certain I wish to qualify as a solicitor or barrister do I want to study another subject at degree level to broaden my education and interests?
- What useful information and guidance can I obtain from my school, teachers, family or friends?

Bearing in mind the answers to these questions, read the prospectuses you have obtained and ask:

What reputation has the course, law school and institution got? Why does it have that reputation and is it one which I find attractive? Some universities have a good overall reputation, but an indifferent law school, some universities have a good law school, but a poor overall reputation. You will need to consider what criteria are of most importance to you. Some factors to consider will be highly subjective (*e.g.* geographic location, desire to live at home or away, *etc*).

The following questions of the law school should be asked:

- How much choice does the course offer me and is the law school of sufficient size to offer a wide variety of optional subjects? (Be suspicious of small law schools that claim to offer a wide variety of subjects. Only a few may actually be on offer in any one year). Does the course offer subjects that reflect my career aims?
- What connections has the law school got with the legal profession and the wider world and what are the career opportunities it considers open to its students?
- What guidance does it offer to students on optional choices and careers? Does it offer to help in selecting courses best suited for my intended career?
- How much flexibility does the course give if my motivations or interests change during my three years at college?
- What type of teaching methods are used and what is the mode of assessment?

Eventually, you will have to decide to which university or college to apply. With a few exceptions, applications to full-time courses of higher education are made through a central "clearing house" called UCAS (Universities and Colleges Admissions Service).

How you can apply through UCAS

You can apply for a full-time, undergraduate course through UCAS in one of three ways, using:

- **apply**, a web-based application system; or
- **EAS**, an electronic application system supplied on a CD; or
- a paper application form.

apply

apply is available through your school, college or careers centre. It is a secure, web-based, on-line application system. You can use **apply** anywhere that has access to the internet and your application can be processed within one working day.

Electronic Application System (EAS)

EAS is available through your school, college or careers centre and can be used on any PC that has the appropriate software downloaded. Your application can be processed within one working day.

Paper application form

Some people prefer to use a paper application form, as you don't need access to a computer or the internet. Paper application forms can take up to four weeks to process.

Whichever method you use, you complete one application form only but can make applications to up to six choices of institution/course: the form is reproduced and copied to the admissions tutor of each course selected. Application forms and UCAS Handbooks, which detail application procedures, universities, colleges and courses, are available free of charge via schools and colleges. Local Careers Advisory Services also have stocks. Completed forms should be received at UCAS by January 15 (October 15 if Oxford and Cambridge Universities are included) for those wishing to enrol at University the following autumn. The address of UCAS is Rosehill, New Barn Lane, Cheltenham, Gloucestershire, GL52 3ZD. Tel.0870 11222 (*www.ucas.ac.uk*).

In deciding where to apply you should bear in mind the examination grades that the institution may expect you to get if you are given an offer of a place (can you realistically hope to get the required grades?). Do not judge an institution's reputation purely by the grades it demands. Obtain guidance on admission policies and examination grade requirements from your school or college.

A few law schools will want to interview selected candidates before deciding whether or not to give them a place. An interview is not only a chance for the law school to find out about the candidate but a chance for the candidate to find out about the law school. Be prepared to ask questions about the aims of the law degree course, the range and nature of the optional subjects available and current interest in such courses (be aware that some optional courses will not run if there is insufficient interest), and the research interests of the staff. Never ask a question that can be easily answered by reference to material that has already been sent to you or which you should already have obtained. Do not, for example, ask what subjects are taught if this is in a faculty brochure which you have been given. Do ask, if the brochure does not tell you, the philosophy behind a particular course and, for example, its emphasis on traditional legal study or on the study of law in its social context. Asking no questions at all shows that you have not prepared for the interview and perhaps have little interest in the institution. Asking questions that can be answered from available information shows the same thing. Use the information that you have been sent as a basis for asking further, more detailed questions. Some Careers Advisory Services and schools will be able to advise on interview technique and often hold workshops to help develop relevant skills.

Most law schools run open days. Open days offer you an opportunity to look at the facilities that both the law school and its host university has to offer. Typically, you will get an opportunity to talk to both staff and students. You may be able to discuss any particular problems that you have with the law school's admissions tutor.

In many degree courses, contract, tort, criminal law, property law, equity and trusts, constitutional and administrative law and law of the European Union (EU law) will be studied as compulsory subjects, in either the first or second year. One reason for this is that many academics see these subjects as being basic to the study of English law. Either they contain principles or concepts that are of importance in a wide range of legal subjects or they are about matters that are themselves of general significance. There is also a pragmatic justification for making these subjects compulsory. Students wishing to qualify as barristers or solicitors must normally study these subjects at degree level in order to be exempt from having to take them in professional examinations. The subjects used to be referred to as core subjects but are now known as foundation subjects or foundation of legal knowledge subjects.

In addition to the seven subjects above, a normal law degree would involve a student in studying another seven or eight subjects. A list of typical subjects might include:

> English Legal System, Labour Law, Commercial Law, Public International Law, Family Law, Jurisprudence, Human Rights and Civil Liberties, Sociology of Law, Revenue Law, Company Law, Law and Medicine, Private International Law and Intellectual Property Law.

There may be scope for a student to write a dissertation (an extended essay) on a subject of their choice under the supervision of a member of staff as an alternative to studying of one of the optional subjects. Prospectuses should be read so as to get an idea of the context of the courses and the different individual emphases and approaches adopted. Choice of course options is dictated by many factors. The student's own interests, career intentions, the way in which the subject is taught and the folk-lore surrounding it within the institution where a student is studying all play their part. Subjects vary both in content and the style in which they are taught. For example international law in one institution may involve different material and be taught in a contrasting way from another course labelled international law in another.

Many optional subjects, with the notable exceptions of subjects such as the sociology of law and jurisprudence, have as their starting point principles, concepts and techniques that are acquired in studying the foundation subjects. The foundation subjects studied tend to place an emphasis on common law rather than statute law, on private law rather than public law and on applying legal principles without considering their origins and social effects in any detail. Some law degree courses seek to redress this balance, as there is an argument that the foundation subjects, with their emphasis on individuals' property and other private rights, perpetuate a narrow vision of English law.

No law school can guarantee that it will still be offering the same subjects in its syllabus three years hence. Lecturers may leave, or may lose interest in something that they have taught. Thus, be wary of deciding to go to a particular institution just because of one course, particularly if it is unusual, and particularly if it is taught in the third year. It may not be there when you reach the third year.

Non-law degrees

It is important to bear in mind that you can qualify as a solicitor or barrister without taking a first degree in law. The qualification process is longer as a non-law graduate but many choose this route. Non-law graduates have to undertake a one-year full-time conversion course, the Common Professional Exam (CPE). This is also the legal qualification needed by non-law graduates wishing to train for the Bar. Once non-law graduates take the CPE, they proceed to qualification in the same way as a law graduate. This process is covered in greater detail below under the section "Academic Stage of Training, Non-Law Degree Route".

Law as a profession

When looking and deciding on your future career, it is vital to make a realistic assessment of the range of career opportunities open to you. This means deciding what are your own aptitudes, preferences and interests, as well as what are the actual jobs on offer. Vacation or other temporary work experience of any sort can be a very useful way in which to test out your prejudices and instincts about different types of work and to help you make an informed choice about them. Such experience will also help you in job applications and interviews for other, more permanent, jobs. Never be afraid to ask teachers and friends about their jobs and career decisions. Use every opportunity to take advantage of careers advice that is available in your school, college or university. Consider whether participating in a placement scheme would help. When you have made a tentative decision and applied for a job, take time in preparing your letter of application, application form and/ or curriculum vitae (resume of your career to date). Get friends and your tutor to read through your applications and ensure that you present yourself in as interesting and as favourable a light as possible. Never hesitate to take advice. Never be diffident about applying for a particular job.

There are a wide variety of jobs with some legal content. The level and kind of prior legal knowledge that they demand (if any) varies from job to job. You will find an extensive list of such jobs, together with addresses to write for more information about them, in the Careers Directory in Appendix I to this book. In the remainder of this chapter we will concentrate on the two areas of the legal profession: solicitors and barristers. The third section of the legal profession, legal executives, is dealt with separately.

Solicitors and barristers

The legal profession in England and Wales is divided into three branches (solicitors, barristers and legal executives) all of which have their own entry and training schemes. The majority of lawyers are solicitors. As at July 31, 2002, there were over 110,000 solicitors in England and Wales (an increase of only 3.5 per cent over the year before) of which over 89,000 held practicing certificates. Over 34,000 of these were women (over 38 per cent) and more than 6,000 were from ethnic minorities (7 per cent). Women accounted for 55.6 per cent of new admissions to the profession, and ethnic minorities over 16 per cent. In terms of professional trainee trends, there were over 5,300 new traineeships registered in the year August 1, 2001 to July 31, 2002 which represented an increase of over 4 per cent in trainee solicitors commencing contracts over the previous year. Of the new trainees registered, 60 per cent were women and 18 per cent were from ethic minorities. There were 20,094 applicants to study first degree courses in law in 2001 of whom 12,606 were accepted. Over half of the 9,248 graduates in the summer of 2001 achieved firsts or upper second classifications. More women graduated with firsts and upper seconds than men; 52.1 per cent as compared to 49.4 per cent.

In 2002, there were over 9,200 private practice firms of solicitors in England and Wales. Although firms of solicitors exist in all large towns, over 41.5 per cent of these firms are concentrated in London and the south-east, with 26 per cent located in London. These London firms employ 42 per cent of all private practitioners. Traditionally, solicitors have been generalists, advising individual clients on a wide variety of legal matters such as conveyancing, probate, personal injury, family law and criminal law. Many solicitors continue to perform this role in small firms. Over 84 per cent of law practices in England and Wales have four or fewer partners. Sole practices accounted for 44.8 per cent of firms and employed 12.2 per cent of all principals and 8.6 per cent of all solicitors. However, there are an increasing amount of private practice firms who advise business and corporate clients on employment law issues, company mergers and acquisitions, contract law and other commercial matters. There are many specialist or "boutique" firms who advise on a particular aspect of law such as insurance, shipping, banking, intellectual property and media and entertainment law to name a few. Some of the larger firms have European and international offices where they advise clients on United Kingdom law, EU law and foreign law. The largest of these firms have become "multi-national" businesses employing thousands of lawyers and staff worldwide. For example, the 0.4 per cent of firms with 81 or more partners employed 14.3 per cent of all principals and over 21 per cent of all solicitors in private practice.

Just over 70,500 or 79.3 per cent of solicitors holding practicing certificates are employed in private practice at various levels of seniority up to partner or proprietor (through share option plans). There are, however, around 18,500 solicitors employed in commerce and industry, local government, law centres and other occupations. Women account for a higher proportion of solicitors in the employed and other sectors than in private practice. In private practice, 36.5 per cent of solicitors are women, compared with 46.7 per cent in these other sectors. The work of solicitors in sectors other than private practice can be broken down in the following way:

Category of Employment	Total
Commerce/Industry	6,081
Accountancy practice	107
Nationalised industry	107
Trade Union	48
Government Department	90
Local Government	3,097
Court	125
Government funded services	210
Crown Prosecution Service	1,697
Advice service	337
Educational establishment	178
Health service	53
Others (Armed Forces, churches,*etc.*)	759
Not attached to an organisation	5,585
Total	18,474

(Source: Law Society Annual Statistical Report 2002)

Barristers

Just under two-thirds of the 11,000 plus practising barristers work in central London. The remaining practice on circuit in cities such as Liverpool, Manchester, Bristol and Birmingham. Barristers have restricted access to clients and can normally only represent a client when instructed by a solicitor. However, some professional organisations may brief the bar directly without having to go through a solicitor (through a scheme called "Bar Direct"). The Bar Council regulates the bodies that have such direct access.

A barrister specialises in giving advice on detailed issues and representing clients in court. The majority work as individual fee-earners on their own account, sharing overheads with other barristers who are members of the set of chambers. However, about a quarter of barristers are not in independent practice but are instead employed by commercial organisations such as the Government Legal Service, the Crown Prosecution Service, local government or the armed forces. Barristers in independent practice have few of the protections that are afforded to solicitors and commercially employed barristers. Their success or failure is linked directly to their own ability, flair, and preparedness to work, luck and connections.

Historically, comparisons have been drawn between the legal and medical professions. Solicitors, in common with general practitioners, are generalists. Barristers, in common with consultants, are specialists. This comparison still has some degree of validity, although it does not give nearly enough emphasis to the highly specialised work undertaken by many firms of solicitors covering such areas as commercial, company and tax law. It also is the case that a considerable number of solicitors currently act as advocates and will do so increasingly due to their rights of audience being extended to the higher courts. Many barristers spend much of their time out of court, advising solicitors and their clients on points of law and drafting pleadings during the initial stages of litigation.

Those primarily interested in advocacy should normally consider becoming barristers. However, the Access to Justice Act 1999 introduced major amendments to the Courts and Legal Services Act 1990 which grant to all solicitors the rights to appear in all courts in all proceedings with effect from July 31, 2000. In addition to solicitors continuing to be able to represent clients in the County Courts, Magistrates Courts and before Tribunals, it is now possible for solicitors to present cases in the higher courts: Crown Court, High Court, Court of Appeal, and House of Lords. Under the Higher Courts Qualification Regulations 2000, solicitors may obtain the award of a higher court qualification from The Law Society. There are a number of different routes by which a solicitor may acquire rights of audience in the higher courts and The Law Society has published Guidance Notes for solicitors or trainee solicitors who wish to apply for rights of audience in the higher courts.

In making a career decision, thought should be given to the relative opportunities at the Bar and in practice as a solicitor. Practice as a solicitor, in the early stages of a person's career, has the attraction of providing some element of predictability and financial security. Newly qualified barristers must be prepared to put up with career uncertainties and fairly modest incomes in their first years of practice.

Choosing between the two branches of the profession is extremely difficult, especially at the present time, when the legal profession is in a state of transition. Changing attitudes towards the function and conduct of the legal profession, the advent of professional advertising, and greater competition between the two branches of the profession, will all change the nature of legal practice and career opportunities within it. Lawyers have less job security than in the past and their range of work and differences in their terms and conditions of employment have grown in recent years. Qualification as a lawyer is no longer (if it has ever been) an automatic passport to a high standard of living or permanent employment.

Legal Executives

Legal Executives often specialise in a particular area of law such as family law, civil disputes, wills and probate, criminal cases, conveyancing or debt recovery. They are most open employed by solicitors in private practice in a support role. It takes five or six years on average to qualify as a Legal Executive, (*i.e.* a Fellow of ILEX), but during this time you will be doing the job, building up your client base, and becoming a valuable fee earner. With a minimum entry qualification of 4 GCSEs (A–C), most people study while they are working — by day release or by evening classes or by taking a distance learning course — combining study and examination with practical experience. In order to become a fully qualified Legal Executive, (*i.e.* a Fellow of ILEX), you must have completed the ILEX Professional Qualification in Law, be over 25 years old, and have five years experience in a legal office. You can qualify as a solicitor via the ILEX training route, taking a further year or two part-time study. ILEX Fellows may be exempted from the two year Training Contract which must be undertaken before admission by The Law Society as a solicitor.

Education and training of solicitors

The Law Society issues a series of helpful guidance notes about becoming a solicitor and careers as a solicitor in local government and commerce and industry. Guidance is also given on financial support for students, together with a list of institutions which offer "qualifying" law degrees, graduate diplomas in law, the Common Professional Examination (CPE) and the Legal Practice Course (LPC). Information is available from the information services department at The Law Society on +44 (0) 1527504433 or email: info.services@lawsociety. org.uk and The Law Society's website is helpful at *www.lawsociety.org.uk*. The Law Society's Education and Training Unit has launched an online reference system entitled Training trainee solicitors which is also essential reading.

The Law Society prescribes the legal education and training required to qualify as a solicitor in England and Wales. This is often updated so you should ask the Law Society for the current version. The main routes to become a solicitor of England and Wales are the law degree route and the non-law degree route. It is also possible to qualify as a solicitor through the legal executive route.

You should be aware that legal education is currently under review. The Government has set up a review under Sir David Clementi to examine the regulation of the legal profession in England and Wales which covers The Law Society and its educational role. The Law Society is carrying out its own Training Framework Review and in June 2004, issued a Statement following its second consultation on introducing a new training framework for solicitors. The Statement sets out The Law Society's Council's agreement to:

- introduce a new qualification framework based on the knowledge, understanding, skills and attributes that all solicitors should be able to demonstrate on admission as a solicitor (known as day one requirements);
- ensure that its regulatory focus is directed towards its public interest responsibility to act as "gate-keeper" to the profession thus requiring new entrants to demonstrate that they meet the required standards for entry;
- consider a formal pre-admission assessment as one possible method of ensuring that only individuals who can demonstrate day one requirements are admitted to the Roll;
- consider whether new and innovative routes to qualification should be allowed to develop given recent major changes in higher education, the diversity of the backgrounds of new entrants to the profession, and the diversity of legal practice. The Law Society acknowledges that the current approach to qualification, based on the academic stage of training, a Legal Practice Course and two years working under the supervision of a solicitor may continue to be the preferred approach to qualification for many but is open to new models being developed by course providers; and
- offer its services, in a quality assurance role in the future, with regard to courses and learning programmes available.

The Council expects to be able to make decisions about how the day one requirements will be assessed together with an implementation timetable, by the end of 2005. To keep up with

Sir David Clementi's review on behalf of the Government and the Law Society's Training Framework Review developments, you should refer to The Law Society's website (see above).

Academic stage of training

(a) Law degree route

This is the quickest and most common way to qualify as a solicitor in England and Wales.

If you decide to take a law degree, you will need to have a good academic record, as competition for places is intense. You should aim for three "A" levels or equivalent. You may study any academic subject. It is important that you try to obtain high grades. Science "A" levels are as acceptable as arts subjects and no one subject is essential for admission to a Law Degree course.

You should study for a qualifying law degree, which covers the foundation subjects required by both The Law Society and the Bar Council, to complete the Academic Stage of Training. These subjects are restitution, contract and tort, criminal law, foundations of equity and the law of trusts, law of the European Union, property law, and public law including constitutional, administrative and human rights. A list of approved degrees is available from The Law Society and the Bar Council and you should check that your degree is approved.

(b) Non-law degree route

This is the second most common way to qualify as a solicitor.

If you have a degree in a subject other than law, you are required to undertake a one-year full-time or two-year part-time course leading to the Common Professional Examination, which covers the foundation subjects that constitute the Academic Stage of Training. The course is offered at around thirty eight academic institutions across the country and a full list can be obtained from the Law Society. A current alternative to the Common Professional Examination course is the Graduate Diploma in Law, which also covers the foundation subjects, and will enable you, for Law Society purposes, to complete the Academic Stage of Training. Other alternatives include completing a "senior status" law degree (a normal law degree condensed into two years) for which an MA or a postgraduate LL.B. is awarded. A list of these alternative courses, which are offered at around thirty institutions, can be obtained from the Law Society or from your local Careers Advisory Service. Courses start in autumn of each year and application is by means of a clearinghouse for most institutions. The closing date for applications is normally in the spring of the year in which the course commences, *e.g.* Spring 2005 for the 2005–2006 course. Competition for places is extremely strong and students who have not obtained an upper second class honours degree or better may find it difficult to gain a place on a course.

Many people ask if they will have problems obtaining employment as a solicitor or barrister if they do not have a law degree. Most employers are keen to recruit law and non-law students and progression in the profession is not normally affected by degree subject.

(c) Student membership

Upon completion of the Academic Stage of Training, by the Common Professional Examination, Diploma in Law, or a qualifying law degree, you must apply for student membership of The Law Society in order to proceed to the next stage of training. Application forms should be submitted to The Law Society no later than March 31 of the year in which you wish to undertake professional training but there is some flexibility about this date. You will be asked a number of questions on the form about such matters as criminal convictions. Particular care must be taken in filling in the forms and making certain that you are eligible for membership.

Vocational stage of training

Professional training for solicitors is by means of the Legal Practice Course. Anyone wishing to become a solicitor must complete this course. The purpose of the course is to ensure that trainee solicitors entering training contracts have the necessary knowledge and practical skills to undertake appropriate tasks under proper supervision during the contract. A full-time Legal Practice Course will run for one academic year; a part-time course for two years. The introduction of part-time courses has increased the flexibility of the training scheme and access to the profession. A list of courses, which are offered at thirty-two institutions, is available from the Law Society (*www.lawsociety.org.uk*).

The Legal Practice Course (LPC) is made up of five elements: core areas, compulsory subjects, electives (optional subjects), pervasive areas and key skills.

There are three compulsory subjects that must be completed by all students: Business Law and Practice, Litigation and Advocacy (including criminal and civil litigation), and Property Law and Practice. In addition to the compulsory subjects students may choose three optional subjects known as "electives" from a range covering subjects in Private Client and Corporate Client work. A student must spend a minimum number of hours on each elective to demonstrate in-depth study.

The Law Society has established a set of pervasive areas and key skills which must be emphasised and assessed as part of the Legal Practice Course. The key skills include Interviewing and Advising, Legal Writing and Drafting, Advocacy and Practical Legal Research. The pervasive areas include Professional Conduct and Client Care (including Financial Services), and Human Rights, Accounts, EU Law and Revenue Law. Each course provider must meet the Law Society's standards in these areas but has the freedom to be unique in its course content and teaching method to reflect an increasingly diverse legal profession.

Pressure from large corporate firms led to a greater degree of business law and practice being incorporated into the LPC and in 2001, eight of the leading corporate firms broke away to set up their own "City LPC" with three providers. This trend towards tailor-made LPC courses continues and course providers now aim to align training more closely to the type of firm for which students wish to work. Recently, three of these firms separately contracted with one provider to run bespoke LPC courses for them from September 2006 in an example of the first-ever firm-specific LPC courses. Furthermore, a new LPC called the

Public Legal Services Pathway has been developed by a provider from September 2005, in conjunction with the Legal Services Commission, for those who want to become legal aid solicitors. Given these developments, it is important that students, when choosing an LPC course, ensure that the course content reflects the type of legal career they wish to pursue.

Further information about the LPC course can be obtained from the course providers. Application forms for the Legal Practice Course can be obtained from the Legal Practice Course Central Applications Board, PO Box 84, Guildford, Surrey, GU3 1YX. Tel: 01483 451080. Alternatively, students may apply online by visiting the CAB's website, *www. lawcabs.ac.uk*.

Practical stage of training

After successful completion of the Legal Practice Course, students have to undertake a two-year training contract with a firm of solicitors or other authorised organisation. This involves working in paid employment under the supervision of an authorised firm. Finding a training contract is up to you, but help can be obtained from a variety of sources. Competition for training contracts is strong at present and many employers recruit two-three years in advance.

During your training contract you will be required to complete the *Professional Skills Course* (PSC). The PSC consists of three core modules: Finance and Business Skills, Advocacy and Communication Skills, and Client Care and Professional Standards. You are also required to take elective courses in two or more of the core subject areas. There is also 24 hours tuition on optional subjects that can be tailored to the firm's practice areas.

Trainee solicitors

(a) Private practice

The profession is competitive and entry into it is not guaranteed to those with law degrees. Market forces impact on the number of training places available within the profession that will therefore fluctuate. The Law Society advises potential trainees in its literature to market themselves effectively with good interpersonal skills to enhance job opportunities.

Most training contracts are served with private firms of solicitors. Firms vary considerably in size and type of work; therefore a trainee solicitor's range of experience and salary may also vary considerably. There are a number of sources students can use to obtain information on law firms that offer training contracts such as John Pritchard's Legal 500 and Chambers Directory of Law Firms. Many large law firms now produce their own recruitment brochures, which should be obtained as they give a good indication of opportunities. Before making an application you need to think of the sort of training you are seeking.

(i) In rural areas, firms will tend to consist of five or six partners at the most, with total staffs often not exceeding fifteen people. Most such firms will be "general practitioners", which means that they will mostly do conveyancing, landlord and tenant, trusts, wills and probate, small-scale commercial and company work, family law, civil and criminal litigation.

(ii) In large towns most firms will also do the kinds of work listed above though there will tend to be some degree of specialisation, *(e.g.* towards property work and conveyancing, or crime). The larger firms do more commercial work. Some of these firms may have around twenty partners (with some specialising in certain types of work) and staffs of one hundred or more. Generally, in inner city areas, the higher the percentage of legal aid work done and the greater the emphasis of welfare law, *(e.g.* family employment, social security and housing law). Such firms have been affected by reductions in the availability of legal aid for many people.

(iii) In London and other major cities, there is the greatest degree of specialisation, with the large firms in the City of London concentrating very heavily on company, financial, commercial and shipping work. Such firms are very large with over one hundred partners and staffs of eight hundred or more and with offices around the world. Smaller specialist firms have developed significantly with "niche", specialist practices covering such areas as intellectual property, employment and media law.

(b) Public service

Legal work in local government covers many aspects of conveyancing and planning and commercial work. Local authorities do a certain amount of prosecuting work both in those areas where they have special law enforcement responsibilities, *(e.g.* weights and measures or public health legislation) and also sometimes, on behalf of the public. Local authorities are involved in childcare law and social services law.

There are also substantial opportunities for legal careers in Central Government and the Crown Prosecution Service (for relevant addresses see Appendix I).

(c) Industry and commerce

A number of companies and other organisations, both in the private and public sectors have their own legal departments, with qualified solicitors who occasionally take on trainee solicitors. While the work tends to be specialised, large commercial organisations can offer valuable experience in property and commercial work and in areas such as employment, insurance and pension law. Once a person has qualified there are considerable opportunities to work in commerce with a large City of London firm. Limited opportunities also exist to work as a lawyer for a range of trade and employer associations, trade unions, pressure groups and charities.

(d) Law centres

In the inner areas of cities in the United Kingdom, there are now 61 Law Centres, offering occasional opportunities for trainee solicitors seeking to specialise in welfare law. All Law Centres provide free legal advice and representation to individuals and groups within their local areas. There are opportunities for solicitors to work for Law Centres and similar agencies, especially where they have had an all-round experience of litigation during their training contract. All Centres employ paid staff from a minimum of four, up to twenty, in the largest centre, but they are managed by voluntary management committees of local people, representing local communities. They are financed in some cases by the Legal Aid Board, but more usually by local authorities. Each centre is responsible for filling its own vacancies but most jobs are advertised in *The Guardian*, local newspapers, and Legal Action, the bulletin of the Legal Action Group (available from 242 Pentonville Road, London, N1 9UW.

Funding

Students can obtain financial support to fund the Common Professional Examinations (CPE), the Graduate Diploma in Law and the Legal Practice Course (LPC). The main sources of funding are as follows:

Sponsorship

Many of the larger firms of solicitors will sponsor students undertaking the Legal Practice Course (and in some instances those taking the CPE or Graduate Diploma in Law). As a general rule students will complete their training contract with the sponsoring firm and will occasionally have to commit to employment over a longer period of time.

Students hoping to gain sponsorship should apply early. Applications should be submitted before the start of the final year of the undergraduate course, although this will vary depending on the firms. Students are advised to check with firms on an individual basis.

Loan schemes

Many of the High Street banks offer loans at favourable rates to fund CPE, Diploma and LPC courses.

Career development loans

These loans are operated on behalf of the Government for students who are unable to fund the course through other means. Interest on the loan is paid by the Government for the duration of the course and for up to three months after completion (this can be extended to 12 months if the recipient goes in to practical training such as a training contract).

Law society bursary scheme

The Law Society has a limited fund with which to award support to students in need of financial assistance. Application forms must be completed by May in the year the applicant hopes to commence the course.

Law society diversity access scheme

The Law Society has also recently launched a Diversity Access Scheme that aims to provide support to talented students who might find it particularly difficult to qualify due to exceptional social, educational, financial or family circumstances or because of a disability.

For information on the above and for further sources of funding contact: Information Services, The Law Society, on +44 (0) 1527504433 or email: infoservices@lawsociety.org.uk.

Legal Executive route to qualifying as a solicitor (The non-graduate route)

If you have four GCSEs (special provisions apply for those over twenty–one who do not have the relevant qualifications), you can become qualified through the Institute of Legal Executive route.

Most people study while they are working in a legal office — by day release or by evening classes or by taking a distance learning course — to combine study with practical experience. The ILEX Professional Qualification in law is set at two levels: the Level 3 Professional Diploma in Law (PDL) which is equivalent to GCE A-Level/AVCE standard, and the Level 4 Professional Higher Diploma in law (PHDL) which is set at degree level. These qualifications take on average four years to complete.

Having successfully passed the Level 4 PHDL, you will become a Member of ILEX. To become a fully qualified Legal Executive, (*i.e.* a Fellow of ILEX) you need to be over 25 years old, and have five years experience in a legal office(two of which must be after becoming a Member).

Once you become a Fellow of ILEX, you can qualify as a solicitor via the ILEX training route, taking one or two years further part-time study. ILEX Fellows must take the Legal Practice Course and Professional Skills Course. However, Fellows may be exempted from the two year training Contract which must be undertaken before admission by The Law Society as a solicitor, provided they are Fellows when they start the Legal Practice Course.

Further information on Legal Executives is contained in Appendix I.

Education and training of barristers

The academic stage of training for solicitors and barristers (the Bar) is to all intents and purposes the same. The Bar is predominantly a graduate profession. Full details of the entrance requirements can be obtained from The Education and Training Department, The General Council of the Bar, 2/3 Cursitor Street, London EC4A 1NE (*www.barcouncil.org.uk*) and *www.legaleducation.org.uk*.

The academic stage

The academic stage for intending barristers will normally be covered in their degree course, provided that they study the seven foundations of legal knowledge which form the academic stage of legal education at institutions and on courses approved by the Bar. If the degree does not cover all of the foundation subjects or if the student is a non-law graduate the relevant parts of the Common Professional Examination (CPE) or Diploma must be completed before entering the Bar Vocational Course.

The vocational stage

Before proceeding to the vocational stage of training, intending barristers must be admitted to one of the four Inns of Court: Middle Temple (Students' Officer, The Honourable Society of Middle Temple, Treasury Office, London EC4Y 9AT. Tel: 020 7427 4800 *www. middletemple.org.uk*); Inner Temple (Students' Officer, The Honourable Society of Inner Temple, Treasury Office, London EC4Y 7HL. Tel: 020 7797 8250 *www.innertemple.org.uk*); Lincoln's Inn (Students' Officer, The Honourable Society of Lincoln's Inn, Treasury Office, London WC2A 3TL. Tel: 020 7831 1839 *www.lincolnsinn.org.uk*); Grays's Inn (Students' Officer, The Honourable Society of Gray's Inn, 8 South Square, Gray's Inn, London WC1R 5EU. Tel: 020 7458 7800 *www.graysinn.org.uk*).

The Inns of Court provide collegiate activities, support for barristers and student members, advocacy training and continuing professional development opportunities. Student members must comply with certain requirements once admitted to an Inn in order to qualify as a barrister. The most noteworthy of these is the need, prior to qualification, to "keep term", which means attending twelve "qualifying sessions" at the Inn of Court during set periods. This involves "dinners" which may be combined with events such as moots, advocacy workshops, talks, concerts and training weekends. Although dining may appear, at first, to be an outdated practice, it encourages a collegiate atmosphere which is vital to the identity of each Inn. This requirement enables judges, barristers and intending barristers to meet and get to know each other. Advice should be taken from careers tutors as to the appropriate Inn to join. The choice of an Inn is an important one as it will be your professional home throughout your career. All four Inns fulfill the same functions but differ in their delivery. Try to assess their individual atmospheres and characters by visiting them. Much will depend on your career intentions, scholarship opportunities, your likely pupillage arrangements and the contacts that exist between your law department and particular Inns.

The vocational stage takes the form of a one-year full-time or two-year part-time, compulsory Bar Vocational Course at one of eight institutions approved by the Bar Council.

The Bar Vocational Course places an emphasis on developing practical skills including casework skills (fact management and legal research), written skills (opinion drafting and drafting documents) and interpersonal skills (conference, negotiation and advocacy skills). Other major elements of the course include developing knowledge in criminal and civil litigation, evidence and sentencing with the student choosing a further two optional subjects.

Students applying for the Bar Vocational Course cannot apply to the institution directly. Applications must be made through a central, web-based recruitment system, known as BVC Online at *www.bvconline.co.uk*.

Pupillage

Students who pass the Bar Vocational Course examinations are "called to the Bar". In contrast to the solicitor's qualification, the Bar qualification does not entail the successful completion of a period of apprenticeship training. However, barristers intending to practise, rather than teach law or to go on to some other career, must complete a period of apprenticeship ("a pupillage") which takes a period of one year. This is split into two six month periods (sixes), the first "non-practising" six, and the second "practising" six. A pupil does not have to stay in the same chambers to complete the second practising six. There are a growing number of opportunities to undertake a pupillage at the "employed bar" (working as an employed legal advisor rather than as an independent practitioner).

When starting a pupillage, all pupils are assigned one or more pupil supervisors, experienced barristers who will organise training, allocate the work and assess progress. Generally the first non-practising six, will consist of assisting the pupil supervisor by undertaking tasks such as legal research, document reading and drafting, and attending court. On successfully completing the first non-practising six, pupils are issued a certificate allowing them to undertake work for a fee. In the second practicing six, pupils may have their own clients, cases and court appearances with the permission of their pupil supervisor. During the pupillage, the Bar Council requires all pupils to attend two training courses outside the chambers giving further training in advocacy and managing a practice.

In selecting pupillage a student must have regard not only to the range of training on offer but also to the future prospects in the set of chambers which offers the pupillage. Students should not only consider pupillage in London, but also in sets of chambers in cities such as Manchester or Birmingham. Regard must also be had to the number and amount of pupillage awards and scholarships given by the chambers, to help off-set the living expenses for pupils. All pupillages are now funded but this ranges from a minimum of £5000 per six months for criminal barristers to £40000 per year for pupil barristers in the top commercial sets. During the second six months, funding can be in the form of guaranteed earnings. Many chambers do a mixture of litigation work covering crime, personal injury litigation and other common law areas. Students wishing to obtain pupillage and to earn a reasonable living at an early stage at the Bar will often choose such chambers. In London, particularly, there is a large number of specialist chambers covering such fields as commercial law, chancery, patents, tax, libel, planning, employment law and so on. Competition is very fierce for places in such sets of chambers. A very good academic record is required and even those students who are offered places are not assured of making a career at the Bar. Even if offered a place for pupillage there is no guarantee that the student will subsequently be offered a position in the chambers ("a tenancy") after its completion.

The "Pupillages & Awards Handbook", published by the Bar Council gives potential applicants much of the information they need when selecting chambers. Alternatively, if a student wishes to meet and talk with members of a specific chamber before applying, they may consider attending a pupillage fair, the largest of which is held in Lincoln's Inn in March every year. For dates and venues, see *www.doctorjob.com/law* or *www.olpas.co.uk*. To get a feel for the profession students may undertake a "mini-pupillage" at a chosen chambers. This consists of a period of work experience, usually a week, which may or may not be assessed. Some chambers require applicants to undertake an assessed mini-pupillage as part of their recruitment process.

Applying for a pupillage has been made easier by the introduction of OLPAS (the OnLine Pupillage Application System), run by the Bar Council. Applicants are asked to complete a web-based application form. Applications can be made to up to 12 selected chambers in each recruitment season free of charge. Prospective pupils will then have to attend an interview prior to being offered a pupillage. Chambers that do not participate in the scheme can be applied to on an individual basis. OLPAS can be found at *www.olpas.co.uk*, and is operational from March to November each year.

Funding

Although all pupillages are now funded to a lesser or greater extent as discussed above under Pupillage, there is less opportunity to obtain financial support when training to be a barrister compared with trainee solicitors although an increasing number of chambers provide Bar Vocational Course sponsorship to their future pupils.

Funding is available for the Common Professional Examination, the Bar Vocational Course and the pupillage year through the individual Inns of Court. Each of the four Inns provide listings of the bursaries and awards available to students who have been admitted to the Inn. In 2003/2004, over £3 million in scholarships and awards was on offer to students from the Inns of Court. However, the majority of students are self-funded. Many of the High Street Banks provide competitive loan packages for intending barristers, including lower interest rates and extended repayment terms. However, students should enquire of banks on Fleet Street and around the Temple, even if they live or practice elsewhere in the country, as these branches are familiar with barristers' practice and are more sympathetic and accommodating of trainee barristers than the same bank's branches elsewhere.

Practical points: solicitors and barristers

- The following points may be of assistance to those considering entering the legal profession:
    Consider when applications need to be made for the various professional examination courses, obtain advice from your tutor, the Law Society or Bar Council and the growing number of institutions offering the professional courses.

- Intending solicitors should give thought to the advantages and disadvantages of different institutions for the Legal Practice Course. Some firms of solicitors will help their prospective trainee solicitors with the course fees and living expenses.
- Intending entrants to the legal profession should assess the total costs of entry, *(e.g.* tuition and living costs, membership fees and other expenses), the possibility or not of obtaining a bank loan, the availability of scholarships from the various Inns, chambers and law firms and the conditions attached to such awards.
- The desirability of obtaining work experience in a solicitor's office or attached to a barrister's set of chambers during student vacations. Many firms of solicitors and barristers' chambers now organise student placement schemes which are referred to as mini-pupillages.
- Advice should be sought to ensure that you obtain a satisfactory period of practice-based training which reflects your career and subject interests either as a trainee solicitor or as a pupil barrister and that the training contract or pupillage is arranged at the appropriate time.
- An assessment should be made of prospects in either branch of the profession and the overall treatment of trainees and new recruits.
- Read regularly the legal recruitment/jobs pages in *The Times* and other national newspapers, the *Law Society Gazette, The Lawyer* and *Legal Week.* These publications provide an accurate barometer of vacancies, salaries and employment trends in the legal profession.
- Students should make every effort possible to explore career opportunities which are open to them and find out "first-hand" what work as a solicitor or barrister is like whilst they are at university. Do not assume that your interest in the law as a degree subject automatically means that you will enjoy working as a lawyer, or that your disinterest in law as a degree subject means that you will not enjoy working as a lawyer. Appendix I summarises other career opportunities open to students who have studied law or have an interest in a career with a legal content.

Qualifying as a solicitor in Scotland

This section reproduces material supplied by the Law Society of Scotland in January 2004.

Entering the legal profession

A law degree is now the accepted means of entering the legal profession. However as an alternative, it is possible to qualify for the solicitor's branch of the legal profession by a combination of the Law Society of Scotland's own examinations and the Diploma in Legal practice.

The academic stage

(a) Law degree route

A Bachelor of Laws Degree can be studied at nine Scottish Universities: Aberdeen, Abertay, Dundee, Edinburgh, Glasgow, Glasgow Caledonian, Napier, Robert Gordon and Strathclyde. This can be completed as an ordinary degree (three years full time) or as an Honours degree (four years full time).

(b) Non-law degree route (Law Society Examinations)

To qualify as a solicitor without a law degree it is necessary to pass the Law Society of Scotland's professional examinations in order to be eligible to sit the Diploma in Legal Practice. Non-law graduates must be in, or find, full time employment as a Pre-diploma trainee with a qualified solicitor practicing in Scotland. Pre-diploma training lasts for three years during which time the trainee will study for the Law Society Examinations and receive training in three prescribed areas of law: conveyancing, court work and either wills, executries and trusts or the work of a local authority. For admission requirements contact: The Law Society of Scotland, Legal Education Department, 26 Drumsheugh Gardens, Edinburgh, EH3 7YR. (*www.lawscot.org.uk*).

The vocational stage

Diploma in legal practice

After completing the degree or the Law Society examinations, all intending solicitors are required to take the Diploma in Legal Practice. This seven month course can be taken in Aberdeen, Dundee, Edinburgh or Glasgow. This course teaches the practical knowledge and the skills necessary for the working life of a solicitor. To gain admission to the Diploma Course entrants must obtain passes in certain "core" subjects in their LLB degree and obtain a satisfactory standard in the performance of their LLB or Law Society examinations

Post-Diploma practical training

After completion of the Degree/Law Society Professional examinations and the Diploma all intending solicitors serve a two-year post-Diploma training contract with a practising solicitor in Scotland. Between six and eighteen months into the training contract, all trainees must complete the Professional Competence Course with an accredited provider. This consists of both core and elective modules dealing in more depth with practical skills required by solicitors. During the training, all trainees complete quarterly performance reviews which are returned to The Law Society of Scotland for monitoring. On completing the first year of training, trainees can apply to be admitted as a solicitor holding a practising certificate. This allows trainees to appear in court for their employer's clients.

Requalifying in Scotland: solicitors from England, Wales and Northern Ireland

Qualified solicitors from England, Wales and Northern Ireland who wish to be admitted as solicitors in Scotland must apply to the Legal Education Department of The Law Society of Scotland. Prior to being admitted, a fee must be paid, eligibility must be proved and three examinations, Conveyancing with Trusts and Succession, Scots Criminal Law with civil and criminal evidence and procedure, and European Community law, must be passed.

For further information: The Legal Education Department, The Law Society of Scotland, 26 Drumsheugh Gardens, Edinburgh, EH3 7YR. Tel: (0131) 476 8155/8126.

Qualifying as an advocate (barrister) in Scotland

An advocate in Scotland undertakes similar work to a barrister in England and Wales. Their primary duty is to represent clients in court and before tribunals. However, advocates train, and often work, as solicitors before going to the Bar.

Intending advocates must obtain a LLB (Honours) Degree in order to proceed with legal training. This must cover the eight core legal subjects. Having completed the law degree it is then necessary to take the one-year postgraduate Diploma in Legal Practice at one of the Law Faculty's Legal Practice Units (Aberdeen, Edinburgh, Dundee, Strathclyde or Glasgow). Intending barristers will then undertake a traineeship for a period of 1–2 years in a solicitors office. Following this period it is recommended, although not essential, to practice as a solicitor before going to the Bar.

On completing the traineeship, intending barristers undertake a period of unpaid practical training with an experienced advocate. Training is completed by successfully completing the Faculty of Advocates' written examinations.

For further information contact: The Faculty of Advocates, Advocate's Library, Parliament House, Edinburgh, EH1 1RF, (*www.advocates.org.uk*), (scott.brownridge@advocates.org.uk).

Qualifying as a solicitor in Northern Ireland

Entering the legal profession

Usually students complete a law degree to enter the profession. However it is possible for students with a degree in another discipline to become qualified.

Academic stage of training

(a) Law degree route

This is the most common way to qualify as a solicitor. When choosing a degree course it is important to ensure it covers the eight core subjects. These subjects are: Constitutional Law, Criminal Law, Land Law, Law of Tort, Equity, Law of Evidence, Law of contract and European Law.

(b) Non-law degree route

Students from other disciplines can commence training as a solicitor if it can be shown a satisfactory level of knowledge has been achieved in the eight core subjects. The Bachelor of Legal Science awarded by Queen's University, Belfast is accepted as sufficient evidence of knowledge of the relevant subjects. For more information contact: The Queen's University of Belfast, 14 Malone Road, Belfast, BT9 5BN (*www.qub.ac.uk*).

Vocational stage of training

Apprenticeship

After completing an acceptable Degree intending solicitors take up a period of apprenticeship. This involves securing both a place at the Institute of Professional Legal Studies and an apprenticeship contract with a qualified solicitor. Applicants to the Institute must sit an entrance examination in the December prior to the year they wish to take up a place at the institute.

The professional education of a solicitor involves a combination of practical in-office training and formal academic instruction. The period of apprenticeship is two years. The first three months of apprenticeship is spent in office, the following twelve at the Institute of Professional Legal Studies and returning to the office for the final eight months. Once the student has passed all the relevant examinations and completed the apprenticeship period, application can be made to be enrolled as a solicitor of the Supreme Court of Judicature in Northern Ireland. Once enrolled, a practising certificate can be applied for. Newly qualified solicitors are restricted from acting otherwise than as employees for a three-year period (reduced to two by attending the Society's Continuing Legal Education programme)

Contact: The Law Society of Northern Ireland, Law Society House, 98 Victoria Street, Belfast, BT1 3JZ. Tel: 028 9023 1614 (*www.lawsoc-ni.org.uk*).

The Institute of Professional Legal Studies, 10 Lennox Vale, Malone Road, Belfast (*www.qub.ac.uk/ipls*).

Requalifying in Northern Ireland: solicitors from England and Wales

Any practising member of the Bar of England and Wales who has been practising for at least three years can, on payment of a fee and subject to satisfactory references, be called to the Bar of Northern Ireland.

Contact: The Law Society of Northern Ireland, Law Society House, 98 Victoria Street, Belfast, BT1 3JZ. Tel: 028 9023 1614 (*www.lawsoc-ni.org*).

Qualifying as a barrister in Northern Ireland

To qualify as a barrister in Northern Ireland it is necessary to attain at least a second class honours degree in law. This must cover the eight core subjects. A non-law graduates who wish to qualify as barrister must complete the Bachelor of Legal Science Studies at the Queen's University of Belfast.

On completing one of the above courses, intending barristers take a one-year Vocational Certificate course at the Queen's University of Belfast before becoming qualified. Barristers then undertake a six-month unpaid pupillage.

Contact: The Queen's University of Belfast, 14 Malone Road, Belfast, BT9 5BN (*www.qub.ac.uk*).

Appendix I

Careers directory

This alphabetical list of careers opportunities summarises a selection of those careers that have some legal content or contact with the legal profession. The materials contained in this book are designed to be of assistance to trainees for the vast majority of these occupations. Students who have studied law will sometimes find that they can negotiate exemptions from law examinations in professional courses. In some cases they will automatically have such an exemption. The 50 or so organisations mentioned in the directory were written to in January 2004, and where relevant, their amendments to previous entries have been included. We are extremely grateful to them for their comments. We are also grateful to Cora Newell (B.A., J.D., Attorney-at-law, Solicitor) who has helped co-ordinate this process. Most academic institutions and professional bodies now consider a wide variety of qualifications such as BTEC, GNVQ, Scottish Highers and SQA National Units.

Accountancy

Accountants are usually thought of in association with companies rather than as independent financial advisors. Whether working for a company or acting as an independent financial advisor, accountants are involved in the day-to-day financial control of businesses as well as larger-scale matters such as the creation of new businesses and the restructuring of established ones.

In recent years the accountancy profession has shown itself to be adaptable and enterprising. Their work as liquidators and receivers, dealing with the closing down of businesses, has expanded, as has the role of auditors. They have also extended their activities into the more general area of management consultants. An area of accountancy ideally suited to law graduates is tax planning as it involves predicting and applying changes in tax legislation. Due to this, some firms specifically take on law graduates as trainees in this area. Over past decades accountants have increasingly worked closely with solicitors and, in recent years, have expanded their business into areas traditionally the prerogative of solicitors. Many of the larger firms of accountants acquired their own legal practices by way of expansion into the legal profession but most of these law firms have split off from their accountancy tied networks in response to difficulties caused by international curbs introduced on the services accountancy firms can offer, such as the US Sarbanes-Oxley Act 2002. Although no specific qualifications are required to become an accountant, it is necessary to obtain a professional qualification to become a chartered, certified or management accountant. Many accountancy firms finance the obtaining of such qualifications as part of a graduate-training scheme.

Minimum entry requirements: Entry requirements vary depending upon the qualification sought, however as a general rule a minimum of three GCSE passes plus two A-levels or equivalent are required. Normally, 18 UCAS points, a UCAS Tariff score of 220 or equivalent are required. The subjects you study at A-level are not as important as the grades. The ACA qualification requires Professional Stage and Advanced Stage examinations.

Training period: To become a qualified accountant, a minimum of three years relevant training is required.

Further information:
Institute of Chartered Accountants in England and Wales, Gloucester House, 399 Silbury Boulevard, Central Milton Keynes, MK9 2HL (*www.icaew.co.uk/careers*).

The Chartered Association of Certified Accountants, 29 Lincoln's Inn, London, WC2A 3EE (*www.acca.org.uk*).

The Chartered Institute of Management Accountants, 26 Chapter St, London, SW1M 4NP. Tel: 020 7663 5441 (*www.cimaglobal.com*).

The Chartered Institute of Public Finance and Accountancy, 3 Robert Street, London, WC2N 6RL (*www.cipfa.org.uk*).

Actuary

Most actuaries work for insurance and pension fund companies. They calculate matters such as the life expectancies of certain occupational groups and assess a wide range of insurance risks.

Minimum entry standard: 2 "A" levels (one being a B in maths or C in further maths) and 3 "GCSE" levels. This is predominantly a maths graduate profession. Training period: 5–6 years for graduates.

Further information:
Institute of Actuaries, Napier House, 4 Worcester Street, Oxford, OX1 2AW (*www. actuaries.org.uk*).

Advertising

There is a wide range of job opportunities for graduates in the advertising industry.

Further information:

The Advertising Association, Abford House, 15 Wilton Road, London, SW1V 1NJ (*www.adassoc.org.uk*).

Institute of Practitioners in Advertising, 44 Belgrave Square, London, SW1X 8QS (*www.ipa.co.uk*).

Banking

The High Street Banks have expanded the range of services they offer to corporate and personal customers. Advice is given on a wide range of services including investments, taxation, securities, loans and leasing schemes. The Banks have substantial trust and probate departments. Merchant banks give specialist advice, manage clients' investments, and advise on company acquisitions, flotations and mergers. They employ a number of lawyers.

Qualifications and training periods depend on the Bank and the relevant traineeship.

Further information:

London Investment Banking Association, 6 Frederick's Place, London, EC2R 8BT (*www.liba.org.uk*).

British Bankers' Association, Pinners Hall, 105–108 Old Broad Street, London, EC2N 1EX (*www.bba.org.uk*).

Barrister

See Chapter 8.

Building society management

At present Building Societies have to deal with solicitors over the granting and drawing up of mortgages. They employ a number of lawyers. It is likely that the scope of Building Societies operations will grow in the future to include more commercial initiatives and the provision of a wider range of legal services for their clients. There is also likely to be a greater degree of overlap between the banking and building society businesses.

No mandatory qualification exists for Building Society Management however there is provision to obtain an Associate of the Chartered Institute of Bankers qualification that covers areas such as lending, management and financial services. Other qualifications relevant to Building Society Management, such as CeMAP and the Diploma in Mortgage Lending, may also be obtained from the Chartered Institute of Bankers.

Minimum entry requirements: no formal requirements.

Training period: 18 months–4 years.

Further information:
British Bankers' Association, Pinners Hall, 105–108 Old Broad Street, London, EC2N
1EX (*www.bba.org.uk*).
The Building Societies Association, 3 Savile Row, London, W1S 3PB (*www.bsa.org.uk*).

Chartered secretary

A typical Chartered Secretary working within a company or charity has a variety of high-level responsibilities including acting as an adviser and confidant to the Chairman, Board and senior management on corporate governance and other important areas. These include Board and shareholder/trustee meetings, the design, management and administration of executive and employee share plans, compliance with legal and stock exchange regulations, and shareholder communication. Responsibilities often include the management of pensions and insurance issues, legal work, including the negotiation of contracts on behalf of the organisation, and acting as the organisation's point of contact for regulatory bodies.

Minimum entry standard: The ICSA International Qualifying Scheme is a post-graduate level qualification, although entry is available via a Foundation Programme for those with no academic qualifications.

Training period: 2–5 years.

Further information:
Student Services Department, Institute of Chartered Secretaries and Administrators, 16 Park Crescent, London, W1B 1AH. Tel: 020 7580 4741 (*www.icsa.org.uk*).

Civil Service (UK and European)

UK Civil Service

The range of jobs in the civil service is enormous. Many have a legal content. The civil service employs a large number of solicitors and barristers. The Government Legal Service employs over 1800 lawyers, working in both major Departments of State and smaller, more specialised public bodies, approximately 40 government organizations in all. Their activities cover virtually every aspect of law and reflect the breadth of government activities. This includes working with Ministers and Parliamentary Counsel on primary legislation, seeing Bills through Parliament, involvement in judicial reviews, and civil and criminal law litigation.

Further information:
GLS Recruitment Team, Queen Anne's Chambers, 28 Broadway, London, SW1H 9JS. Tel: 020 7210 3304 (*www.gls.gov.uk*) (email: recruit@gls.gsi.gov.uk).

European opportunities

European institutions

Regular open competitions are held to recruit staff to institutions such as the European Commission, European Parliament and the European Court of Justice. The majority of opportunities exist within the Commission with the other institutions recruiting on a lesser scale. Open competitions usually consist of pre-selection tests, a written examination and interview. Full details of all competitions run by the European Personnel Selection Office for all European Institutions combined can be obtained from the EPSO website (see below).

Qualified lawyers are also recruited to the European Commission, Parliament and Council of Ministers through the open competitions. Opportunities at the European Court of Justice are usually confined to lawyer linguists and are always advertised.

Minimum entry requirements: Applicants must have good knowledge of two EU languages.

Further information:
General information about recruitment and open competitions can be obtained from: European Personnel Selection Office (EPSO), Info-Recruitment, B1049 Brussels. Tel: +32 2 2993131 (*http://europa.eu.int/epso*) (*inforecruitment@cec.eu.int*).

Stages

To enhance prospects of being successful in the open competitions applicants may decides to complete a five month "stage" with the European Commission. A "stage" is a five-month in-service training programme offered to university graduates and public service employees. It consists of a period of work experience in one of the Commission's services (undertaking tasks such as minute writing, research and assessment of financial, economic and technical co-operation projects) supplemented by lectures and visits to other EU institutions.

Further information and application forms:
The Traineeships Office, European Commission, B1049 Brussels, Belgium.
Minimum entry requirements: University degree or equivalent.
Training period: 5 months.

European Fast Stream

The European Fast Stream Programme is a UK Government initiative designed to increase the number of British graduate securing posts in the EU institutions. It offers a four-year period of work experience designed to increase chances of success in the EU recruitment competitions. European Fast Streamers are full time UK Civil Servants, working in UK Government Departments. Their work has an emphasis on European policy issues, so they learn how the EU machinery works and how Brussels and Member State governments interact. They also get special training to help them get through the EU recruitment competitions. If they pass a competition, they normally resign from the British Civil Service and become employees of one of the EU Institutions.

Minimum entry requirements: A first or second class honours degree, "A" level standard in another EU language. (Must be a British National and no older than 41).

Training period: 4 years.

Further information:

European Fast Stream, Room 74/2, Cabinet Office, Horse Guards Road, London, SW1P 3AL (*www.faststream.gov.uk*).

Recruitment and Assessment Service (CAPITA RAS Ltd), Innovation Court, New Street, Basingstoke, Hampshire, RG21 7JB (*www.rasnet.co.uk*).

Customs and Excise

The Solicitors Office of HM Customs has over 140 lawyers, and 360 staff in total. HM Customs are responsible for the collection of all indirect taxation (*e.g.* VAT, excise duties) and for enforcing the prohibition against smuggling drugs and other prohibited or restricted items (*e.g.* firearms, pornography).

Further information:

The Solicitor, HM Customs and Excise, New Kings Beam House, 22 Upper Ground, London, SE1 9PJ (*www.hmce.gov.uk*).

Engineering

Most professional engineers study aspects of law during some part of their training; generally this will relate to matters such as contract, employment and building law.

Further information:

EMTA (Engineering Marine Training Authority), (*www.eal.org.uk*).

The Engineering Council (UK), 10 Maltravers Street, London, WC2R 3ER (*www.engc.org.uk*).

WISE (Women into Science and Engineering), 22 Old Queen Street, London, SW1H 9HP. Tel: 020 7227 8421(*www.wisecampaign.org.uk*).

Environmental Health Officers

Environmental Health Officers (Practitioners) work in both the public and private sectors. The work includes responsibility for ensuring that certain food, hygiene, health and safety, environmental protection, public health, and housing standards are maintained or improved and that other regulatory provisions are complied with. The job includes some involvement with lawyers and the courts and requires detailed knowledge of a number of Acts of Parliament and related statutory instruments.

Minimum entry standards: 160 points or 200 points at "A" levels and 5 "GCSE" levels (including English, Maths and 2 science subjects). (Provision for graduate entry and alternative equivalent qualification).

Training period: 4 year sandwich course leading to BSc (Hons) Environmental Health. 2 year MSc in Environmental Health for science graduates. Some courses offered on a part-time or distance-learning basis.

Further information:
The Chartered Institute of Environmental Health, Chadwick Court, 15 Hatfields, London, SE1 8DJ (*www.cieh.org.uk*).

Factory inspector

Much of a factory inspector's time is spent visiting appropriate premises advising on safety requirements and ensuring that a variety of statutes are complied with. The job involves some contact with courts and lawyers.

Minimum entry standards: Graduate entry plus further experience normally required.
Training period: 2 years.

Further information:
The Health and Safety Executive, Room 321, St Hughs House, Bootle, Liverpool, 3QY L20 (*www.hse.gov.uk*).

Recruitment and Assessment Service, Innovation Court, New Street, Basingstoke Hampshire, RG21 7JB (*www.rasnet.co.uk*).

Health services management

Health service managers play a key role in the organisation, staffing, equipping and functioning of hospitals. Moves towards privatising some services, (*e.g.* catering and laundering), industrial relations problems, and intricate commercial decisions that have to be taken by hospital trusts have all increased the legal content of the work done.

Minimum entry standards: No set pattern.

Training period: Variable. It is possible to take the Institute of Health Services Management courses but other qualifications such as those in law, accountancy or personnel management may be adequate.

Further information:
Institute of Healthcare Management, (*www.ihm.org.uk*).

Housing

Housing professionals work to develop, supply or manage housing and related services. People who work in housing tend to work for a local authority, housing association or a commercial landlord. The work varies according to the particular functions of the housing organisation, its size and location. Social, legal and other changes have expanded the spectrum of work available and skills required in the housing profession. Much of the work has a legal content due to the statutory framework surrounding the field of housing management.

Minimum entry standards: 1 "A" level and 3 GCSE or equivalent experience.

Training period: 4 years (less for graduates).

Further information:
Chartered Institute of Housing, Octavia House, Westwood Way, Coventry, CV4 8JP. Tel: 024 7685 1700 (email: careers@cih.org).

Insurance

The insurance field offers a wide range of different employment opportunities. The precise nature of insurance contracts and the wide range of specialist legal rules means there are many openings for lawyers in this area.

Further information:
Careers Information Officer, The Chartered Insurance Institute, The Hall, 20 Aldermanbury, London, EC2V 7HY (*www.cii.co.uk*).

Journalism and broadcasting

This is a wide field offering opportunities not just as a broadcaster or journalist, but also behind the scenes in the administration and management of businesses. Many media companies have "in house" legal departments. The BBC's is probably the largest. From the end of 2003, the Independent Television Commission has been merged with four other regulators (BSC, RA, RCA and Oftel) into the new Office of Communications (Ofcom).

Further information:
BBC Recruitment Service, White City, 201 Wood Lane, London, W12 7TS (*www.bbc.co.uk*).
ITV Network Centre, 200 Gray's Inn Road, London, WC1 8XS (*www.itv.co.uk*).
Ofcom (Office of Communication), Riverside House, 2a Southwark Bridge Road, London, SE1 9HA. Tel: 020 7981 3000 (*www.ofcom.org.uk*).
National Council for the Training of Journalists, Latton Bush Centre, Southern Way, Harlow, Essex, CM18 7BL (*www.nctj.com*).
Newspaper Society, Bloomsbury House, 74–77 Great Russell Street, London, WC1B 3DA (*www.newspapersoc.org.uk*).
Periodical Publishers' Association, Queen's House, 28 Kingsway, London, WC2B 6JR (*www.ppa.org.uk*).

Legal career opportunities

Solicitors and barristers are covered in Chapter 8. This entry reproduces updated material originally supplied by the Law Society in January 2000 on other careers in the legal profession.

(a) Legal executives

Legal executives have their own status and role within the legal profession. They work as assistants to solicitors, predominantly in the area of private practice. To qualify as a legal executive they must take the examinations of the Institute of Legal Executives (ILEX). To qualify as a Fellow of the Institute they must also have at least 5 years experience in legal work. They do a wide range of legal work and often develop their own individual specialisations (particularly in the field of conveyancing, accounts, trusts, wills and litigation). It is possible to qualify as a solicitor through the Legal Executive route by taking further examinations. Some people are employed by solicitors to do the same work as legal executives although they are not qualified as such.

Entry qualifications: 4 GCSE levels in approved subjects or the ILEX Preliminary Certificate in Legal Studies or the ILEX para legal training qualification.

Further information:
The Institute of Legal Executives, Kempston Manor, Kempston, Bedford, MK42 7AB. Tel: 01234 841000 (*www.ilex.org.uk*).

(b) Outdoor Clerks

Many large firms of solicitors employ school leavers as Clerks who deliver statements of case or attend court to pay fees and have documents stamped. Careers offices, Job Centres and newspapers advertise vacancies for Outdoor Clerks. Qualifications required range from two to four GCSEs including English Language.

(c) Barristers' Clerks

Barristers' Clerks manage the diaries, court lists and fees of barristers in practice.

Further information:
Institute of Barristers' Clerks, (*www.instbclerks.org*).

(d) Legal Secretaries

Legal Secretaries provide the secretarial and clerical backup for solicitors, barristers, law courts, civil service, and banks. They deal with large amounts of correspondence and the preparation of documents such as wills, divorce petitions and witness statements.

Further information:
Association of Legal Secretaries, The Mill, Clymping Street, Clymping, Littlehampton, West Sussex, BN17 5RN. Tel: 01903 714276.

(e) Legal Cashiers

Legal Cashiers are usually employed in solicitors' practices, and their main duties are to keep solicitors up to date with the financial position of the firm and to maintain accounting records. A cashier often deals with the payment of salaries, pensions, National Insurance contributions and income tax. Cashiers are increasingly using computerised accounting systems.

Further information:
The Institute of Legal Cashiers, 146/148 Eltham Hill, Eltham, London, SE9 5DX (*www.ilca.org.uk*).

(f) Law Costs Draftsmen or Legal Costs Consultants

Law Costs Draftsmen or Legal Costs Consultants are primarily engaged in the preparation of and/or opposing of bills and/or claims for costs on the instructions of solicitors. They provide advice and assistance on all aspects of legal costs, prepare costs estimates and statements of costs as required at various stages in the litigation process and can greatly assist in case budgeting. They work with, assist and advise in all areas of legal costs be they contentious or non-contentious. Fellows of the Association of Law Costs Draftsmen (ALCD) may act as experts in advising litigants in person on legal costs issues. A knowledge of many areas of law and procedure is essential to fulfill the role of a Law Costs Draftsman/Legal Costs Consultant. Membership of the ALCD denotes that a certain standard of professionalism is achieved dependant upon status and that continuing education will be undertaken.

Further information:
Association of Law Costs Draftsmen, Church Cottage, Church Lane, Stuston, Diss, Norfolk, IP21 4AG. Tel: 01379 741404 (*www.alcd.org.uk*).

(g) Licensed Conveyancers

Licensed Conveyancers are specialist property lawyers who have qualified in all aspects of the law dealing with property through the Council for Licensed Conveyancers (CLC) Examinations and are employed under the supervision of a "qualified" person. A qualified person is a Licensed Conveyancer or Solicitor in sole practice or partnership for at least two years. Once qualified, a Licensed Conveyancer may set up in business after being employed for a further three years. Licensed Conveyancers are regulated by the Council for Licensed Conveyancers.

Further information:
The Council for Licensed Conveyancers, 16 Glebe Road, Chelmsford, Essex, CM1 1QG. Tel: 012453 49599 (*www.theclc.gov.uk*) (email: clc@theclc.gov.uk).

(h) Justices' Chief Executives, Justices' Clerks, and Legal Advisers

A Justices' Chief Executive is the principal adviser on policy to the Magistrates' Courts Committee. The role involves the management and administration of the Committee's resources and strategic planning of future developments. Justices' Chief Executives do not have to be legally qualified.

The role of a Justices' Clerk is to advise Magistrates on law and procedure both in and out of court. Justices' Clerks also exercise a number of judicial functions in their own right. Other duties may include training magistrates, general staff management and over-seeing the administration of the courts as delegated by the Justices' Chief Executive. Justices' Clerks need five years experience as a qualified solicitor or barrister. Where several courts are in operation at once, Justices' Clerks delegate much of their work to legal advisers.

Legal Advisers sit in court and advise Magistrates on law, legal practice and procedure. They also undertake administrative work necessary before and after a case. They may also deal with legal matters such as licensing applications, fine enforcement and maintenance payments. Legal Advisers must be qualified as a barrister or solicitor.

Further information:
The Justices' Clerks' Society, 2nd Floor, Port of Liverpool Building, Pier Head, Liverpool, L3 1BY, Tel: 0151 255 0790. (*www.jc-society.co.uk*).

(i) Court Clerks

Court Clerks work in Justices' Clerks' offices and advise lay magistrates on law and procedure in court. They are also responsible for the Licensing and Betting and Gaming Committees, which involves visiting premises with a Magistrate. Court Clerks often have to be on standby at weekends just in case it is necessary to set up an emergency court.

Further information:
The Association of Magisterial Officers, 1 Fellmongers Path, Tower Bridge Road, London, SE1 3LY, Tel: 020 7403 2244. (*www.amo-online.org.uk*).

(j) Crown Prosecution Service

The Crown Prosecution Service is an independent body responsible for the prosecution and review of criminal proceedings instituted by the police in England and Wales (with the exception of cases conducted by the Serious Fraud Office and certain minor offences). The Crown Prosecutors are qualified solicitors or barristers. The Crown Prosecution Service is part of the Civil Service, and all prosecutors are civil servants. Prosecutors have a support staff of executive and administrative officers and assistants to prepare papers for hearings in Court.

Further information:
The Crown Prosecution Service, 50 Ludgate Hill, London, EC4M 7GG, Tel: 020 7273 8309. (*www.cps.gov.uk*).

(k) The Government Legal Service

The GLS consists of around 1,800 qualified lawyers employed in approximately 40 government organisations. The GLS provides training and career opportunities for all its lawyers. The scope of the work undertaken by GLS lawyers is wide reflecting the breadth of activities with which the Government is concerned.

Further information:
Government Legal Services, Recruitment Team, Queen Anne's Chambers, 28 Broadway, London, SW1H 9JS. Tel: 020 7210 3304 (*www.gls.gov.uk*) (email: recruit@gls.gsi.gov.uk).

(l) The Department for Constitutional Affairs

This government office, part of the Civil Service, has various responsibilities, the majority of which it administers through executive agencies. It employs civil servants, some of whom are lawyers, to deal with matters relating to the administration of the courts. The Department also deals with policy matters concerning the legal profession.

Further information:
The Department for Constitutional Affairs, Selborne House, 54–60 Victoria Street, London, SW1E 6QW. Tel: 020 7210 0628 (*www.dca.gov.uk*).

(m) Armed Forces

There are a number of vacancies for lawyers in the armed forces.

Further information:
Army Legal Services, Trenchard Lines, Upavon, Pewsey, Wiltshire, SN9 6BE (*www.army.mod.uk*).
RAF Legal Services, RAF Innsworth, Gloucestershire, GL3 1EZ (*www.raf.mod.uk*).

Library, information and training services

An increasing number of the larger firms of solicitors have specialist departments covering legal information and practice developments, library services, precedents, education and training programmes, research and publications. These departments are often staffed by lawyers.

Further information:
CILIP: Chartered Institute of Library and Information Professionals, 7 Ridgmont Street, London, WC1E 7AE. Tel: 020 7255 0500 (*www.cilip.org.uk*).
The British and Irish Association of Law Librarians, 26 Myton Crescent, Warwick, CV34 6QA (*www.biall.org.uk*).

Local government

Some specific careers in local government are listed in this appendix under the appropriate headings. There are a wide range of careers in local government either as a lawyer or in management. For information about them you should consult the appropriate department of the Town Hall or Council Office in the area in which you wish to work.

Management

Most companies in industry, commerce and the financial sectors have graduate recruitment programmes. A good law degree will often be considered a suitable background to a career in management. Please consult your own Careers' Advisory Service on particular opportunities, when to apply, and to obtain an overview of a career in management.
Some companies will actually come to your university or college to interview prospective trainees and employees.

Patent and Trademarks

Patent agents (also known as patent attorneys) advise on all aspects of the protection of ideas through patents, copyright, designs and trade marks, collectively known as intellectual property or IP. Registration of a patent or industrial design is a way of preventing anyone copying your invention without them first paying an appropriate fee. The job involves a knowledge of both science and law and is particularly suitable for a science or engineering student with an interest in the law.
Minimum entry standard: Science or engineering degree.
Training period: 3–4 years.

Further information:
Chartered Institute of Patent Agents, 95 Chancery Lane, London, WC2A 1DT (*www.cipa.org.uk*).

Personnel management

The continual development of employment law and health and safety legislation over the past decades has resulted in an increased need for some personnel managers to have a specialist knowledge of law so that they can advise their companies on such matters and, if necessary, represent them in employment tribunals.

Minimum entry standard: Varies (provision for graduate entry).
Training period: Variable.

Further information:
Chartered Institute of Personnel and Development, CIPID House, Camp Road, Wimbledon, London, SW19 4UX. Tel: 020 8971 9000 (*www.cipd.co.uk*).

Police

The Police Force offers a variety of careers suitable for law graduates. All entrants to the police force must complete a two year period as a uniformed Constable within a police station. On completion of this period there is scope to progress through the police ranks or work for one of the specialist squads such as the Air Support Unit or the Public Order Branch. Graduates may apply for the Accelerated Promotion Scheme for Graduates (APSG) that provides enhanced career progression.

Further information:
The Police Recruiting Department, The Home Office, 50 Queen Anne's Gate, London, SW1H 9AT. Tel: 0870 000 1585 (*www.police.uk*) or (*www.policecouldyou.co.uk*).

Public relations

Many of the largest firms of solicitors now employ external or internal public relations advisers to help them with their overall "image" and relations with the media, clients and prospective clients.

Further information:
Institute of Public Relations, The Old Trading House, 15 Northburgh Street, London, EC1V 0PR (*www.ipr.org.uk*).

Publishing

Some law publishers, such as Oxford University Press and Sweet & Maxwell, are interested in employing law graduates and newly qualified lawyers in their editorial and marketing departments. If you are interested in working for a particular legal publisher you should contact them directly. Your law tutor should be able to advise you about which law publishers you should approach.

Further information:
The Publishers' Association, 29b Montague St, London, WC1B 5BW. Tel: 020 7691 9191 (*www.publishers.org.uk*).

Sweet & Maxwell, 100 Avenue Road, Swiss Cottage, London, NW3 3PF (*www. sweetandmaxwell.co.uk*).

Recruitment consultants

There is some scope for law graduates and lawyers to work for the recruitment consultants for the legal profession. To obtain an idea of the "market leaders", read the legal job vacancy pages of the national newspapers, the *Law Society Gazette, Legal Week* and *The Lawyer.*

Social work and probation

Social work

The majority of social workers are employed by local authorities. They provide a social work service to families, children, the elderly, the sick, those with disabilities and the community at large. They are employed in a variety of settings; hospitals, residential homes and in the community. Some are specialists working in such areas as mental health or child care where a good knowledge of the relevant area of law is particularly important. Other elements of social work include providing advice and support where a general awareness of the law is frequently required.

Probation

The aims of the National Probation Service (for England and Wales) are:

- protecting the public;
- reducing re-offending;
- the proper punishment of offenders in the community;
- ensuring offenders' awareness of the effects of crime on the victims of crime and the public;
- and the rehabilitation of offenders.

To meet these aims, the service provides pre-sentence reports to the courts, the supervision of offenders and the continuous assessment and management of risk and dangerousness of offenders. In order to provide these services, the National Probation Service employs a range of staff. Probation Officers and Probation Services Officers are the two main groups of staff working directly with offenders.

Minimum entry standard: There is no formal qualification for Probation Services Officers. Staff are recruited directly into these posts by Probation Areas (there are 42 Areas in England and Wales) and receive in-service training to undertake their work. In some Areas the staff work towards the achievement of a Community Justice NVQ at level 3.

Probation Officers are required to hold the Diploma in Probation Studies (DipPS) which is an integrated award combining a Community Justice degree and a Community Justice NVQ at level 4. The DipPS is delivered through programmes run by nine regional probation training consortia (contact details are on the probation website) and the qualification takes two years to complete. Trainee probation officers are recruited annually to these regional programmes and are full-time employees of a Probation Area for the whole training period before transferring to a probation officer post on completion.

Further information:
National Probation Directorate, Human Resources Section, 1st Floor, Horseferry House, Dean Ryle Street, London, SW1P 2AW (*www.probation.homeoffice.gov.uk*).

Stock Exchange

Graduates with either law or law-related degrees may find jobs in firms of stockbrokers working in their research and investment analysis departments. There is no formal training for these positions.

The London Stock Exchange organises and regulates the activities of its 400 plus member firms which range from large international securities houses to small two-partner firms of brokers.

It is the member firms, rather than the Exchange, which employ stockbrokers. You should contact the firms directly as recruiting requirements vary. Most reference sections of business libraries hold the London Stock Exchange Member Firms Book, which gives the names and addresses of stockbroking firms.

The London Stock Exchange itself runs a Graduate Training Scheme. For further information write to: Human Resources at the Stock Exchange, London, EC2N 1HP (*www. londonstockexchange.com*).

There are also a number of securities industry courses and exams. For more information, write to: The Securities Institute, Centurion House, 24 Monument Street, London, EC3R 8AJ (*www.securities-institute.org.uk*).

Surveying and autioneering

Membership of the Royal Institution of Chartered Surveyors requires study of a number of subjects which have a legal content, covering such topics as contract, agency and land law.

Further information:
Royal Institution of Chartered Surveyors, 12 Great George Street, London, SW1P 3AD (*www.rics.org.uk*).

Tax inspector

Those who are interested in tax law or the tax system and who have a good degree or an accountancy qualification may be interested in this career option. Progress in the tax inspectorate depends on both the ability to pass internal revenue examinations and the willingness to be mobile. Some tax inspectors later leave the service in order to start work as tax consultants with firms of accountants.

Minimum entry standard: First or Second class honours degree or equivalent. Training period: 4–7 years.

Further information:
Inland Revenue (HRD), PO Box 55, Mowbray House, Castle Meadow Road, Nottingham, NG2 1BE (*www.inlandrevenue.gov.uk*).

Recruitment and Assessment Service, Innovation Court, New Street, Basingstoke, Hampshire, RG21 7JB (*www.rasnet.co.uk*).

Teaching and post-graduate opportunities

If you are interested in either of the above options you should consult your law tutor or your local Careers Advisory Service. The majority of university law faculties have facilities for post-graduate research and/or run taught post-graduate courses. You normally need a second class honours degree to obtain a place on such a course. Most of these courses can either be studied full-time or part-time. Some are run on a "distance learning" basis. It is very difficult to obtain scholarships or state grants for such courses. Some universities are able to offer scholarships or other forms of assistance. A post-graduate degree is of some assistance to anyone wishing to teach law. The majority of university law lecturers have an upper second class honours degree or better. Many also have a professional qualification, further degree or both. Although opportunities to lecture in law are limited there are more openings than in many other disciplines.

It is possible to pursue post-graduate research in foreign countries, particularly in the United States and Canada and, increasingly, with the European Union.

Further information:
For further degrees and diplomas by examination or research write direct to a range of law faculties. Diplomas and higher degrees can be obtained in a vast array of legal and law related subjects on a part-time or full-time basis at a wide range of institutions.

Study in the United Kingdom:
Grants Information: The British Arts and Humanities Research Board (AHRB), 10 Carlton House Terrace, London, SW1Y 5AH (*www.ahrb.ac.uk*).

Law Commission, Conquest House, 37–38 John Street, London, WC1N 2BQ (for research assistant positions). Tel: 020 7453 1242 (*www.lawcom.gov.uk*).

The Economic and Social Research Council, Polaris House, Swindon, SN2 1ET (*www.esrc.ac.uk*).

Overseas Opportunities:
Association of Commonwealth Universities, John Foster House, 36 Gordon Square, London, WC1H 0PF (*www.acu.ac.uk*).

The British Council, Bridgewater House, 58 Whitworth Street, Manchester, M1 6BB (*www.britishcouncil.org*).

Commonwealth Legal Education Association (CLEA) c/o Legal and Constitutional Affairs Division, Commonwealth Secretariat, Marlborough House, Pall Mall, London, SW1Y 5XH.

For the USA:
The U.S. Educational Advisory Service, The Fulbright Commission, 62 Doughty Street, London, WC1N 2SZ (*www.fulbright.co.uk*).

Trading standards officer

Trading standards officers are responsible for the enforcement of a wide range of legislation including the Trade Descriptions Act 1968, the Consumer Credit Act 1974, the Consumer Protection Act 1987 and other regulatory provisions covering food, drugs, weights and measures. They are also often involved in the provision of advice and assistance to traders and to consumers. They are employed by local authorities.

Minimum entry standard: A Consumer Protection Degree via one of four approved university courses (The Manchester Metropolitan University, University of Teeside, Glasgow Caledonian University and University of Wales Institute, Cardiff) or accreditation of prior experience and learning (APEL).

Further information:
Institute of Trading Standards Administration, PO Box 2714, The Croft, County Hall, Lewes, East Sussex, BN7 1AL.

Appendix II

Abbreviations

The short list below contains some of the standard abbreviations that you will find most frequently referred to in books and case reports. It is not exhaustive. It will help you whilst you are beginning your study of law. The most complete and up-to-date list of abbreviations is to be found at *http://www.legalabbrevs.cardiff.ac.uk/*. This can be searched both by abbreviation, to find out what journal or law report is being referred to, and by journal or law report, to find out what the accepted abbreviation or the journal or law report is:

A.C.	Appeal Cases (Law Reports).
All E.R.	All England Law Reports.
C.L.J.	Cambridge Law Journal.
Ch.D.	Chancery Division (Law Reports).
C.M.L.R.	Common Market Law Reports.
Conv.(n.s.)	Conveyancer and Property Lawyer (New Series).
Crim.L.R.	Criminal Law Review.
D.L.R.	Dominion Law Reports.
E.L.R.	European Law Reports.
E.L.Rev.	European Law Review.
E.R.	English Reports.
Fam.	Family Division (Law Reports).
Fam.Law	Family Law (A journal which also contains notes about cases).
H. of C. or H.C.	House of Commons.
H. of L. or H.L.	House of Lords.
I.L.J.	Industrial Law Journal.
K.B.	King's Bench (Law Reports).
L.Q.R.	Law Quarterly Review.
L.S.Gaz.	Law Society Gazette.
M.L.R.	Modern Law Review.
N.I.L.Q.	Northern Ireland Legal Quarterly.
N.L.J.	New Law Journal.
P.L.	Public Law.
O.J.	Official Journal of the European Communities.

Q.B.D.	Queen's Bench Division.
R.T.R.	Road Traffic Reports.
S.I.	Statutory Instrument.
S.J. or Sol.Jo.	Solicitors' Journal.
W.L.R.	Weekly Law Reports.

Appendix III

Further reading

The number of books about law and legal rules increases each day. They range from simple guides, written for the GCSE student, to thousand-page, closely argued texts, written for the academic. Some are encyclopaedias; others are exhaustive surveys of a very small area of law. This short list of further reading is intended to be of use to those readers who want to take further specific themes raised in this book. The list is not a guide to legal literature as a whole. Readers who have specific interests should consult their library catalogues for books in their area.

Introductory books

J Adams and R Brownsword, *Understanding Law* (2003, 3rd ed) Sweet and Maxwell.
P Atiyah, *Law and Modern Society* (1983) Oxford University Press.
J Waldron, *The Law* (1990) Routledge.

Books on the English legal system

S Bailey, J Ching, M Gunn and D Ormerod Smith, *Bailey and Gunn on the Modern English Legal System* (2002, 4th ed) Sweet and Maxwell.
F Cownie, A Bradney and M Burton, *The English Legal System in Context* (2003, 3rd ed) LexisNexis.
K Malleson, *The Legal System* (2003) Butterworths.
R Ward, *Walker and Walker's English Legal System* (1998, 8th ed) Butterworths.

Bibliographical techniques and dictionaries

Dane, J. and Thomas, P. *How to Use a Law Library* (2001, 4th ed).
Osborn's Concise Law Dictionary (1983, 7th ed) Sweet and Maxwell.

Appendix IV

Exercise answers

Exercise 1

1. Section 1 creates the offence of dishonestly dealing in a tainted cultural object. In addition to the specific offence it is also possible for a person to be convicted of offences of inciting someone to commit the offence in s.1, attempting to commit the offence or conspiring to commit the offence.

2. The Act applies to England and Wales (s.6(3)).

3. The Act came into force on December 30, 2003 (s.6(2)).

4. (a) The offence must appear to the Commissioners of Customs and Excise to involve the importation or exportation of a tainted cultural object (s.4(1)).
   (b) Customs and Excise may also prosecute related offences such as an attempt to commit the offence in s.1, or conspiracy, or incitement, to commit it (s.4(2)(b)).

5. (a) The offence has a number of elements:

   (1) there must be a dishonest dealing (s.1(1), 3(1)–(3));
   (2) the dealing must be with a tainted cultural object (s.2); and
   (3) the person dealing must know or believe that the object is tainted (s.1(1)).

   (1) There has been a dealing with the fireplace: Charles has acquired the fireplace (s.3(1)(a)). Del has arranged for the disposal of the fireplace (s.3(1)(b), (3)). Bob and Del have all arranged with each other that Charles acquires the fireplace (s.3(1)(c)). It is clear that Del is dishonest. Bob may be dishonest.

   (2) The fireplace appears to be a tainted cultural object within s.2:

   (1) It is an object of architectural interest (s.2(1)) and
   (2) It was removed from a building where it had formed part of the structure (s.2(2)(a) and 4(a)).

(3) The removal without permission of the owner would amount to the offence of theft.

(3) Del knows that the object is tainted but it is not clear whether the others are aware of this.

(b) The object must be a tainted cultural object but it is immaterial whether the accused knows or believes that the object is a cultural object. Therefore someone who thinks (or says they think) they are buying a copy can be convicted if the item was an original. (s.1(2)).

6. To find out more about the history of the Elgin Marbles look at the following web sites:

http://www.greece.org/parthenon/marbles/
http://faculty.stcc.cc.tn.us/bmcclure/Links/ElginMarbles.htm
http://www.museum-security.org/elginmarbles.html

(a) Removal of the Elgin Marbles from the British Museum would not be an offence under the Act unless it could be argued that they had formed part of the building or structure (s.2(2),(4)). The fact that a museum was constructed to house an object would not be sufficient.

(b) The Act only applies where cultural objects were removed or excavated after the Act came into force.

(c) The motive for the removal does not seem to be important although it might mean that the person was not dishonestly dealing with the object. The removal (or excavation) must be an offence (s.2(2)(b)). Lord Elgin would have to show that he had permission from someone with authority to allow removal. The permission of a colonial power would arguably not be sufficient, and certainly would be insufficient if it breached the country's laws on removal of cultural objects.

Exercise 2

1. (a) Section 15(1) provides for the Secretary of State to bring ss.1,2,4,5, 7–12 into force by statutory instrument; s.15(2) gives the power to bring s.3 and 6 into force to the Lord Chancellor. Why do you think there are separate powers relation to these provisions? Commencement orders have been made, these are not listed in the 2002 *Current Law Legislation Citator* but it is clear that the courts are applying the Act. The relevant commencement orders are SI 1997/1418 and 1997 SI 1997/1498. These can be found at: *http://www.hmso.gov.uk/stat.htm*

(b) The 2002 *Current Law Legislation Citator* does indicate that s.2 has been repealed in part by 2002 c.30 Sch.8 *i.e.* by the Police Reform Act 2002, sch.8. This can be found at: *http://www.hmso.gov.uk/acts.htm*

There have been further amendment in 2003 and these should be indicated in the 2003 *Current Law Legislation Citator.* 2003 asp 7 is a reference to an Act of the Scottish Parliament. Legislation of the Scottish Parliament is available at: *http://www.oqps.gov.uk/scotlegislation/acts_scotparliament.htm*

Or:

www.scotland-legislation.hmso.gov.uk/legislation/scotland/s-acts.htm

2. Sections 1–7 apply to England and Wales only; ss.8–11 apply to Scotland only. Section 12 applies to England, Wales and Scotland, and s.13 applies to Northern Ireland, (s.14).

3. There is only a partial definition in ss.1 and 7. Harassment includes causing "alarm or distress" (s.7(1)) and the "conduct" which may amount to harassment includes speech (s.7(4)). An offence under s.2 is only committed if the perpetrator knows or ought to know his conduct amounts to harassment (s.1(1)(b),(2)). There is a similarly limited definition for Scotland in s.8(3). Without a definition of harassment in the statute the law must rely on the common sense understanding of the word and may turn to dictionaries to see what it means.

4. The Act creates both criminal liability — the offences in s.2 and 4 in England and Wales and in s.9 in Scotland — and civil liability. In England and Wales the victim may seek damages (s.3(2)) or an injunction (s.3(3)). Breach of an injunction "without reasonable excuse" is a criminal offence (s.3(6)). In addition where a person is convicted of an offence under ss.2 or 4 the court may impose a "restraining order" a form of injunction which can be enforced through the criminal law. These are novel features of the legislation, normally breach of an injunction would only be able to be dealt with as contempt of court and a criminal court would not be able to restrain the offender's future conduct. Similarly, in Scotland the court may make civil orders (s.8(5)) or non-harassment orders under the Criminal Procedure (Scotland) Act 1995, s.234A.

5. (a) Romeo has repeatedly sat in his car outside Juliet's house. This is a course of conduct but does it amount to harassment? Would a reasonable person, knowing that Juliet was Romeo's ex-girlfriend think that this was harassment? The reasonable person's view is not sufficient alone, it only enables satisfaction of the requirement in s.1(1)(b). It is also necessary to satisfy s.1(1)(a). Repeatedly waiting outside somebody's house could amount to harassment.
   (b) Placing flowers in Juliet's arms or bag could amount to harassment because it would involve some direct contact with her.

6. Under s.4(3) it is a defence for a person charged with an offence under s.4 to show that (a) "his course of conduct was pursued for the purpose of preventing crime" and (b) or (c). If the jury is satisfied that Mr MacGregor's actions were reasonable for the protection of his property he must be acquitted. Threatening to "skin someone alive" could be taken just as an expression — not a serious threat. However, if it really were a threat to kill this would not seem a reasonable response to children stealing fruit.

7. The court's sentencing powers in relation to the offence in s.4(1) are set out in ss.4(4) and (5). In addition, under s.5 a person convicted of an offence under either s.2 or s.4 can be prohibited from specific action in the future (s.5(2), (3)). Beach of this order also amounts to an offence, s.5(5).

8. (a) The Criminal Justice and Police Act 2002, s.44 (2001c.16 s.44) has added a new subsection 7(3A), which relates to "collective" harassment. This is relevant to the prosecution of Ed.
   Although Ed does not personally harass Sheila he organised a campaign by

others. Section 7(3A)(a) makes the actions of the other people Ed's actions. Thus Ed may be guilty because of the course of conduct even though he committed none of the break ins. The other individuals may not be liable under the Act if each only committed a single incident, so long as they were not implicated in other incidents though subs.3A. The harassment of Sheila certainly amounts to an offence under s.2. It may also amount to an offence under s.4. It is immaterial that there was no intention to frighten the children. Ed ought to have known that this conduct — letting dogs loose — was likely to mean that they would escape. Small children are frequently frightened of dogs, particularly dogs that are not under control, s.4(2).

(b) Both Sheila and the nursery may be able to claim compensation by bringing an action under s.3. For example Sheila may obtain compensation for the anxiety or the damage to her business as a dog breeder (for example if any of her dogs was injured). The nursery would need to show damage to equipment or loss of business. The law of tort has taken a restrictive view about economic loss; not all such losses are recoverable. The children would also have possible claims if they were injured. They might also be able to claim under the Criminal Injuries Compensation Scheme.

Further Reading

There is a lot of relevant information available on the web. To read the debates on the Protection from Harassment Act 1997 go to the Parliament web site at:

http://www.parliament.uk/hansard/hansard.cfm

Click Bound Volume Debate; click session 1996–97.

You will find the Debate on Second reading in the House of Commons on 17 Dec 1996, vol. 287, Column 781. Similarly the debate can be found at that reference of the printed *Hansard* Commons.

Exercise 3

1. Mr. Donachie. See para.1 of the decision.

2. See the formulation by Lord Justice Auld. in para.9 of the decision.

3. (a) 1. The Manchester County Court, before His Honour Judge Tetlow.
       See para.1 of the decision.
    2. The reported decision is in relation to a hearing before the Court of Appeal (Civil Division).

See the information set out at the head of the report.

(b) Civil proceedings.
(c) 1. In the Manchester County Court, the judge dismissed the claims for negligence and breach of statutory duty (*i.e.* Mr. Donachie lost).
        See para.1 of the decision.
     2. The Court of Appeal (Civil Division) allowed the appeal unanimously (*i.e.* Mr. Donachie won).
        See para.46 of the decision, setting out the conclusion of Lord Justice Auld, together with the following agreements by Lord Justice Latham (at para.47) and Lord Justice Arden (at para.48).

(d) Yes.

4. See the grounds set out in para.8 of the decision.

5. See what is set out at para.8 of the decision.

6. See the formulation by Lord Justice Auld at para.9 of the decision.

Exercise 4

1. (a)   1. High Court (Manchester District Registry).
              See at p.1124j in the report.
           2. Court of Appeal (Civil Division).
              See at p.1122b in the report.
              [See also the "running header" of the published law report].
           3. House of Lords.
              See at p.1122c in the report.
           4. Note also that the case had come before the Appeal Committee of the House of Lords on July 23, 2002 in respect of an application by the Defendant for leave to appeal. See at p.1139j in the report. At the same page it emerges that the case had also come before the Appeal Committee of the House of Lords on October 9, 2002 when leave was granted to the Claimant to bring a cross-appeal.
    (b)   1. Claim dismissed (*i.e.* The claimant lost).
           2. Appeal allowed by 2–1 majority (*i.e.* The claimant won).
           3. Appeal allowed by 5–0 majority (*i.e.* The claimant lost).
Note that the outcome in the Court of Appeal is set out at p.1139g–h, while the final outcome in the House of Lords is set out at p.1166j.

2. 1. As regards the report of the Court of Appeal decision, compare the judgment of Longmore L.J. at p.1139f–g with the judgment of Ward L.J. at p.1137e and the judgment of Sedley L.J. at p.1138c.
    2. In relation to the report of the House of Lords opinions, there is no dissent.

3. See those of Mr Bill Braithwaite Q.C., at p.1128d–f.
Compare them with the arguments of Mr Raymond Machell Q.C., at p.1128f–g.
Then see p.1128h–j for the responses made by Mr Braithwaite Q.C.
4. See p.1137g–h.

Exercise 5

1. The article sets out to see "how doctors themselves see their ethical and legal responsibilities" (p.260). This is put in the context of a general consideration of why doctors might or might not engage in Good Samaritan behaviour and what the law with regard to this matter is.

2. Good Samaritan behaviour is action that is undertaken for purely altruistic reasons. If you are uncertain as to the provenance of the phrase "Good Samaritan" you could either enter the phrase in to an internet search engine such as Google (*http://www.google.com*) or look it up in something like the Encyclopedia Britannica.

3. The study is based on a questionnaire administered to doctors in the Sheffield Health Authority and doctors working in the Sheffield Hospitals NHS Trust (p.261). The overall response rate was 36 per cent. Do you think this is sufficient to mean that those responding are representative of the survey population? Is the survey population representative of doctors taken as a whole? The next matter to consider is whether the responses given are significant and therefore worth considering. On p.262 and 263 Williams uses the Pearson chi-square test of statistical significance when analysing his data. Elsewhere he simply reports the data, usually giving the results as a percentage.

4. First you should note that this study does not look at doctors' knowledge of the law. Instead it assesses doctors' knowledge of the law in a very specialized area that relates to their professional responsibilities. Secondly, what the study reports are doctors' answers to a series of questions about the law (p.269). Even when the correct answer is given this does not necessarily indicate knowledge of the law. As Williams notes the responses are so poor that random chance would produce more rights answers. The respondents may simply be guessing. Some respondents did indeed indicate that they were guessing (p.268). The study should thus not be read as report on what doctors' knowledge of the law is but, rather, as a report of some information relating to doctors' knowledge of the law.

5. The implicit premise in this remark is that all doctors should be in a position to give emergency assistance. This may be true because it would widen the number of people available to help when accidents occur. However there are converse arguments. For example, some doctors pursue very specialized areas of work. Why should they also have the general knowledge pertaining to medicine that may be necessary to give assistance in Good Samaritan type situations? Indeed is it possible for doctors to have this knowledge. Even if they received initial training in medical school would they still retain

that knowledge when faced with a Samaritan type situation that occurs perhaps many years after their training?

It is inevitable that any piece of writing will contain within it implicit points that the author is assuming to be true. What is important is that you should understand what things are being assumed and what are being argued and that you can see the alternative possibilities to the things that the author is assuming.

Index

Acts 4–5
  application 4
types of
  General 4
  Local 4
  Personal 4
Advocate
  qualifying as in Scotland 221
Assignments
  writing 184–189
Barristers 207–208
  education and training of 215–218
    academic stage 216
    funding 218
    pupillage 217–218
    vocational stage 216–217
  qualifying as advocate in Scotland 221
  qualifying as in Northern Ireland 223
  statistics 206

Career opportunities
  accountancy 225–226
  actuary 226
  advertising 226–227
  armed forces 237
  auctioneering 242
  banking 227
  barristers' clerks 234
  building society management 227–228
  chartered secretary 228
  court clerks 236
  Crown Prosecution Service 236
  customs and excise 230
  Department for Constitutional Affairs 237
  engineering 230
  environmental health officers 231
  European 229–230
    European Fast Stream 229–230
    stages 229
  factory inspector 231
  Government legal service 237

Career opportunities—*contd*
  health services management 231–232
  housing 232
  insurance 232
  journalism and broadcasting 232–233
  justices' chief executives 235–236
  justices' clerks 235–236
  law costs draftsmen 235
  legal advisers 235–236
  legal cashiers 234
  legal costs consultants 235
  legal executives 233
  legal secretaries 234
  library, information and training services 237–238
  licensed conveyancers 235
  local government 238
  management 238
  outdoor clerks 234
  patent and trademarks 238
  personnel management 239
  police 239
  probation 241
  public relations 239
  publishing 240
  recruitment consultants 240
  social work 240
  stock exchange 241–242
  surveying 242
  tax inspector 242
  teaching and post-graduate opportunities 242–243
  trading standards officer 243–244
  UK civil service 228
Case law 6
  application 6
Cases
  finding 31
  internet, on 38–39
  reading 45–53, 181–182
    cases referred to 49
    contents of law reports 45

Cases—*contd*
  reading—*contd*
    exercises 76–137
    headnote 49
    history of proceedings 49
    "judgment of the court" 51
    judgments 49–50
    multiple judgments 51
    names of counsel 49
    obiter dictum 52
    processes 50
    ratio decidendi 50
    "second matter" 51
    time available 52
  references 33
  up-dating 35–36
Civil law
  emphasis 13
  meaning 12
  procedure 13
  standard of proof 13
Commentaries 58
Common law 6
  equity, and 9
Courts
  structure of 7
Criminal law
  meaning 12
  objectives 13
  procedure 13
  volume of 11
Customary law 14–15

Degrees
  non-law 205

Electronic retrieval facilities 38
Encyclopedias
  using 40–41
Equity
  common law, and 9
Essays 184–189
European Union law 16–17
  application 17
  basic framework 16
  decisions 17
  directives 17
  finding 41–42
  foundation of EU 16
  information and notices 42
  internet, on 43
  legislation 42
    transposed in to UK law 43
  regulations 16
  using material on 41–42
Exams 189–192

Halsbury's laws, consulting 49

Independent learning 169–170
International law 14–16
  changing 15
  creation of 14–15
  difference from national law 14
  organisations 15
  scope and interpretation 15
  UK obligations under 15–16
International students
  study skills 192
Internet
  cases on 38–39
  European Union materials on 43
  law reports on 34
  "on-line" services 38
Interviews 139–140

Judicial review 20
Judiciary
  case law, application 6
  importance 8
  influences on decisions by 24
  law made by 6–8
  obiter dicta 7
  principles used by 5–6
  ratio decidendi 7

Law
  action, in 21–22, 25–27
  books, in 21–22
  divisions of 11
  meaning of 3
  profession, as 205
  sources of 3–9
Law courses 201–202
  application through UCAS 202–205
  non-law degrees 205
Law reports 33–35
  case references 33
  contents. *see* Cases
  internet, on 34
Lectures 172–174
Legal executives 208, 233
  route to qualifying as solicitor 215
Legal rules
  binding nature of 4
  content 21
  sources of 3–4
Legislation 4, 5–6
  application 5
  delegated 4
  effect 5
  local 4
  statutory interpretation 5

Libraries
  electronic retrieval facilities 38
  non-electronic research facilities
    31–33
    uses 31–32
  using limited facilities 37–38

Newspapers
  case reports 33
Northern Ireland
  qualifying as barrister in 223
  qualifying as solicitor in. *see* Solicitors

Obiter dicta **7, 52**
Observation 140–141
On-line services 38

Parliament 4–5
  Acts 4
  role of 4
Private law
  meaning 17
  origins of 19
  purpose 18
Problem answers 184–189
Public law
  enforcement 19
  individual rights 19–20
  judicial review, and 20
  meaning 17
  origins of 19
  purpose 18

Questionnaires 139–140
Questions
  answering 24–25
  different kinds 21, 23–24
  nature of law, about 25
  source of answers 25
  treatment of suspects, and 22–23

Ratio decidendi **7, 50**
Reading
  cases. *see* Cases
  research, for 180–182
  statutes. *see* Statutes
Record reading 139
Research materials
  interviews 139–140
  observation 140–141
  questionnaires 139–140
  reading 139
    exercises 145–167
  record reading 139
  research findings 141–144
  sampling 141

Sampling 141
Scotland
  qualifying as advocate in. *see* Barristers
  qualifying as solicitor in. *see* Solicitors
Seminars 175–176
Solicitors
  education and training of 209–215
    academic stage 210–211
    funding 214
    law degree route 210
    non-law degree route 210
    practical stage 212–214
    student membership 211
    vocational stage 211–212
  legal executive route to qualifying as 215
  qualifying as in Northern Ireland 221–223
    apprenticeship 222
    entering legal profession 221
    law degree route 222
    non-law degree route 222
    requalifying 223
  qualifying as in Scotland 219–221
    diploma in legal practice 220
    entering legal profession 219
    law degree route 220
    non-law degree route 220
    post-diploma practical training
      220–221
    requalifying in Scotland 221
  statistics 206
  trainee 212–214
    industry and commerce 213
    law centres 213–214
    private practice 212–213
    public service 213
Sources of law 3–9
  Parliament 4–5
Statistics
  law in action, on 25–26
  official, limitations 26
  sources of 26
  uses 26–27
Statutes
  finding 39–40, 53
  reading 53–58, 181
    chapter number 57
    citation 57
    enacting formula 57
    exercises 61–75
    finding 53
    long title 57
    marginal notes 57
    royal assent 57
    sections of main body 57–58
    short title 57
  up-dating 39–40

Statutes—*contd*
   using 58–60
      commentaries 58
Statutory instruments 60
Statutory provisions 14
Study skills
   assessment 189–192
   essays 184–189
   exams 189–192
   exercises 194–197
   independent learning 169–170
   international students 192
   lectures 172–174
      listening 172–174
      notetaking 172–174
   problem answers 184–189
   reading for research 180–182

Study skills—*contd*
   recording research 182–184
   researching topic 177–180
   seminars 175–176
   studying effectively 169
   time management 170–172
   tutorials 175–176
   writing assignments 184–189

Treaties 14–15
Tutorials 175–176

UCAS
   applications to law courses 202–205
      Electronic Application System (EAS)
         203
      paper application form 203–205